The Myth *of* Experience

The Myth *of* Experience

Why We Learn the Wrong Lessons, and Ways to Correct Them

EMRE SOYER *and*
ROBIN M. HOGARTH

PUBLICAFFAIRS
New York

PublicAffairs
Hachette Book Group
1290 Avenue of the Americas, New York, NY 10104
www.publicaffairsbooks.com
@Public_Affairs

Printed in the United States of America

First Edition: September 2020

Published by PublicAffairs, an imprint of Perseus Books, LLC, a subsidiary of Hachette Book Group, Inc. The PublicAffairs name and logo is a trademark of the Hachette Book Group.

The Hachette Speakers Bureau provides a wide range of authors for speaking events. To find out more, go to www.hachettespeakersbureau.com or call (866) 376-6591.

The publisher is not responsible for websites (or their content) that are not owned by the publisher.

Print book interior design by Jeff Williams

Library of Congress Cataloging-in-Publication Data

Names: Soyer, Emre, author. | Hogarth, Robin M., author.
Title: The myth of experience : why we learn the wrong lessons and ways to correct them / Emre Soyer, Robin M. Hogarth.
Description: New York : PublicAffairs, 2020. | Includes bibliographical references and index.
Identifiers: LCCN 2020011530 | ISBN 9781541742055 (hardcover) | ISBN 9781541742062 (ebook)
Subjects: LCSH: Experiential learning—Social aspects. | Experience. | Social psychology. | Social sciences.
Classification: LCC BF318.5 .S69 2020 | DDC 153.1/52—dc23

LC record available at https://lccn.loc.gov/2020011530

ISBNs: 978-1-5417-4205-5 (hardcover) 978-1-5417-4206-2 (ebook)

LSC-C

10 9 8 7 6 5 4 3 2 1

To the memory of Hilly Einhorn

"If history repeats itself, and the unexpected always happens, how incapable must Man be of learning from experience!"

—GEORGE BERNARD SHAW
Man and Superman

CONTENTS

INTRODUCTION

Experience Is a Great Teacher—
Except When It Isn't

Do you trust your experience?

Most people do. Our personal experience shapes our preferences, educates our intuition, and guides our decisions. It's our treasured teacher, whose lessons stay with us for a long time. Society at large venerates experience. We want our doctors, judges, politicians, and managers to have plenty of it. The more, the better.

Great. What can go wrong?

Unfortunately, an excessive or unthinking reliance on experience can lead to distressing results. In fact, things can get bloody—very bloody.

Two weeks before the start of the nineteenth century, the sixty-seven-year-old George Washington fell ill. The first president of the United States was feverish. He had a severe inflammation in his throat, which had started interfering with his breathing. His aide promptly called his three physicians.

There was little doubt about the required treatment: bloodletting. The doctors and Washington himself immediately urged the widely used procedure. Abundant and repeated bloodletting was a key ingredient of health care of the day, often accompanied with blistering, enemas, and purging. Washington had access to the best health care available, and not applying bloodletting thoroughly was inconceivable. Hoping to quickly heal the ailment, the physicians pushed the procedure to its limits. Reports suggest that, during the course of twelve hours, nearly half of Washington's blood was drained. He died after a few hours.[1]

Washington's condition was serious even before his doctors arrived, and he may have been beyond saving with the methods available at the time. But because of the treatment he endured, Washington lost his blood when he needed it most. As a result, he likely suffered more *because* of the well-intentioned attempts to help him.[2]

Generations of practice and clinical experience supported the use of bloodletting. For millennia, it had been considered a cure for all kinds of disorders. In his first-century medical treatise *De Medicina*, Roman scholar Celsus declared that "to let blood by incising a vein is no novelty: what is novel is that there should be scarcely any malady in which blood should not be let."[3]

The Greek physician Galen of Pergamum avidly advocated the procedure in the second century and ended up profoundly shaping Western medical practice for centuries to come. William Harvey, the English physician who was among the first to discover the blood's circulatory system, still maintained in the seventeenth century that "daily experience satisfies us that bloodletting has a most salutary effect in many diseases, and is indeed the foremost among all the general remedial means."[4] So we kept on bleeding.

Benjamin Rush was a contemporary of Washington, a highly respected physician and a cosigner of the Declaration of Independence. He strived to improve the conditions of his community by opposing slavery, advocating for prison reform, and supporting better education for all.[5]

When a yellow fever epidemic took Philadelphia by surprise in 1793, Rush—driven by a fervent desire to heal the sick—both championed and practiced an intensive regimen of bloodletting and purging. Extreme circumstances required extreme remedies. When he himself contracted fever, he instructed that he also be bled plentifully.[6]

He survived. "I have proved upon my own body," Rush declared in a letter afterward, "that the yellow fever when treated in the new way, is no more than a common cold."[7]

A few decades later, Lord Byron was a bloodletting skeptic. When he fell ill, he reportedly exclaimed to the doctors trying to bleed him that "many more die of the lancet than the lance." His doctors disagreed. He was bled repeatedly amid multiple health problems, during what turned out to be the final days of his life.[8]

Why did people and knowledgeable experts insist for so long that bloodletting was a cure-all, a belief we now know to have been misguided?

The procedure owes its origins to inaccurate assumptions about human anatomy and the biology of disease. It was thought that illnesses were due to an imbalance of bodily fluids and that letting blood was a way of restoring balance. The tools and methods necessary to reveal the real causes of diseases were lacking. The starting point was off.

Fair enough. Even smart, knowledgeable experts can embrace flawed ideas when a field of science is in the early stages of development. It happens. But then, repeated experience over countless cases across many centuries in such a vital context should have helped our ancestors promptly learn their lesson, recognize the errors in their thinking, and revise their ways.

It didn't. It actually made things worse.

Around 2,400 years ago, in his first and most famous aphorism, Hippocrates warned us about learning from experience: "Life is short, and Art long; the crisis fleeting; experience fallacious, and decision difficult."[9]

He was right. Experience in the form of personal observations and oft-repeated anecdotes was indeed fallacious in the case of bloodletting. It fueled the procedure's persistence as a panacea by confirming inaccurate assumptions and encouraging well-meaning healers, physicians, and even barbers to use the procedure liberally when "treating" their patients, often in unsanitary conditions. Even the best educated and most reputable were vulnerable to the deceptions of experience. They were up against a teacher that was extremely hard to deny, even when it conveyed the wrong lessons.

Let's consider the various ways learning from experience could have led them astray.

In many cases, the body could recover after minor doses of bloodletting, sometimes administered through cupping and leeching. Some fevers and inflammations also diminished. It was easy to conclude that effective healing had occurred in the presence of such soothing of symptoms and possible placebo effects.[10]

It was also possible for patients to recover even from excessive blood loss. And some of these people may have been misdiagnosed and have not actually had the presumed disease. Their endurance could, however, be interpreted as further proof of the treatment's curing prowess.

While happy survivors could testify loudly to bloodletting's supposed benefits, the deceased were promptly filtered out of experience. Their absence made it easy to blame the disease for their demise rather than implicating the procedure.

The inability to discern the real causes of diseases merely from observation made it hard to devise appropriate preventive measures, potentially encouraging the further spread of illnesses. And it made sense to intensify a conventional cure during a sudden epidemic.

Also, many influential experts, who personally experienced and survived the procedure, acquired an unshakeable confidence in it. They often felt licensed, even obligated, to propagate it to the masses. These experts then went on to mentor their successors, preserving and spreading the established school of thought. In fact, two (out of three) of Washington's physicians and two (out of three) of Byron's, had all attended the same medical school— the same one Benjamin Rush himself attended. And Washington's third doctor had been Rush's student. This kind of closed circle of expertise, with entire generations of practitioners imbibing knowledge from the same source, made it even easier for flawed lessons to endure and spread.[11]

And finally, as all these lessons based on experience pointed in the same direction, it became increasingly difficult for decision makers to even consider alternative notions. One way of challenging the prevailing belief, for instance, would have involved *not* bleeding a random group of patients, and then tracking how their health differed from those who were bled. But denying an established cure to patients in need would have felt cruel and unusual, especially when they themselves demanded the treatment. Hence, years of experience proved hard to unlearn and the resulting traditions too strong to overturn.

During the nineteenth century, the popularity of bloodletting finally started to subside, due to a combination of randomized trials, autopsies, and advances in biology. Medical historian W. Mitchell Clarke confirmed Hippocrates's 2,400-year-old wisdom: "Experience must, indeed, as Hippocrates says in his first aphorism, be fallacious if we decide that a means of treatment, sanctioned by the use of between two and three thousand years, and upheld by the authority of the ablest men of past times, is finally and forever given up. This seems to me to be the most interesting and important question in connection with this subject."[12]

Indeed, it is. The potential of lessons of experience to mislead, sometimes with fatal consequences, is a significant problem with the way we humans learn and think. That's why we've chosen to write a book exploring this phenomenon.

There's little doubt that experience is indispensable for our decisions in most aspects of our lives. And it can indeed be a reliable teacher. The problem, however, is that it isn't *always* reliable. Yet we tend to remain convinced that it is.

In certain circumstances, relying strongly on experience can perversely endow us with "knowledge" that makes us unwise, while deceptively making us feel wiser. Instead of giving us the right answers, experience can reinforce the wrong ones. We can make the same mistakes over and over again, and for a long time, without even realizing that we have a problem.

In the chapters that follow, we'll focus on instances when experience unexpectedly becomes a foe and a trickster, rather than a friend and a teacher. We'll discuss when and how experience can betray competent decision makers by depriving them of their full capacity to perform, while falsely reassuring them about their competence. We'll explore under what conditions we tend to learn the wrong lessons, and what we can do to go beyond available experience to discover the right ones instead.

We have much to gain from nurturing a healthy constructive critical attitude toward the lessons of experience. If we fall ill today, except for a few rare conditions, we won't be bled excessively. Although the procedure still persists, it's more restricted and less mainstream. It wasn't easy, but we ultimately managed to unlearn it and refine our practices.[13]

Yet, how else does experience deceive us today in other important areas of our lives? When is it unreliable without us being aware? What sorts of new habits and thinking tools could help us recognize its flaws, see beyond its misleading lessons, and make better-informed decisions?

These are the questions this book will explore.

Experience—A Powerful Teacher

Experience is a complex concept. The simple term denotes something with several aspects and qualities.[14]

Experience is a *process*. It's the moment-to-moment interaction with our current environment. We observe and participate in events or do both simultaneously. We experience a rock concert or a ski trip. If we are managing a business, we worry about optimizing the customer and user experience when we design our stores, websites, and mobile phones.

Experience is also a *product*. It accumulates over time based on our numerous past interactions. We gain experience through practice and by engaging in a task multiple times. Because we value its lessons, we worry about employing people with the appropriate experience given the jobs we want them to perform.

And experience is *personal*. We try things out and learn if we like or dislike them by relying on our experience. We then plan our future decisions and behavior accordingly. Experience also plays a key role in shaping our tastes. Many Americans like baseball, while many British prefer cricket—but most Turks or Spaniards don't really care for either. We typically learn to like the games, the kinds of books, and the particular food we grew up with.[15]

Ultimately, experience is a fundamental source of knowledge that we constantly rely on in life. When we face a decision, we welcome and even require some experience to be able to make sense of the situation and act according to our preferences and goals.

Luckily, learning from experience has many advantages.

It's *automatic*. We rarely think about how we learn from experience. It just happens. Many members of the animal kingdom naturally learn about various conditions, patterns, risks, and rewards in their surroundings through experience.[16]

It's *quick*. Experience swiftly feeds our intuition, our gut feelings, our unconscious perception of a wide variety of situations we have to face on a daily basis. Even a single encounter can be enough for us to form an opinion, which in many cases helps us deal with life's circumstances more or less effectively.[17]

It's *encouraging*. Experience informs us about the reality we live in and helps us build the confidence necessary to engage it. We feel that by gaining more experience, we stand to become more competent.

It's *durable*. Many skills that we learn from experience eventually become second nature to us. They remain with us a long time and become easier to retrieve. Their durability provides us with time and energy to learn other skills.

Riding a bicycle is the quintessential skill everybody learns from experience. If you can ride one, you've learned it by doing—one cannot master it by reading books or watching videos. It doesn't take hundreds of hours to learn it, and the more you ride, the more you feel in control. You don't need to think about what you are doing while riding a bicycle. Nor would it be easy to explain to someone who has never ridden one. They need to experience it to understand. Even if you don't ride for some time, you pick it up quite rapidly when you try again. The same goes for many other motor skills, like driving, typing, skiing, or performing surgery.[18]

As a result, extensive experience can lead to *expertise*. Deliberate practice that involves reliable feedback helps people perfect their skills in many complex tasks.[19]

Take playing tennis. The consequences of every movement and shot in tennis can be immediately observed by all players on court. Hundreds of interactions in each practice session and match between opponents provide reliable and actionable insights on what strategies lead to which potential outcomes in almost every possible situation. A coach can also observe this whole process from outside, further enriching the players' experience. Recently, equipment makers have also started building smart rackets. Microchips and sensors provide minute data on how the ball was hit, which can be analyzed to improve learning and boost performance.[20]

Given their conditions for learning, it should be no surprise that those who play at Wimbledon seem to have superhuman abilities. Reliable experience helps them develop their talents to the limit.

Beside physical skills, experience is also a great help in learning concepts. Repeated exposure to ideas can greatly reduce the need for effortful thinking. Experience is much more than a tedious list of things that are happening or have happened to us. It's an intricate bundle of memories, interpretations, and associations that helps us remember and connect a wide variety of concepts without much effort.

Psychologists like John Dewey, Kurt Lewin, Jean Piaget, and, more recently, David Kolb and Ronald E. Fry have envisioned learning from experience as a cycle. We first experience, then reflect, produce abstract lessons, and finally try these lessons out to build further experience, thereby restarting the learning cycle.[21]

This cycle is a chief source of our understanding of *causes and effects*. We make certain decisions and observe others make theirs. We then detect connections and consequences. We subsequently use these insights to revise our decisions and increase the chances of obtaining the outcomes we desire.[22]

On the tennis court, for example, different strategies can provoke different responses from opponents and lead to different outcomes, allowing players to gradually optimize their game plans.

Likewise, memories of past relationships—in family and social life, on the job, in the community—can shape one's behavior in subsequent ones.

Experience in one domain can also inform us about related processes and problems in other domains. It enriches the types of dots we can connect and enhances the potential of *knowledge transfer* from one field to another.[23]

Playing tennis can provide insights on the nature of hard work, competition, patience, defeat, confidence, and talent, which can also prove valuable off court. A successful project in one sector can provide an entrepreneur with the tools necessary to succeed in an upcoming project in a different sector.

Finally, we can learn from *others' experience.* While these lessons are often less vivid than those we gain firsthand, they can guide us as we build our own competences. And mentors can save apprentices great amounts of time and effort by sharing with them the lessons they've derived from experience.[24]

In tennis, watching opponents play others can give a player valuable clues about how to compete against them. Coaches can steer players toward strategies that would personally suit and benefit them. Similarly, tips from a seasoned business adviser can help decision makers better chart their desired paths.

For all these reasons, experience *can* be a great teacher as we form our intuitions and make our decisions in all aspects of our lives. It can help us adapt to new surroundings, improve our performance, and survive difficult situations.

All these virtues, however, end up hiding its darker side. Experience can deceive, without us being aware.

Wicked Learning Environments: What's Missing? What's Irrelevant?

Because experience is personal, automatic, quick, encouraging, and durable, it's extremely hard to ignore. The concepts experience installs in our intuition feel reliable. Unfortunately, this is also true when it teaches the *wrong* lessons.

The default mode in our thinking is to assume that our experience reflects a clear and complete picture of the situations we face. Whatever we learn through observation and participation appears to be the reality. Psychologist and Nobel laureate Daniel Kahneman dubbed this syndrome WYSIATI: what you see is all there is.[25]

This assumption is generally valid for activities like cycling and tennis. These involve *kind learning environments*, where decision makers receive abundant, immediate, and accurate feedback on their actions and the rules of the game remain largely constant. Under these controlled and limited circumstances, the lessons of experience are typically reliable.[26]

Modern life, however, is rarely like cycling or tennis. What we see isn't necessarily all there is.

As psychologist Thomas Gilovich warns us in *How We Know What Isn't So*, "the world does not play fair. Instead of providing us with clear information that would enable us to 'know' better, it presents us with messy data that are random, incomplete, unrepresentative, ambiguous, inconsistent, unpalatable, or secondhand."[27]

For instance, we may not always get to observe the consequences of our decisions or only observe them after considerable delay. Rules can change quickly and unexpectedly, rendering hard-earned experience obsolete. And we often don't have coaches or microchips that can help us dissect and correct our personal interpretations of what has taken place.

In most life circumstances, we are up against *wicked learning environments*, where our experience is constantly subject to a variety of filters and distortions. As in Plato's famed allegory of the cave, we may merely be observing some shadowy representations of what's actually taking place in many relevant contexts. And while experience still leads to learning, there is no guarantee that its lessons accurately represent the reality of a situation.[28]

Indeed, sociologist and organizational behavioral scholar James March argues in *The Ambiguities of Experience* that we often fail to learn the right lessons when they involve missing evidence and irrelevant details. We are also easily swayed by subjective interpretations and make swift generalizations based on limited information. As a result, more experience can reinforce misleading beliefs while making us think that we are getting wiser.[29]

Hence, it becomes essential to question and then adjust the lessons of experience in a timely fashion, especially in complex situations where we truly wish to make informed decisions. In particular, there are two crucial questions that can be invaluable to us when grappling with wicked learning environments:

- Is there something important *missing* from my experience that I need to uncover if I hope to fully understand what is happening?

- What *irrelevant* details are present in my experience that I need to ignore to avoid being distracted from what is happening?

Here's a simple example of how what's missing can render our experiences misleading.

In his television special *The System*, illusionist Derren Brown tosses a coin ten times in a row, getting heads each time. The coin he uses is a real one, and there are no camera tricks. The ten tosses take him less than one minute.[30]

When you watch him do it, the whole event seems supernatural. Brown looks confident and in control. After the sixth toss, he even foreshadows his achievement: "Four more to go . . . then I'll stop." It's as if he has found a way to cheat nature and exert his will over the coin.

Indeed, he has. Yet he does it not by manipulating the coin but by hiding part of the bigger picture from the audience. He eventually reveals later in the program that the segment with the ten tosses we witnessed was merely the last minute of a long footage. Brown's camera crew had to film him for hours tossing the coin and start from scratch whenever he got tails. After enough trials, however, he eventually tossed ten heads in a row, which was the only part that was initially shown to viewers. Over time, what at first seemed impossible became inevitable. Brown's achievement is thus not due to a psychic talent but is a mere consequence of the probabilistic nature of coin tosses.

In this case, while the impressive outcome is readily available, the intricate process that led to it is missing from experience, making the outcome look more extraordinary than it is.[31]

A similar effect could also be created in a scenario where, instead of one person tossing a coin many times, thousands of people are tossing coins simultaneously. A few of them will actually manage to toss ten heads in a row. Once again, however, this would not be due to their coin-tossing skills but a consequence of luck. But if one could observe only those who tossed ten heads in a row, this becomes a case where certain outcomes are missing from experience (those who failed to toss ten heads in a row). As a result, the successful few would look once again more extraordinary than they actually are.[32]

Unfortunately, much of our experience in life is based on such selective samples of information. For example, we typically don't get to observe what would have happened had we made another choice. Also, unprecedented disasters and disruptive innovations are by definition missing from our experience. This makes it really easy to discount or ignore certain relevant details that should inform our important decisions. Out of sight easily becomes out of mind.[33]

The opposite happens as well: what we are able to see shapes our experience and the conclusions we draw from it, even when what we see may be irrelevant.

A favorite family excursion for one of us (the authors), who grew up in Scotland, was to a hillside called the Electric Brae. Situated a few miles south of the town of Ayr on the southwest coast, this remarkable slope is near the village of Dunure. If you place a ball on the ground or spill some water, you will observe the ball or water start to move—*uphill*. Is the law of gravity not valid in this part of Scotland?

There's a stone near the slope, inscribed with the following explanation:

This runs the quarter mile from the bend overlooking Croy Railway Viaduct in the west (286 feet above ordnance datum) to the wooded Craigencroy Glen (303 feet A.O.D) to the east. Whilst there is this slope of 1 in 86 upwards from the bend to the glen, the configuration of the land on either side of the road provides an optical illusion, making it look as if the slope is going the other way. Therefore, a stationary car on the road with breaks off will appear to move slowly uphill. The term "electric" dates from a time when it was incorrectly thought to be a phenomenon caused by electric or magnetic attraction within the brae.[34]

The contours of the surrounding countryside interfere with our judgment about the slope. Although our visual experience suggests that the brae is electric, it certainly isn't.

Throughout this book, we'll return to the two crucial questions: *What's missing? What's irrelevant?* They're invaluable tools that help us challenge the easy and obvious lessons that experience teaches—lessons that, in wicked learning environments, all too often lead to conclusions that are incomplete or flat wrong.

Learning from Experience—Then Struggling to Unlearn

Once we've learned unreliable lessons from experience, they are hard to unlearn or amend. And they often get further solidified with more experience. This is why, even when circumstances change, we can find ourselves trapped by our experience and fail to adjust appropriately.[35]

Destin Sandlin, the creator of the YouTube channel Smarter Every Day, tested this notion with an unusual experiment. He reversed the way his bicycle's handlebars operate so that when you rotate them to the left the wheel turns right and vice versa. He then asked people, who can easily ride a normal bike, to try and travel a few feet in what he called "the backwards brain bicycle."

How hard can it be? Extremely. Because people are familiar with a normal bike, they simply cannot adjust to this new situation.

Impressively, after much practice, experience, and trial and error, Sandlin eventually learned to ride the bizarre bike. But then he discovered that he was unable to ride a normal bike, proving that learning to ride a regular bicycle can teach the wrong skills for riding the backward brain bicycle and vice versa.[36]

If you don't wish to mess up your bike, you can experience the same effect by inverting the keyboard of your computer. Now try typing your name. You'll find your hands hovering over the keys awkwardly as you search for letters in places they used to be, frustrated to realize they are not there.[37]

Experience can thus constrain us to prefer certain choices, processes, or actions even when they become obsolete or irrelevant, partly because we have a hard time unlearning our lesson and relearning something else.[38]

In his classic book *Future Shock*, futurist Alvin Toffler likened the ability to unlearn and relearn to being literate. In a constantly evolving social, technological, and global world, irreversibility and unreliability of the lessons from experience can render us "illiterate" in this sense for a long time, while leaving us oblivious to that illiteracy.[39]

For centuries, in fact, we humans arrogantly thought that we were at the center of the universe. We simply assumed what we saw must be what is. The lens of experience constantly confirmed and reinforced our belief that planet Earth is flat and everything revolves around it. We had to develop methods and technologies that let us see beyond our experience to grasp our actual situation—to discover that we are, in fact, not at the center of the universe but merely a small part of a much larger system. Without an accurate assessment of our actual place, we were stuck with the wrong know-how, derived from experience and further reinforced by more experience.[40]

The good news is that with the right tools, we can avoid or escape such experiential traps. This is essential for our progress in important domains such as medicine, technology, education, politics, economics, and business. The bad news is that, unless we acknowledge that experience can occasionally be a terrible teacher, we can be trapped despite abundant evidence against its lessons.

Escaping the Delusions of Experience

It's a myth that experience is always a great teacher. When we (the authors) first met more than fifteen years ago, we set out to study instances where experience helps people learn valuable insights and make better decisions. In time, however, we started to notice many relevant contexts where more experience complicated things rather than clarifying them, without people's awareness.

Cognitive psychologist Hillel Einhorn, one of the fathers of behavioral decision research, asked: "If we believe we can learn from experience, can we also learn that we can't?"[41]

There's much ongoing debate in today's contentious world about when and how one should challenge the received wisdom, whether it comes from academic and scientific experts, political and social "elites," or powerful organs of the news media. Building on Einhorn's question, we argue that a similar rigorous and thoughtful scrutiny should also be applied to the wisdom generated by experience. After all, self-deception is just as bad as being deceived by others—and it tends to be even harder to overcome.

We don't mean that experience should be ignored. But developing a timely and healthy skepticism toward our experience would allow us to discern when it is and isn't reliable. As decision makers, we would be better off considering its lessons as assumptions that need to be tested rather than verdicts that can't be denied. In this way, we can hope to effectively learn, unlearn, and relearn.[42]

In *On Becoming a Person*, humanistic psychologist Carl Rogers elaborates eloquently on such skepticism. He declares personal experience to be "the highest authority" and the "touchstone of validity" as we learn about the world around us and make decisions. Nothing else may feel as convincing as the lessons we derive from our experience. But this authority should not stem from an assumption that it's infallible. On the contrary, Rogers argues that we should value its lessons precisely because they can be checked and corrected.[43]

An inquisitive attitude toward the lessons of experience would also keep in check the experts and leaders we rely on. Understanding when experience leads to reliable expertise and when it doesn't would allow us to select better managers, specialists, advisers, and administrators, further improving our long-term well-being.

This book aims to improve how we learn from experience. It never presumes to know or dictate what one's ultimate decision should or shouldn't be. Instead, it strives to expose instances where experience is unreliable and envisions creative ways to educate intuition, without bleeding needlessly.

1

STORIES THAT LIE

*When Experience Becomes an
All-Too-Simple Narrative*

CONSIDER THE FOLLOWING SHORT FILM.

On the screen is a circle, motionless and slightly to the right of center. A triangle then enters from the left and slides toward the circle. When the two shapes meet in the middle of the screen, the triangle stops moving, and the circle starts sliding toward the right. It eventually falls outside the screen. The triangle remains on the screen, motionless. The end.

Please think about what just happened. What could this sequence of events represent?

During some of our talks and workshops, we show this film and ask the audience members this question. They usually react, surprisingly quickly, with a wide range of responses. A few see and interpret the film rather literally: "A triangle pushes a circle out of the picture."

Other responses are more colorful and metaphorical:

"Change is inevitable."

"Solutions evolve to fit problems better."

"Order wins over chaos."

"Those who have a clear set of principles trump those who don't."

"Reason beats emotion."

After collecting numerous responses, we ask a follow-up question: What will happen next? Once again, we get many answers, but now most are based on the previous ones:

"A square will come and push away the triangle."

"The return of the circle . . . It will come back and take revenge."

"A better solution will replace this one . . . perhaps it will have more colors."

"Emotion will eventually prevail."

This exercise is based on the work of psychologists Fritz Heider and Marianne Simmel, themselves inspired by the psychologist Albert Michotte. They would show certain shapes to audiences, make them move around, and then study people's perceptions.[1]

The story of the triangle and the circle reveals important clues about the way we learn from experience.

First, *experiences quickly become stories*. People are able to effortlessly generate narratives based on their observations, often linking their interpretations to their previous experiences, beliefs, and knowledge.

Second, *the chronology of events often leads people to perceive cause-and-effect relationships*. The film simply shows two objects moving in various ways, but based on the sequence of events, viewers quickly conclude that one thing *causes* the other to move and ultimately to fall.

Third, *people can easily use a perceived story to generate a prediction of what will happen next*. Because one object pushed the other, now it's time for the latter to take revenge on the former. Or because change is inevitable, the newcomer will be replaced in turn by something else. The content of the initial story paves a path for guesses and expectations regarding what lies ahead.

Hence, this little exercise suggests that we humans are able to quickly and proficiently generate stories based on our experience and then use them in our future judgments about the situation. This is a rather complex task, yet we excel at it. Perhaps we've become so good at storytelling, in part, because stories provide us with such powerful, valuable tools for dealing with experience.

Stories help us *understand* our experience. They provide a way to attach meaning to complicated yet important events that affect our lives. They allow us to create order out of chaos.

Stories help us *remember* our experience. Memorizing a list of a dozen words or concepts and remembering their order sometime later would be difficult. But if we connect them through a unifying story, they are easier to recall when needed.

Stories help us *communicate* our experience. We can convey them easily to others, making sure that the learning becomes collective. We can also learn from others' experience through their stories.

Stories help us *predict* the future based on our experience. We can use them to educate our guesses about what will take place at a later time. Stories about the past and the present shape the ones about the future.[2]

In *Sapiens,* historian Yuval Harari emphasizes the importance of the human ability to create, believe, and spread stories for our dominance as a species on earth. Stories helped us collaborate, defeat our adversaries, survive deadly dangers, build massive cities, maintain complex systems, and invent new things. Countries, for example, are built on and supported by stories that vividly encapsulate the shared experiences of their fellow citizens. By contrast, failing to see a story can deprive us of valuable lessons, collaborations, and opportunities.[3]

Given that stories helped us evolve to become what we are today, one can argue that we are programmed to see stories automatically in what we experience.

Great. What can go wrong?

Unfortunately, our storytelling proclivity can also create serious problems. If our perception of events is shaped by filters, distortions, missing details, and irrelevant information, then the stories we generate would be too simplistic and unrealistic to capture the nuances of the actual situation—or to prepare us adequately for the future. Such misleading stories, however, may still be influential and durable. In *Human, All Too Human*, philosopher Friedrich Nietzsche argues that "partial knowledge is more often victorious than full knowledge: it conceives things as simpler than they are and therefore makes its opinion easier to grasp and more persuasive."[4]

The nature of history itself makes partial knowledge inevitable. When we learn from history, we get to observe the unfolding of just one of many possible outcomes. And what occurred might not even be the most probable version. When it comes to learning from history, the learning environment is, by definition, wicked. In *Everything Is Obvious: Once You Know the Answer*, sociologist Duncan Watts warns that "when we look to the past, we see only the things that happened—not all the things that might have happened but didn't—and as a result, our commonsense explanations often mistake for cause and effect what is really just a sequence of events."[5]

What we see isn't necessarily all there is.

In the story of the triangle and the circle, for example, there may be more than what meets the eye. It may be that the departure of the circle is what prompts the triangle to arrive, so the latter event is actually causing the former. The story could also be probabilistic: one event leads to the other only some of the time, and we simply observed a particular sequence where it happened. Or maybe there is no causation but only correlation: one event happens after the other but not *because* of it.

To make things even more complicated, what if there's no meaningful story? No pushing, no pulling, no pattern, no lesson, no cause, no effect, nothing to predict. What if events from our experience, or from the history we learn, have a large element of randomness? We humans run the real risk of seeing stories when none really exist.

When we interpret random events as meaningful, psychologists say that we are under the spell of a clustering illusion. Author and skeptic Michael Shermer refers to "our tendency of seeing mean-ingful patterns in meaningless noise" as "patternicity," while psy-chiatrist Klaus Conrad named it "apophenia." Generating elaborate stories based on randomness gets a name too; applied statistician and author Nassim Taleb calls it the "narrative fallacy."[6]

It's much easier for us to write a story based on our experience than to ignore it. And when operating under complexity and un-certainty, it's awfully easy to write the *wrong* story. We can thus inadvertently compose, learn from, believe in, act on, and tell others stories that either don't exist or that are severely inaccurate. And once we're hooked on a particular story, it can be hard to change our minds. The lessons learned can stick and determine what we do next.

In the case of bloodletting, for instance, a faulty belief about the cause of illnesses led to the specific treatment. Our subsequent experience, which seemingly reflected an illusory cause-and-effect relationship, reinforced and propagated that wrong story for a long time. On occasion, it drove us to take things too far, harming patients in need and people we loved.

If not handled with care, our experience can make us believe in the wrong causes, expect unrealistic consequences, evaluate per-formances inadequately, make bad investments, reward or punish the wrong people, and fail to prepare us for future risks. Worse, we may not even notice that we are acting upon faulty stories and fail to revise them in a timely and appropriate way. As a result, we may end up solving the wrong problems, using inadequate methods, and failing to achieve our objectives.[7]

Only by acknowledging these potential weaknesses and going beyond the available experience can we identify mechanisms to help us develop more accurate representations of many complicated situations we face. We can even use our storywriting prowess to our advantage by considering these as theories to be questioned and improved, rather than actionable truths, no matter how compelling they may sound. A timely and healthy skepticism regarding our experience-based stories can help us judge which causal links are stronger than others and which may be absent altogether.

Throughout this book, we will feature a wide variety of stories that lie, leading to an illusion of learning as we tackle important decisions in different domains of life. Let us start in this chapter with a few specific examples that will lay the foundation for the chapters to come.

Stories That Discount Randomness

The following events all happened in 2015.[8]

Serena Williams, one of the all-time tennis greats and the world's number-one women's player, was expected to win what's called a "calendar Grand Slam." This happens when a player wins all four of the Grand Slam tournaments in the same year: the Australian Open, the French Open, Wimbledon, and the US Open. It's an exceptional accomplishment, and Williams was dominating the tour at the time. So, she was prominently featured on the cover of *Sports Illustrated's* August 31 issue, under the headline "THE SLAM: All Eyes on Serena."

Then the unexpected happened. In a thrilling semifinal match at the US Open tournament in September, heavy favorite Williams lost to unseeded Roberta Vinci.

Baseball star Daniel Murphy was having a great season for the New York Mets, where he "set a major league record with homers in six straight postseason games and was batting .421 with seven home runs and 11 RBI through 9 games headed into the World Series." So, Murphy was promptly featured on the cover of *Sports Illustrated's* November 2 issue. The headline dubbed him "The Amazin' Murph."

Then the unexpected happened. Murphy's batting performance declined, and he missed a groundball in the eighth inning of the pivotal fourth game of the World Series, which was reportedly one reason that the Mets lost the series to the Kansas City Royals.

Actor Will Smith was nominated for a Golden Globe for his portrayal of forensic pathologist Dr. Bennet Omalu, who had discovered a link between football and brain damage. As this is an important development for the sports world, *Sports Illustrated* featured

Smith and the film *Concussion* on its cover in the December 28 issue, bearing the headline, "Will Smith shines a light on football's darkest corner and the future of America's game."

Then the unexpected happened. Despite the popularity of the film and the praise Smith received for his performance, he was not nominated for an Oscar. In fact, the film was completely excluded from the nominations list for the prestigious event.

All of these incidents happened within a few months and featured a similar sequence of events: Person produces a great performance. Person appears on the cover of *Sports Illustrated*. Person's performance suffers. What emerges is a simple story: the person was jinxed by the cover. The magazine *caused* the failure.

The cover of *Sports Illustrated* is thus cursed, and something bad will happen soon to any athlete or team featured on it. Belief in this so-called *Sports Illustrated* cover jinx is based on this recurring sequence of events, which sports fans have, over the years, repeatedly observed. The most up-to-date resource for the extent of the jinx is its Wikipedia entry, which chronicles hundreds of cases. The magazine itself also explored the phenomenon in their January 2002 issue, which revealed that 37 percent of the covers up to that point (913 out of 2,456 since the first issue in August 1954) had indeed been followed by subsequent and substantial decline in performance.[9]

This is a case where it's particularly easy to generate a simple narrative based on experience. When an athlete or team fails to meet expectations, fans are desperate to understand exactly what happened. After a while, they notice that prior to many disappointments, a magazine cover had featured the athlete or the team in question. There *has* to be a connection. Perhaps the athlete or the team could not cope with the pressure of being publicly named great. Maybe they were distracted by the heightened media scrutiny and the increased adulation from fans. Maybe they got complacent and stopped working hard.

All these scenarios are possible. But let's give those on the cover some credit. Pro athletes work hard to achieve success. Certainly, not many of them would bend that much under pressure and get spoiled that easily. The question, *Why* does going on the cover of *Sports Illustrated* lead to a decline in performance? may not be the correct one to ask. Instead, it would be wiser to begin the investigation into the phenomenon by asking: *When* does an athlete or a team go on the cover of that magazine? The answer: When they are at the very top of their game!

If the magazine does its job right, many of those on the cover would be the best of the best at that moment. The headlines they've been earning by their remarkable achievements have propelled them to that status. There would be little room to improve beyond that extreme point. And if their remarkable achievement is a combination of skill and some events that are outside their control (as it always is in sports and many other walks of life), then there is a good chance that performance will decline toward a relatively more "normal" level the next time around. And although this decline might happen soon after their appearance on the cover, it wouldn't be *caused* by it—it would merely be part of the natural course of events.

In fact, it would have been a bad sign for *Sports Illustrated* if many of those featured on the cover did *not* subsequently do worse. That would mean that the editors were not really doing a good job in identifying and singling out the best performers at their own best. Here, we are dealing not with a jinx but mainly with the statistical phenomenon of regression to the mean, or, as *Sports Illustrated* itself described it, "water seeking its own level."[10]

Of course, one may argue that no harm is done by the existence of such an urban legend. After all, this is a peculiar faulty story about certain rare and extreme events limited to the world of sports.[11]

But this example actually represents a much bigger and widely prevalent phenomenon. Regression to the mean exists in all domains and situations where an outcome is partially determined by luck or random events. The greater the role luck plays in an extreme outcome, the greater the likelihood that events will soon revert to more normal levels. This is, of course, true for both positive and negative extremes. And we care deeply about extreme events across many domains of life—which means that our tendency to overlook the phenomenon of regression to the mean often leads us to craft flawed stories that misidentify the causes and overstate their effects on the outcomes we experience.

In medicine, for example, if a drug or treatment is mostly administered in extreme cases, its curative effects could be overestimated. Bloodletting, in fact, may have benefited from regression effects if some patients opted for it when they felt really bad. Their conditions would have improved after a while anyway, but bleeding got most of the credit along the way. The same is also true for many alternative health therapies, sometimes dubbed snake oil remedies. And, as in the case of the *Sports Illustrated* cover jinx, the right question to ask wouldn't be *Why* does snake oil heal? but *When* would one use snake oil?[12]

Similarly, regression to the mean may cause consultants, in any context, to get more credit than they deserve, especially if they are consulted when the performance of their clients is uncharacteristically poor. Part of the subsequent improvement would be thanks to them and part due to luck, but they would often receive the whole glory.

Any type of evaluation would be incomplete without a consideration of possible regression effects. Suppose a company gives bonuses to its best performers and penalizes its worst. Makes sense ... but regression to the mean would ensure that some of the best will do worse and some of the worst will get better next time, independent of rewards and penalties. Taken at face value, that experience would falsely reinforce the belief that penalties work much better to motivate people, while bonuses are detrimental.[13]

The so-called Peter principle is partly due to regression to the mean as well. It asserts that people "are promoted to their level of incompetence." If people get promoted when their job performance is at or near its best, their subsequent performance is likely to decline due to regression effects.[14]

An analogous situation occurs in leadership changes, too. Managers or administrators who experience a streak of bad performance may be replaced—and the organization's performance may subsequently improve. Yet was this improvement purely because of that change? What if the decline was partly due to particularly unlucky circumstances? Because we never see what would have happened had the change not occurred, this alternative explanation is rarely considered.[15]

In *The Drunkard's Walk*, physicist Leonard Mlodinow offers examples from the movie industry, where producers have been fired because they successively selected several films that did not perform well. Upon the arrival of the new executive, the studio's improvement in performance is considered proof that indeed it was previous management that caused the slump and that the new one was a good choice. Ironically, however, this perception occurs even when the subsequent successes were actually selected by the fired executive and already in the pipeline.[16]

Speaking of the film industry, movie sequels are also cursed by regression effects. It shouldn't really be a surprise if the second installments that are made after an original blockbuster get relatively worse ratings. The bigger the first hit, the more "cursed" will be the follow-up. This doesn't mean that a sequel would be objectively bad, of course, and data suggest that movie sequels tend to generate substantial returns. Hence, there's no risk that we'll have a shortage of them anytime soon.[17]

Ultimately, a faulty understanding of regression to the mean based on experience prompts us to generate the wrong story, which leads us to misplace blame and praise. Why, then, don't we hear much about such possible regression effects around us? Despite its prevalence, the concept is missing from most classroom discussions and journalistic analyses. We never see a headline in the sports or finance section exclaim, "Performance Is Down: Regression to the Mean Strikes Again!"

This is partly because accepting regression effects means assigning a crucial role to chance in important outcomes we experience. We humans aren't comfortable with randomness. We are reluctant to admit that we don't have complete control over the results we work hard or pay good money to obtain. Instead, we make up stories to explain both good performance and bad, hoping that this will enable us to consistently obtain the first and avoid the second.

Discounting the role of chance and reading too much into random fluctuations is only one way stories may mislead. There are more ways in which our experience-based narratives can be at odds with the complex underlying causality. And these don't need to involve extreme events at all.

Stories That Warp Time

When we plant a seed, we don't expect to harvest the fruit immediately. We have to plan things ahead, make the investment, stay the course, and wait for the outcome. We know it'll take time.

When we go to school, we don't get the returns immediately. We have to think about what we'd like to achieve, use our knowledge, make the investment, and build toward an outcome. Education and its benefits, too, take time.

If we wish to have a healthy body, we don't get to achieve it immediately. We have to eat well, commit to regular exercise, make the investment, and gradually reach a certain level of desired fitness. Good health also takes time.

Almost everything worthwhile in life takes will and effort—as well as time. And when a treatment or intervention requires a considerable and uncertain time to show its effects, it becomes easier to get confused about what really caused what.

The economy, for instance, is a complex system where processes are imperfectly understood and often take longer than we'd like to show their effects. If measures are taken by the government and other agencies to improve economic conditions, their consequences won't likely present themselves immediately.

What's more, many policies may need a costly upfront investment to yield desired results later, leading to "worse-before-better" dynamics. For example, if the government seeks to reduce unemployment by adjusting its education policies, any possible consequences of today's costly actions would not be seen for some time. Policy makers and managers plant the seeds, and the fruits take time to grow. Yet, we're often inclined to simplify the story, skipping impatiently over the time required for real change to happen and drawing from experience a story that is drastically shortened and therefore oversimplified.[18]

As a result, we risk reaching false conclusions. If an action does not promptly produce a certain projected consequence, it may be deemed ineffective. When an outcome does emerge, we tend to attribute it to actions taken recently. A newly elected politician can thus easily claim credit for positive changes in economic or social conditions that were in fact initiated by actions of previous administrations. The same goes for a newly hired executive in any type of organization. In fact, the case of movie executives fired (or rewarded) primarily based on the current situation is also an apt example of stories that warp time. We end up making faulty choices if we don't recognize the time it takes for water to find its own level and for extreme situations to regress to the mean.

Generating stories with this sort of flawed sense of time raises a barrier against a better tomorrow. People in positions of authority are usually aware of the human tendency to learn from immediate experience—many of them possibly share it and may act accordingly. To secure their positions and statuses, they are often incentivized to opt for quick fixes that produce fast and predictable results, even though longer-term solutions may be more desirable.

Unless we learn to have our stories accurately reflect the element of time necessary to grow things, we shouldn't really be surprised if we reward and then get stuck with inadequate strategies, time and time again. This may even lead those with executive power to gradually become more shortsighted, as they learn to take advantage of our fallible story-generating prowess.

Like randomness, the time delay between a cause and its effect leads us to embrace false stories that prove to be unhelpful guides to future decisions. But the story doesn't end there . . .

Stories That Overgeneralize

What images, characteristics, and emotions immediately emerge in your mind as you read these words?

Democrat.

Republican.

CEO.

Teenager.

People from [insert a country name here].

People who are [insert a profession here].

Chances are, you didn't have to spend much time and effort to generate a short story for each.

Our intuition likes to save time and energy, so it tends to categorize things and to construct simple stories about each of these categories. The resulting *stereotypes* often feature a set of images, a list of characteristics, and a mix of emotions attached to them.[19]

Many of the stereotypes our brains contain have been imported from the broader culture—from stories, beliefs, assumptions, and attitudes we encounter in our families, in our communities, in our schooling, and in the media. But personal experience is also a stereotype-generating machine. It only takes us one or a few encounters with a particular category of people or a particular type of situation to reach conclusions, develop overarching stories, and incorporate them into our view of reality.

Stereotypes can indeed prove useful. As social psychologist Lee Jussim reports in *Social Perception and Social Reality*, many generalizations can be statistically accurate and guide predictions appropriately when time and information are scarce.[20]

Problems arise, however, when stereotypes based on limited personal experience gloss over relevant nuances and lead to absolute conclusions. Experience also doesn't effectively warn us when stereotypes are unreliable, only partially true, purely subjective, or obsolete. Worse, once stereotypes based on faulty stories take hold, more experience can trap us in them, sometimes against our own best interests.[21]

For example, author Malcolm Gladwell discusses in *Blink* the career problems long faced by female classical musicians. Historical practices, unchallenged traditions, and the personal views of

decision makers created powerful stereotypes defining the characteristics of orchestral instrumentalists—many orchestra leaders
believed that only men could play well enough. As a result, orchestras rarely hired women performers. As economists Claudia
Goldin and Cecilia Rouse observe: "Not only were their numbers
extremely low until the 1970's, but many music directors, ultimately in charge of hiring new musicians, publicly disclosed their
belief that female players had lower musical talent."[22]

For centuries, as a result, many women were denied the opportunity to perform music in public, and many more were likely
discouraged from becoming musicians in the first place. And by
excluding a specific talent pool, orchestras ended up reducing their
ability to achieve their own objective, which was to assemble the
talent needed to perform music of the highest possible quality.

One variant of stereotype is the so-called *halo effect*—our tendency to extrapolate from stereotypical stories based on personal
experience to draw additional unwarranted conclusions about a
given situation. A famous example is the common use of attractiveness as a predictor for other desirable features like reliability and
trustworthiness, despite the lack of any objective or necessary link
between them. Similarly, experts' subjective confidence in themselves is often taken as an indicator of their competence. The halo
effect leads us to assume that someone who looks, acts, and sounds
infallible really is infallible.[23]

In *Moneyball*, author Michael Lewis depicts how confident experts tend to draw erroneous conclusions about how ballplayers will
perform based on irrelevant factors in their physical appearance.
They trust their eyes too much, even if "there was a lot you couldn't
see when you watched a baseball game." They are also quick to
base their predictions about someone's future performance primarily on a few recent observations. Unaware of their own unconscious reliance on stereotypes, scouts may then persist in making
these unreliable judgments for years, actively harming the efforts
of their teams to assemble the best possible roster of talent. And
these self-delusions lead to inefficiencies that can be leveraged and
turned into financial opportunities by others.[24]

It's terribly difficult to get experts like these to recognize the flaws in their own thinking—after all, they can truthfully say that their beliefs are based firmly on their personal experience. These experience-based stories then affect their future choices and thus their subsequent experience, further fueling the initial stereotypes and halo effects. Hence, we can get to a situation where faulty stories based on experience eventually become the reality *because* we generate, believe, and act on them. They become self-fulfilling.

Stories That Self-Fulfill

In the 1999 film *The Matrix*, Neo, the hero, visits the Oracle hoping to uncover the future that awaits him. As he enters the room, the Oracle tells him not to worry about the vase. This sudden warning prompts Neo to flinch and turn anxiously around, causing him to bump into the vase and break it. He apologizes and asks how the Oracle knew what was going to happen.

"What's really going to bake your noodle later on is," the Oracle responds, "would you still have broken it if I hadn't said anything?"[25]

The Oracle's warning caused the very outcome it predicted. It was a *self-fulfilling prophecy*.

The mythical Oedipus is the unwanted son of the king, exiled and abandoned to die because of a prophecy that he would one day kill the king. His banishment, however, becomes the very trigger that leads him to return to the kingdom and kill his father.[26]

In the Harry Potter series (spoiler alert in this paragraph!), the evil Lord Voldemort acts on the prophecy that a young wizard will grow powerful and destroy him. So, he tries to kill baby Harry, whom he believes to be the chosen one. He wipes out Harry's family, but ultimately fails to eliminate his main target. This tragic event then creates the circumstances that lead Harry to eventually become the hero that destroys Voldemort, thus fulfilling the prophecy.[27]

Such convoluted events don't occur only in arts, myths, or literature. They have led to confusion in real life as well. In *The Youngest Science*, physician and essayist Lewis Thomas describes the diagnostic prowess of a certain early twentieth-century doctor,

who enjoyed a reputation for being particularly skilled in diagnosing typhoid fever, a widespread ailment in the New York of
that era.

When examining patients, the physician paid particular attention to the appearance of the tongue, which he scrutinized with
great care, palpating it at length to assess the possibility of disease.
After these inspections, he would often declare the presence of typhoid fever in its earliest stages. In many cases, this prophecy was
proven subsequently and tragically to be right.

Nobody realized, however, that the doctor was actually the agent
responsible for transferring the disease from one person to another.
Unbeknownst to the physician himself, his diagnostic procedure
was the reason many people contracted and eventually died from
typhoid fever. As Thomas writes, "He was a more productive carrier,
using only his hands, than Typhoid Mary."[28]

Both the physician and those who observed his work consistently learned the wrong lesson from the experience. Everyone assumed that the doctor was merely a brilliant diagnostician, failing
to realize that his own behavior ensured the accuracy of his self-
fulfilling predictions. They all got the story fatally wrong.

When those who make predictions are able to act on their expectations and thereby influence the course of events, they can
sometimes end up making their predictions come true. If they lack
awareness of the self-fulfilling nature of their prophecies, more
experience doesn't bring understanding but instead further rein-
forces their misguided belief in their own gifts of foresight.[29]

Self-fulfilling stories can exist across many domains. For example, if some administrators regard certain underprivileged people as lazy, ignorant, or otherwise contemptible and then act on
those stereotyped opinions (consciously or not), their behavior can
deepen the degree to which the underprivileged are trapped in that
situation, further exacerbating the problem.

Business managers with prior opinions about the strengths or
weaknesses of their employees may treat them in ways that reinforce those opinions. They can assign particular workers easier or

harder tasks, provide them with different levels of resources, interpret their accomplishments under different lights, and give varying kinds of positive or negative feedback. Such discriminatory behavior can fuel dysfunctional reactions that may lead, in turn, to future discrimination.[30]

Also, hiring and promotion processes provide the selected employees with opportunities and advantages that are not available to the employees that weren't selected. Hence, when their selections turn out to be successful, managers would be mistaken to attribute this outcome solely to their extraordinary ability to pick and hire talented employees and promote the right people.

Some people believe that, overall, they are good at judging others quickly. They pride themselves on their ability to accurately assess another person's character and abilities after a brief meeting. Yet such confidence can be based on a self-fulfilling story. If the way they treat others depends on their first impressions and pre-existing stereotypes, then their behavior can help make their own assessment come true. If they like someone the minute they meet him or her, they may go out of their way to treat that person well—eliciting behavior in response that is likeable and friendly. "I knew it all along!" is the self-congratulatory conclusion.

Every time this cycle is repeated with a new acquaintance, the same story is reinforced: "I've always had a sharp eye for what people are really like!" It's a simple and pleasing thing to believe about oneself—and very likely inaccurate.

Luckily, self-fulfilling prophecies don't happen all the time, and they may not always cause harm. But, when they do, experience doesn't adequately alert their presence and can further reinforce their lessons rather than challenging them. Such events also tend to evolve at a slow pace, continuously boosting one's personal convictions. This makes it even harder to doubt the lessons of experience. But if we don't doubt them, we can't realize we have a problem. Hence, we run the danger of increasingly believing that we possess oracle-like abilities for diagnosing situations and judging other people.

Crafting Truer Stories:
Story Skeptics and Story Scientists

We humans are indeed remarkably capable of generating stories based on what we experience. It's a practice so deeply ingrained in us that we carry it out almost unconsciously. It thus becomes crucial to recognize when the stories we spin from our experience are deceptive due to oversimplifications, flawed perceptions of cause and effect, and misleading overgeneralizations.

What can we humans do to transform our innate gift for storytelling from a potential weakness into a more consistent and reliable strength? A first step is to become a *story skeptic*. This simply entails not falling in love with the stories that we immediately and impulsively produce based on experience. Unfortunately, it's easier said than done.

Have you ever written an actual story, crafted a love letter, drafted a speech, built a structure out of Legos, created a tune in your mind, or sculpted an object out of clay? We bet you really liked it afterward. We like what we create. And that applies to the stories we generate from experience. To doubt those stories is tantamount to doubting ourselves.

Storytelling also has persuasive and team-building properties. The ability to craft evocative and convincing stories and to share them in elegant and vivid prose is often touted as an important skill for leaders and entrepreneurs. Yet the attractiveness of a story does not guarantee its accuracy. In fact, the relationship could be negative, especially when stories reach levels that are too good to be true.[31]

Although relying on stories as depictions of realities can be useful and appropriate in simple situations and predictable circumstances, those we apply to important decisions in life, work, politics, and other complex fields can be deceptively misleading.

As a remedy, we suggest using the human tendency to fall in love with neat, elegant, and simplistic stories as a trigger. If a particular story is *too* attractive—too powerful, too convincing, too magnetic—that should be a cause for alarm, not inspiration. It's likely that a more complex reality lurks behind the story. Particularly if we feel tempted to base any significant decision on the lesson conveyed by a persuasive story, we would be better off looking twice before we leap and be on the lookout for the kinds of storytelling pitfalls outlined in this chapter.

The cover of a magazine causing the decline of an elite athlete? Probably not.

The leader who quickly fixed a complex problem with a simple action? Not likely.

We are great judges of other people based on our first impressions? Doubtful.

Of course, like any thinking strategy, story skepticism can be carried too far. Historians of science, bemused by the many faulty stories and theories that were widespread merely a hundred years ago, sometimes adopt a hyperskeptical attitude that has been called "the pessimistic meta-induction from the history of science." That is, will our current stories be judged and exposed in a hundred years in a similar way? Taken to its limit, this type of skepticism can become counterproductive. We may start to think that we are always getting things wrong anyway. So why even bother to search for truth?[32]

But in moderate doses, story skepticism can be a powerful tool, leading to subsequent discoveries fueled by consistent curiosity. Story skepticism is about asking questions, being willing to revise assumptions, and constantly seeking to identify which of the causal links we perceive through experience should be embraced and which need further scrutiny. The story skeptic sees narratives as routes to better understanding experience, rather than definitive shortcuts to truth.

In *Being Wrong*, journalist and author Kathryn Schulz argues that, through such constructive story skepticism, we can transform a pessimistic meta-induction into an optimistic one. We develop a constant urge to improve our stories to more closely approximate reality and thereby improve our important decisions, particularly through the analysis of the lessons we draw from experience using scientific methods.[33]

The story skeptic then naturally evolves into a *story scientist*—a decision maker who treats the lessons of experience as theories to be investigated through experimentation where possible.

Experimentation, however, doesn't come naturally to humans. The more our experience seems to reinforce a story, the more deeply we believe in it, and the more reluctant we are to challenge it through testing. Even highly educated experts are likely to feel this way, as the story of bloodletting reminds us.

To counteract this innate tendency, it's helpful to adopt a counterbias—a readiness to test assumptions when circumstances allow. In *The Why Axis*, economists Uri Gneezy and John List advocate the use of randomized controlled experiments as a means of moving "beyond anecdotes and urban legends" in social and economic decisions. We can have a clearer idea about how causality really works only by changing a key part of our stories for a representative sample within a larger group and then carefully tracking the effects of this change on the outcomes we experience. This is a nutshell description of the experimental method that is at the heart of most important scientific discoveries. With a bit of ingenuity, it can be applied to situations in everyday life.[34]

For instance, most leading orchestras have found a way to apply the experimental method to overcome the faulty stories that led to the exclusion of women. First, instead of relying on the judgment of one man during a hiring audition, multiple members of the orchestra were appointed as judges to minimize the impact of individual biases. Second, applicants' names were replaced with numbers to hide their genders. Third, a curtain was placed between judges and applicants to remove irrelevant visual cues. Such simple but effective testing protocols help orchestra managers set aside the faulty and self-fulfilling stories that biased their decisions. The result: many of the world's leading orchestras today feature a higher percentage of women instrumentalists than ever before.

Unfortunately, conducting such experiments may not always be possible. For instance, the event may not be repeated. It may involve a one-off decision. Because we can't observe parallel universes where different choices are made, we're forced to rely on other methods of thinking that would help reveal the things that we *don't* get to experience (often called *counterfactuals*).

Counterfactual thinking is about asking what-if questions. What would be the effect, were the supposed cause absent? What would have happened had a decision maker done things differently? Would a given outcome occur all the time? If not, what do the data suggest about its probability? What kinds of new information would confirm a given story? What sorts of evidence would refute it?[35]

In *Farsighted*, author Steven Johnson reviews the possible roles of various forms of counterfactual thinking, including scenario planning, simulations, and the appointment of a devil's advocate to espouse otherwise-ignored narratives. All these are practices that people can use to map out their knowledge and experience while preparing to make important decisions. They force decision makers to imagine alternative explanations to their current situations and different predictions about what might happen in the future. They all induce a timely and healthy dose of story skepticism, coupled with the objective research and imaginative rethinking that a story scientist would employ. The aim is to motivate people to challenge experience-fueled convictions and to prevent faulty causal stories from becoming superstitions and traditions.[36]

For example, just to provide an alternative story to its cover jinx, *Sports Illustrated* could demonstrate that it can do more than curse athletes and teams. It can, in fact, *charm* them as well. Consider a design where the magazine, along with the best of the best, sets out to identify the most disappointing athletes and teams at any given time—NFL teams that were seemingly bound for the Super Bowl that ended up with losing records and high-flying pro golfers who suddenly lost their putting stroke and missed the cut in a string of tournaments. These "failures" could then be featured on the inside back cover of the magazine. What would happen to them in subsequent weeks and months? The test would have to be conducted in reality to know for sure. But the phenomenon of regression to the mean suggests that a healthy share of these failures would bounce back to see their performances improve. Fans and pundits would begin talking about the "*Sports Illustrated* back-cover charm."

Another way the would-be story scientist can test the validity of stories is by taking advantage of the new availability of tools for gathering and analyzing statistical evidence—*big data*, as it's generally called.

We earlier quoted Michael Lewis's *Moneyball* for its analysis of how baseball scouts have historically been misled by flawed stories when analyzing athletes' skills. In baseball and other sports, the use of statistical analysis to measure the real skills of athletes and optimizing strategies have recently transformed the nature of competition. In today's sports world, the familiar old stories told by grizzled scouts and experts based on their individual experience are being replaced by new, more accurate evaluations shaped by computer-aided statistical analysis.

So, are we approaching a time when machines can do all our learning and thinking using big data? Should we trust machines to generate stories in the first place and interpret the world for us?

In *The Book of Why*, computer scientist Judea Pearl and author Dana Mackenzie discuss how machines do indeed excel in finding patterns in vast amounts of data and in making predictions based on that information. But they cannot generate intricate causal stories, as they don't know *why* some patterns and combinations of variables lead to better predictions than others. It still falls on us humans to identify possible causes and effects, detect inaccuracies in them, and resort to data when needed. Hence, we can strive to ask the right questions when learning from experience, and machines can then help us test them.[37]

When it comes to self-fulfilling prophecies, for instance, we can try to determine how much a given situation is conceptually different from one where self-fulfilling prophecies are practically impossible.

One such domain is meteorology. This is a complex field, but it's a relatively kind learning environment, as meteorologists can always learn the right lessons from feedback. They predict the weather, and then observe what happens. Unless some of them have developed special powers to influence environmental conditions, their predictions cannot affect future weather. As a result, their stories can't be self-fulfilling. So, whenever we learn from the outcome of a prediction we made, we could ask: Is this activity like meteorology? Or is this a situation where we can partly influence how our predictions play out?

Leading, governing, managing, hiring, and meeting new people are not meteorology. Once we realize that they are not, we can then investigate what role we might have played in the outcomes we experienced and thereby avoid the risk of being deceived by a self-fulfilling prophecy.

What's Missing? What's Irrelevant?

As storytelling creatures, we humans habitually use stories to help us understand cause and effect: What happens in a given situation and why? Stories are a powerful way to summarize, share, and remember the lessons of experience. But, under complexity and uncertainty, stories tend to oversimplify or distort reality, leading us to make flawed decisions.

Irrelevant patterns in randomness. We love to identify "causes" even when dealing with phenomena that are random or shaped by factors too complex to identify. As a result, we may end up learning and reinforcing a lesson that doesn't really exist.

Missing element of time. Our experience-based stories tend to underestimate the time it takes for things to take effect. Delays between causes and consequences complicate making valid inferences, misplacing rewards and punishments.

Irrelevant overgeneralizations. It's easy to develop false stereotypes and inaccurate halos based on our limited personal experience. Yet, in the real world of highly variable and rapidly changing circumstances, such overgeneralizations often risk being unreliable and obsolete.

Irrelevant self-fulfillments. At times, we can fulfill our own expectations and predictions by acting on them. Failing to consider this possibility can bias the way we see our own decision-making prowess. To detect possible self-fulfilling prophecies, it's good to ask: Is this like meteorology?

Missing counterfactuals. It pays to question immediately emerging, experience-based stories. But it's more constructive to be a story skeptic than a story cynic, as it can help us become a story scientist. This approach would involve using experiments, counterfactual thinking, and data to challenge and test the premises underlying existing narratives and formulate new ones that are more complete and accurate.

The urge to turn experience into stories, and then to codify those stories into lessons that control our future behavior, is powerful. But we can also transform this storytelling instinct from a dangerous pitfall into an effective method of getting close to the world's complex and elusive realities.

2

LOST INSIGHTS

When Experience Limits Creative Potential

THINK OF A POPULAR AND SUCCESSFUL IDEA.

Harry Potter is one example. So is Google. The personal computer is another one. There would be little disagreement that these are massively popular and acclaimed creative concepts that have helped to shape the life and culture of the twenty-first century.

Now try to list various factors behind the success of whatever idea you thought of. There will inevitably be many reasons. Notice the surprising ease with which you are able to come up with them.

The Harry Potter books, for example, transport us to a magical world, telling the tale of an underdog hero who grows and develops together with the reader. Audiences of all ages can find something for themselves in this saga: friendship, adventure, struggle, love, hate, good, evil. The whole series is well written, with elements of suspense, thrills, wonder, and humor. The author J. K. Rowling's own quest for success as a single mother and a long-struggling writer is inspiring. And the list goes on . . .

Google's search engine lets us find exactly what we are looking for on the web in a matter of seconds. From this simple yet incredibly powerful service, Google has expanded into offering a wide variety of essential online services, from email and storage space in the cloud to marketing and advertising tools, document creation and sharing, mapping tools for travelers, and much more. And the list goes on . . .[1]

The modern PC is indispensable and ubiquitous. The graphical user interface, with its intuitive icons, its easy navigation via clicks and links, and the mouse or trackpad that puts it all within easy fingertip reach, can be mastered by anyone from a small child to a retiree. Coupled with the Internet, the PC makes accessible a world of communication, information, entertainment, and experience that includes music, imagery, literature, art, video, science, and personal connections, redefining how people around the world work, play, and communicate. And the list goes on . . .

All these reasons feel obvious given our experience with these ideas. They emerge without effort. In fact, this is true for any popular and successful idea. We can often understand, analyze, explain, and communicate creative success stories with relative ease, and so, we should strive to learn from them.

Great! What can go wrong?

Unfortunately, such experience with innovative ideas ends up distorting our intuitions about creativity, thereby hurting our own creative potential.

To find out how this happens, travel back to a time when that experience didn't exist, to the moment when each of these ideas had been conceived but had not yet revealed its prominence. And try to imagine what most experienced professionals in the domain would have felt when they first heard about the idea. Surely, if multiple reasons for the popularity and success of an idea are that obvious to us now, many of these same reasons ought to have been immediately evident to such experts. Their experience should have helped them better foresee the eventual outcome, make better decisions, and profit.

Not really.

Whatever the idea you were thinking of at the beginning of this chapter, the more innovative and creative it was, the more likely that it clashed with people's experience in that field. And this clash ensured that the idea was rejected or ignored by many experts in the field, right before the moment it hit big.[2]

Publishers did not line up at the entrance of the café in Edinburgh where part of the first Harry Potter book was written. Instead, Harry Potter got relentlessly rejected, not once, not twice, but about a dozen times, by reputable editors and publishers who stood to gain a worldwide reputation and make a fortune from the ultimate success of the series. Not even the publisher who eventually accepted the book was sanguine about its prospects. The London-based publisher Bloomsbury reportedly paid J. K. Rowling a modest advance and printed a mere five hundred copies of *Harry Potter and the Philosopher's Stone*. (Those rare first edition copies are now worth some thousands of dollars each.) Experience in publishing was a poor guide to the amazing potential of Harry Potter.[3]

In the late 1990s, when Sergey Brin and Larry Page came up with the search methodology behind Google, the Internet giants of the era agreed to meet with them. These investors and experts, who were driving the market for web search at that time, had the opportunity to bid for the idea that would soon put them out of business and dominate the scene for decades to come. Google would be worth billions of dollars in just a few years, becoming one of the most valuable companies worldwide.[4]

But when the founders of Google asked them to pay $1.6 million for their technology, the offer was promptly refused by every potential buyer. Experience in Internet and search technology was a poor guide to the amazing potential of Google. Even Google's own visionary creators must not have fully appreciated its promise, since they would have been willing to let it go for a tiny fraction of what it would be worth in a few years.

Back in the late 1970s, when the Palo Alto Research Center (PARC), one of the R&D departments of the document technology giant Xerox, designed the first personal computer with a graphical user interface, including a mouse and interactive icons on its screen, top management of the company did not celebrate the invention. Rather than moving quickly to commercialize the project and use it to achieve dominance of the emerging marketing for computers, they treated it as a mere curiosity. They even demonstrated it in detail to a group of outsiders that included a young Steve Jobs—who proceeded to adapt its key innovations in the first Apple computers. Experience in business machines was a poor guide to the amazing potential of the modern personal computer.[5]

But let's be fair to Xerox. A generation earlier, they'd been brilliantly foresighted about a previous technological breakthrough. When physicist and patent attorney Chester Carlson first developed photocopying technology in the 1940s, Xerox was the only company that saw the idea's potential, after dozens of big, powerful business machine manufacturers, including GE and IBM, declined. Experience in business technology, it turns out, was a poor guide to the amazing potential of photocopying.[6]

The Xerox case also suggests that experience in identifying a groundbreaking technology in the past does not guarantee the ability to identify another groundbreaking technology when it presents itself. And in this case, the personal computer with a graphical user interface did not present itself to Xerox. It was Xerox that pioneered it.

Thus, in the context of creativity, our learning environment is wicked. Experience in a given domain doesn't endow us with an ability to recognize the potential of new ideas. Innovations in any field can bring about disruptive changes that contradict the lessons taught by the past, rendering experience unreliable.[7]

But poor foresight based on experience due to a discrepancy between past and future is only part of the problem. There's also the issue of missing details on how ideas evolve that further mystifies perceptions on how an innovative idea actually comes about.

Many of the particulars and processes involved as ideas become popular and successful are crucially missing from the experience of consumers of those ideas. The "overnight success" becomes legendary—the preceding months or years of painstaking collaboration, experimental stumbling, failure, and redesign tend to be hidden from view. As a result, we often fail to appreciate that creativity, innovation, and entrepreneurship are more complex and unpredictable than they seem to be. This, in turn, adversely affects the way we design our innovative processes in schools, offices, and social lives, which can perpetually limit our creativity.

We are worse judges but better creators of ideas than our experience suggests. Once we recognize the different ways experience can get in the way of recognizing opportunities and generating ideas, we can hope to devise mechanisms to harness its powers rather than fall into its traps.

Failures of Foresight When Judging Ideas

The less the past resembles the future, the less useful experience about that past will be for predicting what may lie ahead. Given that innovation itself is a main driver of the difference between past and future, the more groundbreaking an idea, the less likely its future impact can be assessed accurately based on what happened in the past.

Consequently, many creative projects are bound to be rejected by gatekeepers with poor foresight. We've seen a few examples of how this works—Harry Potter, Google, the modern PC, and photocopying. But there are many others.

The founders of the leading online accommodation-sharing platform Airbnb recently published the rejection letters they received from five potential investors. All five felt that the idea didn't have much potential. Two others didn't even respond.[8]

Every experienced investor has at least a few such errors of judgment in his or her past, though most are reluctant to publicize them. One exception is Bessemer Venture Partners (BVP), which valiantly features its "Anti-Portfolio" on its corporate website. The page lists the investments BVP decided to pass on after careful consideration. These include Apple, eBay, Facebook, FedEx, Google, Intel, PayPal, and Tesla. Experienced investors felt that these ideas weren't really destined to succeed—shortly before they became successful.[9]

The situation is actually even grimmer than these scattered examples would suggest. We only know about the companies that became successful despite being rejected. What about the ideas with potential that were not pursued after being turned down? Countless such "failures" are missing from our observation—and therefore they don't become part of available experience. And what about ideas that were accepted and funded, which then failed soon after? In most cases, both the creators of those ideas and the investors who supported them are happy to bury those stories. As a result, many such "successes" that never really succeeded are also missing from our experience.

These distortions inevitably lead us to overly glorify the ideas that were eventually successful. We thus end up ignoring the reality that the visible successes may not be so different from many previous failures.

In fact, as we've seen, creators themselves are not immune to poor foresight. Not even visionaries like Google and Xerox could clearly see the potential of their own ideas. It happens that these two companies still prospered—but what about other creators who had several initial ideas but didn't develop the one with the highest potential? Recent research suggests that we are not really good at prioritizing among our own projects.[10]

One famous example is Kodak, which pioneered the digital camera in 1975. But Kodak managers didn't prioritize this project. Instead, they relied too much on their experience in analog photography as they assessed the potential of this new technology and the speed with which it would take over the market. Not only did they miss out on an opportunity, but they also ended up suffering massive losses as victims of a technology they themselves had invented.

For all these reasons, experience based on our observations and knowledge of the past is an unreliable guide for judging how an innovative idea might shape the future.

To alleviate the problem of poor foresight, some creative industries have started to seek ways to reduce the influence of experienced gatekeepers. For example, there has been an explosion of self-publishing, where new digital outlets allow the consumers to decide a book's potential rather than leaving the decision about whether to publish in the hands of a few editors. Platforms like DADA.nyc and Choon have been experimenting with blockchain infrastructures to decentralize such judgments for artists and musicians. Crowdfunding websites are also giving would-be entrepreneurs access to small sums of investment money from hundreds of thousands of people, making it possible for them to launch products or businesses without relying on professional investors. By bypassing the experience-shaped intuitions of a few selected decision makers, creators in all these fields are attempting to gain more control over their fates.

Undervaluing Processes When Judging Ideas

We know in great detail about the evolution of the Harry Potter franchise after the popularity of the first book. We have a good idea about what happened after Google set up their website for the first time. And many of us have personally witnessed the explosive growth of the personal computer industry. Lessons from experience highlight with extreme clarity all the events that happen after an idea becomes widely popular and successful. Final achievements feel vivid, inevitable, and obvious in hindsight. But that's just the visible tip of the iceberg. The rest is largely hidden from observation.

What was the initial concept? How did it evolve over time? Who was involved, and how did they contribute to that evolution? The lessons of experience gloss over these specifics, which actually make up most of the creative processes. Ideas almost never stay the same as when they were first imagined. Failure to acknowledge the complexity of their development biases our perceptions about creativity and what really pushes certain ideas to their highest potential.

Take Pixar. The success of their animations is undeniable. They have been producing blockbuster after blockbuster, revolutionizing a whole industry. No doubt about that. But are their ideas really great?[11]

Imagine hearing the concept for a film that involves a rodent cooking gourmet French food by pulling the hair of a clumsy fellow. Does that sound like a blockbuster success? We'd bet that most of the people who actually liked the 2007 animation *Ratatouille* would have been skeptical of the idea's potential. The same goes for the adventures of a grumpy old man whose house is flying with the help of party balloons (*Up*, 2009), or a speechless box-like robot that collects garbage on a now-abandoned Earth (*WALL-E*, 2008).[12] These may not sound like great screenplay ideas at first sight. They took their impressive Oscar-worthy final forms through a meticulous creative process that the audiences didn't get to experience and that a superficial glance at the creative genius of Pixar tends to obscure.[13]

This is why Ed Catmull, computer scientist and the former president of Pixar and Walt Disney Animation Studios, argues that ideas don't matter nearly as much as the processes they subsequently go through. It's not trivial to build and maintain a work environment where people with different skills can perform together in harmony, communicate openly with one another, improve upon each other's ideas, prevent problems before they occur, and learn the right lessons from past projects. Pixar's real achievement lies in creating and nurturing that intricate ecosystem.[14]

Yet most of us don't observe that part of the iceberg. Instead, our experience with creativity generally leads us to inappropriately glorify the ultimate successful outcomes and a few flashy creators, discounting the importance of the underlying complex and iterative processes conducted by scores of innovative individuals and risk-taking entrepreneurs. But without those processes, the ideas that we love wouldn't exist.

What happens before an idea reaches popularity and success is often missing from experience, while what happens after gets constantly highlighted. As a result, creativity can seem more mysterious and exclusive than it actually is, which in turn can hurt our own motivation to create and develop ideas.

Going beyond the lessons of experience would instead suggest that we might not be that much less gifted than those associated with groundbreaking ideas. So, we shouldn't worry much about how our ideas would be judged. Instead, we should concentrate on designing and implementing better creative processes.

Illusions of Originality When Creating Ideas

Suppose you are trying to solve a problem that might eventually lead to a new enterprise, a new method, or a new product. You may be interested in designing an app that helps people learn something new, a system that improves the performance of employees in a company, or a service that will help people solve a common problem quickly and easily. What's key is that you are trying to do things in a new way. You want to ensure that your innovation is unprecedented. It has to be yours; it has to be original.

But as you research the subject, you realize that the issue has been explored and solved by others before you. Nothing you come up with seems to be truly original. It's quite a disappointment— and it leaves you feeling rather depressed and inadequate.

Yet, when creating any idea or solution, how relevant should originality be? The notion of originality implies that the origin of the idea is central to the process. The creator should be a main source of insight, thus strive to conjure up something that others have yet to imagine. The lessons of experience further reinforce this view, as we constantly observe the flashy outcomes of some selected visionary creators.

But the fact is that most of the world's important unsolved problems are quite complicated, and typically a large number of people are simultaneously and independently working on them. The more complicated the problem, the less likely one's personal experience and knowledge will be enough to solve it in an original manner.

The assumption that originality is essential to creativity creates a false constraint on would-be problem solvers. It pushes them to rely mainly or exclusively on their own perspectives. Under a regime that requires such an approach, the discoveries of others are needlessly discounted. Creators feel the need to reinvent certain aspects of the solution that may have already been invented and improved upon by other specialists.

As a result, an overemphasis on originality, though seemingly supported by our experience with creative ideas around us, is actually countercreative. R&D practitioners and other creativity experts have even given this tendency various names, including the "not-invented-here syndrome" and the "let's-reinvent-the-wheel syndrome." Whatever you call it, it leads people to needlessly ignore or reject worthwhile innovations merely because someone else thought of them first.

In *The Little Book of Plagiarism*, jurist and author Richard Posner discusses how people have been borrowing ideas from others throughout history. He mentions how, in Shakespeare's time, creativity was more associated with imitation and improvement rather than with originality.[15] In fact, psychologist and author Adam Grant observes in *Originals* that "nothing is completely original, in the sense that our ideas are influenced by what we learn from the world around us. We are constantly borrowing thoughts, whether intentionally or inadvertently." He thus considers originality as "introducing and advancing an idea that's relatively unusual within a particular domain, and that has the potential to improve it."[16]

Similarly, in his documentary series *Everything Is a Remix*, Kirby Ferguson explores the extent to which everything around us is an intricate reshaping and redesigning of what came before. He shows that a wide variety of groundbreaking ideas and solutions couldn't have existed had they not been based on previous insights.[17]

Examples are legion. Yes, Gutenberg's printing press was revolutionary. But the components used to create the first mechanical printing machines had existed for many years.

Cars and the assembly lines that led to their mass production for the first time were not really invented by Henry Ford. The various elements of the modern assembly line had been devised by other engineers and entrepreneurs at various times over the preceding century. But Ford managed to combine these in the most effective way, which eventually led to the Model T and the transformation of the automobile from a custom-built luxury good into a standardized product that millions of ordinary people could afford.

Edison's light bulb wasn't the first one, but it was an improvement on many designs that had come before and it was the most commercially viable. On the other hand, Edison did invent the phonograph, which in its original design was not of much use. But other inventors, including Alexander Graham Bell and Emile Berliner, improved it to become the first gramophone, thereby ensuring the eventual fame of the Beatles and Beyoncé.[18]

These examples represent the norm for groundbreaking ideas: most of their main components and mechanisms are not necessarily new. Great innovators are usually those who carefully adopt others' insights and combine or transform them in ways that generate novel solutions to pressing problems.

Isaac Newton, one of the most creative thinkers of all time, expressed this notion in a famous letter when he wrote: "If I have seen further it is by standing on the shoulders of Giants." And to make this eloquent point he actually borrowed that notion from a text that had been published five centuries earlier—only making it better.[19]

Compatible with Newton's wisdom and Ferguson's analysis, entrepreneur and author David Kord Murray discusses in *Borrowing Brilliance* the process of benefiting from others' experiences when innovating. He argues that one of the important aspects of such knowledge transfer is distance.[20]

If one borrows from nearby—a close competitor, for example—one can be blamed for stealing. When Windows adapted the Mac's design for its graphical user interface, Apple sued for copyright infringement. Led Zeppelin, one of the most influential rock bands of all time, was accused of borrowing melodies and lyrics from other musicians without always providing appropriate attribution.[21]

But if one borrows from far away—another domain of knowledge, for example—one can be hailed as a creative genius. Charles Darwin's ideas on evolution were inspired by the works of Charles Lyell and James Hutton, who were geologists. Google's initial PageRank algorithm analyzed the links to a web page to determine its relative importance, a system similar to the counting of academic citations to measure the intellectual value of a work of scholarship.[22]

While originality depends on our limited personal experience, creativity doesn't really have to. Accordingly, to be able to borrow others' insights and experiences legitimately and effectively, we may need to divert our attention away from the problem we are focusing on, scanning the distant horizon for fresh connections and hidden opportunities. Our experience, however, may also get in the way of such creative exploration by affecting the rigidity of our focus.

Tunnel Vision When Creating Ideas

Could more experience and familiarity in a certain field hinder us in noticing unexpected opportunities by rendering our focus and methods less flexible? The answer is not straightforward.

Our attention is a limited resource. This can cause so-called *inattentional blindness*—a phenomenon in which we observe something with intense focus, often heightened by experience, but miss a visible detail because we are not specifically looking for it. This concept was made famous by psychologists Daniel J. Simons and Christopher F. Chabris through their invisible gorilla experiment.[23]

In that study, participants are asked to view a video in which two groups of students wearing different colored shirts are passing basketballs. Their task is to count the number of passes made by one of the groups. Midway through this exercise, a person in a gorilla outfit walks across the screen and even makes gestures to the camera. It turns out that most participants count the passes correctly, and yet many fail to notice the gorilla. They are simply not looking for it.

The opposite also seems to be true. We have asked people attending our workshops to look for the gorilla as it passes through the screen (while also counting the basketball passes). As a result, they had more difficulty counting the number of passes correctly. Focusing on one detail hides the other.[24]

In follow-up studies, researchers showed that people with experience and expertise in basketball are actually more likely to notice the gorilla even as they accurately count the passes. Compared to novices, they seem to be able to focus more freely beyond the specific task. So, in some circumstances, experience may actually help us flex our focus and recognize unexpected details. Good news. But does it always work? What happens when we're confronted with a real problem?[25]

A recent experiment compared groups of radiologists and non-radiologists. Both groups viewed stacks of lung screenings with a small black-and-white gorilla figure drawn on some of the scans. Thankfully, radiologists were much better than novices in spotting cancerous tissues. They were also better at spotting the gorilla, but not by much: twenty out of twenty-four experts missed the gorilla as they inspected the scans for cancer. Eye tracking further revealed that many did so despite looking at the area featuring the gorilla.[26]

How do these studies shed light on the nature of focus in relationship to creativity?

When we're engaged in a creative endeavor—whether it involves artistic imagination, problem solving, or resolving a dilemma—our breadth of focus is continually being tested by the intrusion of "gorillas." These are not literal animals but rather unexpected connections or unforeseen opportunities that could help to shed fresh light on the creative challenge. Experimental results suggest that more experience in a given domain may help broaden our focus and thereby increase the chances that we'll make a serendipitous discovery—but that result is far from guaranteed.[27]

What's more, there are at least two other ways experience can work against creative insights by making our focus more rigid.

One is our tendency toward what's called *functional fixedness*, which refers to becoming psychologically committed to the ways in which certain objects or tools are primarily used. The most famous example involves an experiment in which people are asked to attach a candle to a wall using a bunch of miscellaneous items delivered to them in a cardboard box—string, thumbtacks, matches, and so on. It's not intuitive to realize that the box in which the items were delivered could also serve as a platform to support the candle. Functional fixedness makes it easy for us to overlook that a specific object can have a variety of functions.[28]

Especially in domains that change quickly, if experience makes us focus exclusively on particular aspects or functions of things, we can fail to adapt effectively. In a world where ideas can have wildly unexpected consequences, the usual ways we think and behave can prevent us from noticing the unexpected as an opportunity. Thus, a laser-sharp focus on the things that experience has trained us to concentrate on may prevent us from realizing the full potential of ideas.

Experience can further limit our inventiveness by generating so-called *competency traps*. In their study on learning from experience, management scholars Hazhir Rahmandad, Nelson Repenning, and John Sterman explain that "repetition and practice build competence, but can also impede exploration of untried and possibly better options through habit, inertia, and, paradoxically, through improvement itself."

As we get better at something, the opportunity cost of experimentation and trying out alternative solutions inevitably increases. But if the environment changes rapidly and dramatically, we may be stuck with our experience-based routines and expertise, reducing our long-term performance. Such traps can make adaptation more difficult by "turning core capabilities into core rigidities."[29]

In many circumstances, inattentional blindness, functional fixedness, and specialized competency all have important advantages. They render decisions efficient and effective. And they all get reinforced with more experience.

But there are important trade-offs. These tendencies can also restrict creativity. When the lessons of experience are learned too well, they can make us oblivious to creative opportunities by narrowing our focus, limiting us to the familiar functions of objects and ideas, and trapping us in our competency by making exploration more costly.

Uncovering Insights:
Some Time and Space for Autonomy

There's no doubt that some amount of familiarity with a problem or a task is indispensable to come up with novel solutions and valuable improvements. J. K. Rowling had been writing for many years before the first Harry Potter was finally published. Those years of honing her craft helped her develop the skills that enabled her to write a book with characters, themes, and settings that millions of fans would love. Similarly, the technology experts who developed the graphical user interface at Xerox PARC and the Google search engine were using skills sharpened through previous careers of study and experimentation. Experience can increase our creativity—provided we use it, organize it, and think about it in optimal ways.

How, then, can we optimize our experience for creativity?

To identify the problems we care about, come up with better solutions by adding others' experiences to our own, and regulate our focus to recognize unexpected opportunities, we need some time and space that we can manage autonomously. Ideally, this should also involve the ability to set our own goals, explore different ideas, and receive personal feedback. Then things can get really interesting.

Have you ever lost your sense of time and space while engaging in an activity you enjoy? Completely forgot to check your phone or your messages? This can occur while playing sports, engaging in an artistic pursuit, or even writing an intimate letter to a loved one. If you've had this sensation, you've experienced what psychologist Mihály Csíkszentmihályi originally called *flow*.[30]

Flow happens in situations where one has a high interest in a demanding task that provides frequent and accurate feedback across time. It has been studied in a wide variety of situations, most notably in sports, where athletes can achieve extreme levels of concentration and performance. It's also widely considered the pinnacle of the creative process. Psychologists link flow to higher life satisfaction and refer to it as *optimal experience*. Flow is the sort of experience that nurtures creativity. And it happens most often when people are deeply engaged in an activity for which they feel an intense passion.

In *The Element*, education scholar Ken Robinson and author Lou Aronica explore the lives of individuals who have managed to find a major passion in life (their element), which they have been pursuing happily ever since. They show how successful creative people from different backgrounds, such as songwriter Paul McCartney, comic actor and author John Cleese, cartoonist Matt Groening, dancer and choreographer Gillian Lynne, and musician Mick Fleetwood, were not necessarily good students or considered creative by their educators. They were clearly talented but also fortunate to have discovered and honed their abilities and passions in life often despite facing resistance from institutions they attended.[31]

Robinson and Aronica quote Nobel laureate economist Paul Samuelson, who says that we should "never underestimate the vital importance of finding early in life the work that for you is play. This turns possible underachievers into happy warriors." Success is still not guaranteed, but the quest becomes more personal, interesting, and enjoyable.

Unfortunately, however, many of us haven't had much time and space to look for, discover, and pursue our various passions in the first place, even if doing so would have made us better at what we currently do, whether as students, artists, scientists, employees, or entrepreneurs. Such a vital exploration, which often requires experimentation, trial, error, rejection, and failure, is missing from many people's experience, to the detriment of not only their creative potential but their overall happiness as well.

One strategy to counter this problem is to provide some personal time and space in the settings where we seek to be creative, including in our social lives, in our jobs, and in the classroom. People would be free to use (or not to use) that time and space for detecting problems, trying things out, noticing connections, and making serendipitous discoveries. To accomplish this, the administrators of these environments (teachers, managers, owners) would need to yield some control over their operations to encourage the unexpected opportunities that would emerge, while still keeping most of the established operation intact. That's tricky, but it's possible.[32]

Years ago, one of us (the authors) participated regularly in aikido classes. Training sessions in this martial art involved people with a wide range of proficiency, from masters to novices. Except for those wearing black belts, the differences in levels among students were not immediately evident.

The class provided an unexpected lesson. At first sight, things looked quite ordinary. We were all in a spacious dojo, aiming to learn from a master of the domain (our *sensei*, or teacher) and also from one another. When the session started, however, something unusual happened: nobody in class, including the instructor, was talking.

In aikido, you redirect an attacker's momentum to use their aggression against them. Its logic is beautiful. But to be effective, all the parts of a move need to work in sync, or else the redirection breaks down and the momentum is lost. One has to understand and then apply the techniques carefully until, over time, they become second nature. Like riding a bicycle, one can learn aikido only by doing. Unlike riding a bicycle, however, one has to interact with another individual, who is also simultaneously learning by doing.

Teaching such a complex set of skills in an interactive setting without constant verbal instruction may seem odd at first. Instead of describing the methods, the sensei points to someone in the class, calls the name of the technique for everyone to hear, and then performs it several times on that selected student at various speeds and angles, without much explanation. The rest of the class observes in silence.[33]

Once the demonstration is over, everyone randomly finds a partner and starts practicing, once again without any significant dialogue. This method helps students concentrate solely on how they and their partners approach the move, paying attention to all sorts of subtle nonverbal feedback. They dive into the task without any external interruptions. The sensei constantly observes and sometimes intervenes to perform the move once more with certain couples. When the session ends, the class members disperse and proceed with life as if nothing out of the ordinary had happened.

Not all aikido sessions are conducted in silence, but when they are, students have personal time and space to flow and hone their skills. Such sessions respect to a healthy degree each student's unique approaches to the art. The sensei doesn't try to claim complete control over everyone's learning or performance. He ensures that the fundamentals are correct but doesn't run around correcting every little deviation from the norm. It is left to the participants to refine their skills, each in his or her own unique way, through continuous interaction.

Allowing for some autonomous personal time and space is even more crucial to escape the traps of experience outside the dojo.

Such an approach to learning would potentially increase the number and diversity of ideas, improving innovators' chances of being in the right place at the right time. It would let people observe and better appreciate the intricacies of their own and others' creative processes. It would facilitate learning from and building on others' experiences. It would give people the opportunity to redirect their focus to seemingly unrelated issues, which may lead to unexpected discoveries. And it would enable people to identify the domains or methods they are passionate about, and then invest in these to achieve their potential.

There have been many attempts to offer some slack for autonomous learning in modern organizations and institutions. Innovative companies have been experimenting with a wide range of strategies. Companies like 3M and Google, for example, have popularized practices where managers let employees use part of their time to work on problems and solutions that they identify. The companies then listen to and invest in some of these ideas, which allow them to better adapt to a complex and uncertain business world.[34]

Notice that actually implementing some of the ideas is a crucial element. Xerox PARC gave plenty of such autonomy to its employees, which eventually led to the discovery of the personal computer with graphical user interface, among other groundbreaking projects. However, the administration then failed to heed and develop the ideas that resulted. Mere generation of ideas does not guarantee their implementation or success.

Hackathons are ubiquitous in many industries, especially in software. These are usually one- or two-day events where developers build ideas in teams to be presented at the end of the event. Corporations and organizations often sponsor such meetings with competitive prizes for selected ideas and projects.

Other structured approaches to creativity like kaizen events and Six Sigma projects allow organizations to improve their products and services by reconsidering their processes in detail. These can be redesigned specifically to welcome diverse opinions, borrow external ideas, and combine different concepts to increase the quality of outcomes and the welfare of the employees in the long run.

Large organizations have also been adopting innovative approaches like agile and lean startup methods as they develop their products and services. These involve building reliable experience by prototyping, experimenting, and iterating, instead of a strictly controlled implementation of a final and finished version of a project.[35]

All these practices reduce the likelihood that experience will limit creativity. Unfortunately, they remain outside the norm. The majority of businesses, schools, and other organizations are not designed to leave much personal time and space to their members. Most managers and administrators don't have much room to build new ideas or consider those created by others. Instead, the systems in place constantly strive to define "optimal" ways of conducting operations and to manage them under strict controls. The underlying assumption is that one best form of employee experience can be defined and imposed, which then leads to the desired performance. This assumption, however, is flawed in wicked learning environments.

Hence, in the spirit of this chapter's main theme, let us attempt to build on the existing innovation-prone practices to envision three mechanisms within three different domains—social life, school, and work. Our primary aim is to provide a pocket of autonomous time and space within the current systems for countering the unwanted distortions and filters experience may bring to idea creation, selection, and development.

Hobby Hacking:
The Productive Value of Messing Around

Caresse Crosby, also known as Mary Phelps Jacob, was an author and a publisher in the United States during the early 1900s. A socialite, she often attended or organized parties where she liked to dress up and dance. Yet this hobby presented her an unexpected challenge. When attending parties, ladies in those days wore corsets, which were not made for comfort. Even worse for Crosby, they restricted her movements while she was dancing.

One day, she had an idea. She procured a couple of handkerchiefs and sewed them together using a ribbon. She used that contraption as an undergarment instead of her usual tightened corset. Reportedly, she danced so beautifully and freely that other women attending the party questioned her about it.[36]

Crosby went on to design and later patent a modern version of the brassiere, partly because she wanted to dance better while being fashionably dressed. She just used rudimentary sewing methods and materials that had been around for centuries to solve her problem. Her hobby was instrumental in her being in the right place at the right time with the right idea.

George de Mestral was an engineer who enjoyed trekking and hunting in the Alps. He had a loyal dog that followed him on these trips. He loved his hobby, yet it presented him with an unexpected challenge. After excursions, de Mestral often found himself pulling burs from the belly of his dog. He was puzzled. Neither the dog's fur, nor the burs that got entangled in it, were sticky. Nor were they magnetic. So how did the burs cling to the fur?

Using a microscope, de Mestral studied the issue and saw that the two materials were forming tiny hooks and loops to stick together. This discovery eventually led him to develop modern hook and loop fasteners, marketed under the commercial name of Velcro. This product has found uses in many domains, including fashion, medicine, the military, and space exploration.[37]

De Mestral invented Velcro partly because he loved walking in the wild with his dog. He used his skills as an engineer and existing materials to solve a problem in another domain—the engineering of fasteners. His hobby was instrumental in him being in the right place at the right time with the right idea. Today, de Mestral's approach would be described as biomimicry, which entails taking inspiration from nature's forms and processes.

Biomimicry also played a role when Japan's *shinkansen* or so-called bullet train faced problems in the 1990s. Its technical development manager Eiji Nakatsu reportedly found a solution thanks to his personal interest in birds. Trains traveling at high speeds caused sonic booms as they went through tunnels, creating great inconvenience, especially in residential areas. Nakatsu changed the nose of the locomotive to resemble a kingfisher's beak, which allows the bird to dive from air into water with very little friction and splash. He transferred an observation from his hobby to train design, transforming its shape, which reduced the noise significantly and made the trains more efficient.[38]

Most creative processes are hidden from our experience, which can make us underappreciate the usefulness of such interdisciplinary approaches. Everything is indeed a bit of a remix. Brilliance is often borrowed, combined, and transformed. Yet we need some personal time and space to experience these connections and then to cultivate them.

Hobbies offer that luxury. They lie outside the control of forces that guide most of our lives, like career or family. They push us to divert our focus away from our comfort zone and from what's routine. They lead us to encounter people and visit places that we normally wouldn't. And they feature challenges of their own. Actively analyzing these problems and striving to adapt a solution in one domain to another can help us to be in the right place at the right time with the right idea.[39]

Escape to Passion:
Free-Range Creativity for Students

If we want to increase the frequency of optimal experience in our society, and thereby enhance our creativity, we ought to make it easy for young people to discover their personal passions during their school years. Unfortunately, this hardly happens. Standardized curricula, typically characterized by one-sided delivery of information followed by standardized testing of its retention, leave little space for free-range exploration of ideas and experiences outside the prescribed classroom regimen.

The Internet will probably be a main driver of a possible transformation of the educational system. Ever-increasing online initiatives like Khan Academy and Coursera will undoubtedly be a larger part of future education. They allow people to have more control over their schooling, content, and pace of learning.[40]

There are also several out-of-the-mainstream classroom-based models. For example, certain education initiatives like Montessori provide students with opportunities to interact with different situations and with one another. These methods allow students to progress in ways and at speeds that they are comfortable with. Similarly, MIT Media Lab's Lifelong Kindergarten project has been envisioning learning methods borrowed from kindergartens, which emphasize projects, peers, passion, and play. Some institutions have recently started to feature flipped classrooms, where students learn the material before the class and then apply their learning during classroom sessions in an interactive fashion. The whole Finnish education system is known for its philosophy of equal opportunity and its research-based design.[41]

Reports and anecdotal evidence suggest that alternative approaches like these can indeed have positive effects on students' learning and abilities. However, due to political, logistical, economic, and bureaucratic reasons, it is unlikely that they will soon replace or transform standard schooling on a large scale in most countries. It therefore may be unrealistic to expect a quick revolution in the standard knowledge-based method of instruction.[42]

Accordingly, we would like to propose a mechanism that doesn't involve a revolution. Instead, we suggest a mechanism that provides students receiving a standard education (first to twelfth grade) with some time and space where they can have exclusive control over their own learning experience.

The ultimate goal is to help students explore their elements, interests, passions, and talents early on in life and allow them to manage their own creative development. The challenge is to motivate them to use their pocket of autonomous time and space to generate ideas, borrow insights, build on existing efforts, hone their skills, engage in a variety of creative processes, benefit from flow, and contact other like-minded individuals on different activities, whether curricular or extracurricular.

To generate that motivation, enthusiasm, and action, we would start by asking students about a subject in their curricular program that they *don't* like. Was there, for example, a class you deeply disliked in school during a given semester? Geography? History? Math? Physics? Literature? No matter the reasons for your dislike, we bet you didn't learn much from that class. Perhaps the teacher was boring or confusing. Or maybe the way it was taught didn't suit you. Or maybe you simply didn't have much interest in the topic. That sentiment may have changed over time. But it is safe to assume that, in any given semester, students have to attend a class they like the least.

Accordingly, we'd like to give students the option to drop one such class during a semester but only after they have acquired fundamental information on the topic. Before they can avoid a significant portion of the class, they must attend the first part of it and prove through a midterm exam that they are knowledgeable in certain main concepts. Once having proven their basic proficiency, these "escaping" students can sit in a separate room, where they can work on a project of their own in whatever way they wish.

What projects can they do? It's up to them. They can opt for a project that is about another curricular topic, say physics or literature. Or they can choose to improve their prowess in an extracurricular activity, such as chess, writing, photography, dancing, design, or aikido. They could do research on the subject of their choice, practice skills that can be practiced in the available space, or talk to each other about their ideas. They would continue their quests outside of the school too, as much as they wish.

Be it curricular or extracurricular, such additional efforts are currently not incentivized enough by the traditional, standard education systems. But under this mechanism, the students would be promptly rewarded through the option to escape part of a course they don't wish to attend.

What would happen with these projects?

One possibility could be that, at the end of each semester, students give a presentation to small committees of teachers, other students, and parents, discussing what they did. But they would not be judged for it. There would be no grades, no decisions, and no reports on these projects. That time and space belongs to the students. Audiences, if they wish, can only provide constructive feedback and contacts that may help students further their ideas.

Ideally, many students would use this opportunity to escape from a painful learning experience and engage in one of their talents or interests, since that would be the least costly activity for them. This mechanism would then eventually help them naturally explore and discover their various passions. Of course, they may guess wrong and opt for an activity that they don't end up enjoying. But given that they will have the same opportunity in the upcoming semester, they can switch to another domain. Once they like what they experience, they can keep advancing in that particular field.

Some students might choose to exploit the mechanism and fail to be productive. They may pretend to have worked on something and get away with it. That's their choice too.

Those who use this pocket of freedom to explore their passions and work to hone their skills would more than make up for those misuses. Our bet is that we'd eventually start seeing people who are passionate, creative, and lucky, simply because they were given the chance, choice, and responsibility, when they were young, to improve themselves by generating their own opportunities.

This escape-to-passion mechanism uses the rigidity of the current education system to incentivize students to identify their passions through reliable experience. It aims to unleash their potential—all without disrupting most of the traditional classroom system. (More details on the possible operational issues are in the notes.)[43]

To further support students, a national and even international database of projects could be established by an oversight committee so that students all around the world can check who has been doing what types of activities and projects during their escapes, first to get inspired, and then to be able to contact them, benefit from their experience, and build on their ideas.

This learning environment would produce a community-based learning experience within a strict knowledge and assessment-based education system. It's a concept built by borrowing, connecting, and transforming several other practices and alternative approaches. Hence, it needs to be tested, tweaked, adapted, revised, and further improved. It's tricky, but it's possible.

Senate of Managers:
A Problem-Solving Forum for Business Leaders

Many people spend a significant proportion of their adult lives at their jobs. Those who own their businesses may have relatively more control over their time and space at work. But what type of a mechanism could provide a pocket of autonomous experience to those who don't?

Consider a medium- to large-size firm or a department within a big corporation, with several mid- to high-level managers handling a dozen different duties, all of them reporting to a general or department manager. These people are usually well educated and have a wide range of experience in different companies, departments, or processes. Some of them may one day be promoted to lead a department or the whole company.

These managers are busy. They play important roles in a strictly designed operation. They typically don't have much time or space to generate, exchange, test, and implement ideas. On the contrary, new ideas often mean more work and responsibility, for which they will usually not get much recognition but would likely receive blame if things go wrong.

Of course, these managers likely have multiple ideas, not only about their own processes but also about others' problems. Yet because they often lack a venue to creatively discuss and develop these ideas, they are not able to bring their full potential to the operation. All of this is a hidden cost to the company.

One approach to consider in such a situation would be to establish a senate, which would sustainably provide its members time and space to combine their diverse experiences and openly discuss their various ideas. Over the years, we have had the opportunity to implement versions of such a senate in different settings.

Here's the basic protocol in a nutshell.

We ask the general manager to convene a meeting of the relevant mid- to high-level managers. We explain the need to improve creative problem-solving processes and how managers' experiences are not fully appreciated under a regime of strict controls and numbing routines. Given that they know the company's critical processes inside and out, we argue that they are the best people to identify and solve a variety of issues—even though their latent creativity may lie dormant in realms outside their formally recognized "managerial experience." Typically, everyone in the room agrees.

We then ask the general manager to leave the room. This is vital. If a representative of upper management remains in the room, people don't speak or even think freely. Worse, when the boss says something, others stop providing their own perspectives. General managers don't even have to talk for this to happen. Their face and body language are often enough for observers to guess which comments they favor and which ones they oppose. They roll their eyes and it's all over.

Once the top administration is out, we go around the room, identifying problems to be tackled. Each manager expresses several issues he or she faces and deems important. We ensure that everybody contributes, ultimately generating a short list of clearly defined problems. We ask managers to think about each item—both theirs and others'—and schedule to reconvene.

When we next meet—again with upper management excluded—the gathering has now morphed into a senate. We often observe that the participants have jotted down possible approaches to most of the problems raised in the earlier meeting. They find it easy to borrow and adapt solutions from other companies they worked for, or from other domains they are familiar with. The collective experience of the senate leads to previously unavailable ideas flowing in the room.[44]

In one case, we witnessed a human resources manager resolve a pressing problem of the sales manager, mainly because she had experienced a similar situation during her previous employment. She had had no idea about the sales manager's problem before. They had never interacted in a way that would have allowed each other's useful ideas to surface.

In another case, the senate was surprised to hear about the existence of a specific outdated procedure in one of the departments. It was an irrelevant yet costly practice that had remained in place for no good reason. Nobody had discussed or scrutinized it before it was raised on the senate floor. Another manager promptly provided a walkthrough on how to update the procedure based on experience from his own department.

Of course, some problems are trickier, with their proposed solutions decidedly more expensive. After a few meetings, we discuss how we would prioritize the solutions, and then take the final version approved by the senate to upper management. Usually, general managers fall in love immediately with some of the ideas and are filled with an irresistible desire to apply them immediately companywide.

We stop them. The proposed solutions need to be tested and revised before they can be successfully implemented. There's always the possibility that some of them sound great but are actually useless. Some can even be potentially dangerous—like excessive bloodletting procedures that generations of physicians favored.

We help test these ideas on a small scale within the company and report back with results. The senate meets again to discuss potential implementations, this time together with the general manager. Finally, the ideas get implemented.

Through this process, the senate ensures that managers' diverse experiences are harnessed for creativity. They define and solve their problems in their own ways, while benefiting from others' insights. They are also able to show their efforts directly to upper management and be appreciated appropriately. Their ideas don't fall on deaf ears. Some get implemented; some don't. General managers get to have a healthy view of the processes, problems, and ideas of their management team as well. Everyone gets reliable feedback on the issues they raise.

Establishing such a senate doesn't jeopardize the existing operations. A few hours of time and space each month devoid of administrative control can eventually generate a pool of relevant problems and valuable solutions. And once the upper management understands how the protocol works and learns to give autonomy to the senate in discussing their problems, the method ceases to require any outside moderators. Managers can update and address periodically their issues and solutions. The senate becomes sustainable.

In its essence, this protocol is designed to unlock the creativity hidden within employees' personal experience. By momentarily breaking away from conventional lines of responsibility and organizational silos, it allows managers to think in fresh ways about the challenges they and others face, and the unexpected connections to be drawn to past experiences, on the job or elsewhere. The value of such a forum derives not from skills learned by passively participating in ordinary work but rather from the opportunity to examine one's experience in a new light, stimulated by the diverse ideas and questions raised by colleagues from throughout the organization. It's tricky, but it's possible.

What's Missing? What's Irrelevant?

Creativity is indispensable for both individuals and organizations to efficiently navigate uncertainty and complexity. And some experience is indispensable for creativity.

Yet it's important to recognize that experience also involves subtle filters and distortions that deceptively lead us to misjudge ideas and creative processes, both of others and our own.

Irrelevant past. Innovations lead to a break from the past. Hence, experience based on that past leads to poor foresight when judging the potential of new ideas. Their value becomes obvious only in hindsight, once they are experienced.

Missing creative processes. We observe successful outcomes, but we don't necessarily see and understand the details of the underlying processes that generated them. Our experience thus prevents us from appreciating how creativity really works.

Missing others' experience. When seeking originality, we are constrained to our own experience. But progress is more likely when we build on the experiences of others and "stand on their shoulders" as opposed to "in their faces."

Irrelevant focus. Experience can render our focus more rigidly fixed on what's relevant. But if what's relevant changes, such experience can lead to inattentional blindness, functional fixedness, and competency traps, preventing us from seizing unexpected opportunities.

Missing flow. Flow facilitates creativity. Unfortunately, much of our daily experience is devoid of it. Fortunately, there are ways we can reorganize our lives and the practices of our organizations to encourage the free-range thinking and passion-driven exploration that makes flow possible.

Missing autonomy. People need a certain amount of time and space where they are free to engage in problems and develop passions. Institutions can design specific mechanisms to yield some control within their strict operations, incentivizing students and employees to enrich their personal creative experience.

Creativity is about seeking and developing ideas that will lead to positive surprises—new concepts that will benefit individuals, companies, industries, societies, and humanity in general. Going beyond the immediate lessons of experience can help us identify and then harness the power of our latent creativity.

3

BLINDED TO RISK

When Experience Conceals Danger

IMAGINE YOU ARE A DINOSAUR.

A *Velociraptor, a Sauroposeidon*, a *Triceratops*, a *Stegosaurus*, or a *Tyrannosaurus rex*, if you wish. Try and feel it in your bones.

You live a normal life—dodging risks, feeding, reproducing. Your experience has taught you well how to survive. You innately remember the places where easily accessible food can be found. You have developed a sense as to whether a certain area would be dangerous for your life at a given time. In fact, experience has been your ally for ages. It's in your DNA. Most of your instincts are the products of the collective experience of your whole species. For millions of years, your ancestors have adapted to the environment, which helps your survival.

But one day, you wake up from your sleep and something feels off. The environment around you is changing too rapidly for you to adapt. Your experience did not warn you that such a change could be possible. Nothing that you or your ancestors have learned seems to be effective in this new setting. The skills required are not in your DNA. Soon, life gets so difficult that there's no way to survive. You die, along with the rest of your species and many others. You did nothing to cause this situation. Nor was there a way for you to foresee or prevent it.

Rest in peace.

This is based on a true story from roughly sixty-six million years ago, when scientists believe a massive asteroid impact devastated the ecosystem of planet earth. Many victims died right after the blast, while others suffered for a while as a result of cataclysmic changes in the environment before perishing forever. From the perspective of dinosaurs and many other forms of life that existed back then, we are living in a postapocalyptic world.[1]

We know that disasters of various kinds and scales have happened and will continue to happen to us, as a species, as a nation, as organizations, and as individuals. To better understand, predict, and then deal with the disasters that await us, we'll need all the help we can get. Like dinosaurs, we humans also learn from and trust our experience. We record the past and observe the present. These should help us to sense what dangers may lie ahead and to cope with them as effectively as possible.

Great. What can go wrong?

Unfortunately, experience is not a reliable teacher when it comes to surviving disasters. Relying strictly on what we have learned from experience can make us vulnerable to certain catastrophic events by hiding crucial information from us while feeding us irrelevant details. It can render us as helpless as the dinosaurs were. Worse, unlike the dinosaurs, we may even be exposed to disasters that we ourselves have instigated. Only by acknowledging the various filters and distortions in our experience can we hope to identify potential disasters and then make informed and timely decisions about how to tackle them.

A main problem is that many really big unprecedented events with fatally destructive consequences are deceptively missing from our experience. And such looming disasters often come with few or no recognizable warning signs.

In *The Black Swan*, Nassim Taleb describes how such rare yet impactful episodes develop—typically not in a simple, linear fashion, which can allow people to learn to manage them over time, but rather by appearing dormant or progressing very slowly until suddenly there is, in effect, an "explosion" with unexpected outcomes and irreparable consequences. The slippery slope leading to such disasters can be quite flat and easy to get used to. And the tranquil and seemingly familiar present becomes a mere distraction from imminent destruction, leaving the victims tragically unprepared.

So the mere fact that one may have observed only white swans in the past doesn't mean that the next one would definitely not be black. Also, experience not only fails to inform us about the existence of rare events, but about their impact as well. When it comes to unprecedented disasters, reliance on experience leaves us comfortably asleep at the wheel.[2]

Luckily, unlike dinosaurs, we have scientists who provide warnings. These people don't rely on limited personal experience but are instead able to offer educated guesses based on cold statistical analyses. Their insights are potentially a great advantage to us when it comes to preparing for tomorrow's catastrophes.

Yet warnings by experts often clash with our current comfort and daily observations. We hear the alarm but don't sense the problem. We have a hard time deciding what to believe. The contradictions between experts' opinions and our own experience end up interfering with our readiness to take necessary precautions.

The one thing that makes us realize that we can't really afford to learn about disasters from personal experience is when we live through a disaster ourselves. It's devastating. We mourn and are traumatized. We vow to remember and to do all we can to prepare for similar events in the future or to prevent them if possible. Yet over time the memory fades, and so does the urgency of our concern. As we adapt to the aftermath and to the resulting new conditions, the present experience inevitably engulfs our intuition.

It's even harder to learn from disasters that happen to others. Unless we make an effort to imagine a scenario where we are the victims, our personal experience mainly teaches us that others are the ones who suffer. This can even lead to feelings of unwarranted confidence, a belief that we are less vulnerable than we actually are.

Finally, there are some situations in which disasters are accurately forecast and prevented. Good news. Yet these preventions often remain hidden from observation. By their nature, they don't lead to an outcome we can learn from. We may never hear about the precautionary measures, and we don't get to experience first-hand what would have happened had a disaster not been averted. The resulting absence of destruction may in turn induce a delusion that the danger never really existed.

For all these reasons, while experience improves our chances of survival in everyday life, its lessons can paradoxically sabotage our ability to predict and deal with disastrous events. The learning environment is wicked. Hence, it would be wise to ask: Are there any potential terrible surprises that are simply too costly to learn about from experience, foreseeable only through clues that are hidden from our daily observations? Sadly, there are plenty.

Catastrophes We Can't Afford to Experience

Nature can be a dangerous place, and not only for dinosaurs.

Epidemics are candidates for a potential catastrophe with unpredictable timing and consequences. The high levels of connectivity and communication we enjoy in today's society can help infectious diseases to travel easily and to rapidly become global threats to our survival. Just one hundred years ago, the so-called Spanish flu ended up infecting one-third of the world population, killing tens of millions within months. The lessons of such events seem to have faded. If things get out of control with a new bug, it may be too late for humanity to recognize its devastating effects.[3]

As we finalized this chapter during 2019, such a disaster felt hypothetical and remote. Sadly, as we are copyediting the book in spring 2020, a novel coronavirus is causing a global pandemic and holding the whole world hostage. It caught every health care and economic system by surprise, with deadly consequences.

Our experience not only failed to warn us about the existence and impact of this type of disaster, but it also keeps deceiving us as we try to mitigate it. In a situation where the number of cases increases exponentially, it becomes difficult to comprehend that millions can be infected in a matter of weeks. And we fail to appreciate the value of crucial interventions when these take some time to show their effects due to transmission and incubation periods. As a result, we delay precautions, causing the disease to spread quickly, which in turn makes mitigation even more costly.

Coronavirus disease 2019, also known as COVID-19, might not wipe us out as a species, as the asteroid did for the dinosaurs. But the damage goes beyond our immediate health, proving to be a long-term threat to the global economy and well-being. Once we survive it, we would be wise to identify other possible sources of pandemics so that we can avoid their destruction in the future. And we can hopefully view in a new light many other potential catastrophes that we simply can't afford to experience.

For instance, climate change has long been at the center of many environmental, political, and economic disputes. Is the planet warming in a manner that could prove to be catastrophic? For most people, it doesn't really feel like it.

A strict reliance on personal experience would make it hard to embrace the notion of systematic global warming and, as in the case of epidemics, get in the way of essential mitigations. True, we may have recently suffered a summer or two that seemed unusually hot. In recent years, there may have been more hurricanes and fires than usual. But, for practically all of us, the cold days of winter followed autumn as usual, and hurricanes only struck during limited periods in a year. For most people, it's business as usual, which is one reason why it has been difficult to prioritize the issue of climate change among competing social, political, and economic problems.

However, analyses by organizations like NASA and the US Global Change Research Program suggest that things *are* changing. The polar ice caps and Himalayan glaciers are melting rapidly, and CO_2 emissions are at an all-time high, among other alarming deviations. And as global average temperatures continue to rise gradually, most climate scientists agree that the problem will become increasingly hard to reverse. It is conceivable that we will soon reach a point after which negative consequences like heightened sea levels, a greater frequency of extreme weather events, lower air quality, and recurrent droughts will be both physically and economically devastating for large populations and effectively permanent in terms of human lifespans.[4]

Another analogous candidate is a catastrophic spread of antimicrobial resistance (AMR). Under certain conditions, harmful microbes evolve to become resistant to the medications that are currently in use to treat them. It's a process that renders our medicines less useful or, in some cases, useless.

AMR is not new. It existed before humans invented antibiotics—and even before humans existed. Many microbes evolved over time to become resistant to their biological foes, as we humans also did. But AMR started accelerating at an unprecedented rate after humans discovered antibiotics. Their excessive and inappropriate use by individuals and industries can lead certain microbes to evolve at a record rate against our biological defenses.

The World Health Organization (WHO) reports that there's evidence to suggest an abrupt and potentially dangerous increase in AMR. However, like global warming, it has not really affected most people's everyday experiences. On the contrary, people currently experience good outcomes with antibiotics. Even using them to excess (taking them needlessly) or inadequately (not taking the full dose) leads to limited or no harm for many individuals. Such experience leaves us with the belief that AMR is not a serious issue.

Yet, we can't afford to learn about widespread AMR from personal experience. AMR is especially disastrous for people with conditions that are vulnerable to drug-resistant microbes or those who need intensive life-saving cures, such as major surgery or certain cancer treatments that require heavy antibiotic regimens.[5]

Human history shows us that war is always a real possibility. Tensions and divisions usually escalate slowly to a point where military conflict breaks out. Nuclear war would be the ultimate global version of such a disaster. Yet daily experience does not necessarily prepare us to do whatever we must to avoid such a catastrophe. On the contrary, two generations of experience with nuclear arms races and the slow advance of nuclear proliferation can lead to a perverse feeling of safety.

The evolution of economic crises is largely hidden from experience, too. The 2008 global financial crisis developed with little advance warning, especially in the eyes of the general public, who ended up paying for most of its damage. As of spring 2020, we still don't know how deep and long the economic depression due to COVID-19 will be. We simply can't afford to learn about the consequences of these events from experience. But relying strictly on our daily observations distracts us from taking such matters seriously until the dam breaks.[6]

Things get even more complicated with new developments in fields like computer technology and genetics. We cannot clearly fathom what kind of unpredictable risks they may involve. Could artificial intelligence or genetic engineering eventually lead to planet-wide economic or social upheavals, perhaps with consequences as big as the asteroid impact was for the dinosaurs? There's much to discuss and speculate about, but we need to acknowledge that these discussions and speculations cannot be based on either our personal or collective experience.

There may be more candidates for a worldwide catastrophe, but disasters don't have to be global. Local and regional cataclysms can also be devastating for thousands or even millions of people. And we have the same tendency to become complacent about the risks we face from these smaller-scale events. Because most everyday experience remains unaffected by them, the tranquil present starts dominating intuition, and preparedness may dangerously suffer.

When considered one by one, many disasters might seem unlikely to happen. But when considered together, the probability that *none* would happen sometime in the near future becomes quite small, especially given that we are now living longer and progressing faster than in previous periods of human history. Unfortunately, COVID-19 has proved this reasoning right.

When it comes to preparing for disasters, we have to admit that our experience is unreliable for evaluating their likelihood, their

importance, or their possible impact. To manage such terrible surprises adequately, we have to find ways to go beyond our experience.

Probability Blindness and
the Expert-Experience Gap

How can we plan for a potential disaster that roams outside our experience? A first step would be to try to estimate its likelihood and
possible effects. Unfortunately, however, the lessons of experience
can distort our perceptions of probability.

After all, we don't get to observe probabilities. An event either
happens, or it doesn't. A coin toss yields heads or tails. Although we
understand intellectually that the probability of either outcome is
50 percent, we do not experience that probability when we observe
the outcome of a single toss.

Our intuitive sense of probability is clearer when an event
happens frequently. This lets us collect a lot of outcomes, look at
them all together, and, given the frequency of one specific outcome among all the outcomes we've observed, assign it an appropriate probability. Toss a fair coin a thousand times, and about half
of the outcomes will be heads, plus or minus some sampling error.
And that error will get smaller as you toss more and more times.
It then becomes easy to grasp intuitively that there's a 50 percent
probability of observing heads (or tails).

Yet disasters are not frequent events. They are often complicated
and unprecedented. That's partly what makes them disastrous.
Hence, we don't have enough experience about them to form such
a clear aggregate view.

Experts enter the scene. These are statistically sophisticated individuals who study evidence that embraces a much wider range
of events than those included in any individual's experience. They
provide us with descriptions and recommendations based on their
analyses. Yet research suggests that our perceptions based on our
experience and the descriptions by experts can be quite different.
In particular, there's a clash when the two sources of information

tell different tales. A probability of, say, 1 percent, may not feel the same when described and when experienced.[7]

Consider, for example, an investment that has a 1 percent probability of failing. A financial adviser tells you that "the chance of losing your total investment is one in a hundred." How does that description make you feel?

The chances are slim, yes, but a total loss is still possible. One can clearly imagine it. For most people, it's hard not to focus on that one case, to identify with it, and to feel anxious.

But how would you feel if instead you learned about the same situation strictly from experience? Nobody has told you about the 1 percent probability. You can only form a sense of its likelihood by either personally investing or observing the results of several similar investments over time. Here they are: win, win, win, win, win, win, win, win, win.

We created this sample of nine outcomes through a simulation where the probability of loss was set at 1 percent. The disaster is unlikely enough that it doesn't arise in this relatively small sample. If this is your experience as an investor, it would seem to provide a crystal-clear personal lesson. And because a loss is a rare event, many others will share your experience and perception. When you compare notes with fellow investors over drinks, you're likely to encounter mainly other individuals with unbroken winning streaks.

Under these circumstances, although descriptions based on analyses may cause undue anxiety, experience that relies on a limited personal sample can lead to undue comfort. With each win, the investor gains more confidence. The investor is then tempted to risk increasingly more resources, to forgo precautions, and to fail to appropriately insure against a potential unbearable loss.

Something similar also happens with disasters. People's experience-fueled gut feelings can underestimate the likelihood of a catastrophe, which then leads them to act irresponsibly. The probabilities that experts describe can sound unreasonable in comparison. And when the issue is complicated, the data and analyses will be complicated as well. Experts' explanations will tend to be opaque and involve considerable uncertainty. Given that a future event is being discussed, there may be no way to know for sure exactly when and where a certain disaster would occur. There may be no certainty about its impact, either. All of this makes the experts' judgment hard to digest . . . while the lessons of experience remain simple, vivid, and easy to believe. [8]

Consider, for example, the notoriously mind-boggling birthday problem from two different perspectives: expert versus experience. It begins with this question: What's the probability that, in a random group of twenty-five people, two or more celebrate their birthday on the same day?

Our personal experience would suggest that this isn't very probable. We meet with a lot of people in life, but we know only few, if any, who share our birthday. We also don't witness many cases where multiple people celebrate their birthday on the same day. Shared birthdays thus seem relatively rare, and a random group of twenty-five people seems too small for there to be many coincidences.

On the other hand, an expert tells you that, in a room with twenty-five people, finding at least two who share a birthday is more likely than not; in fact, the chance of a shared birthday is about 56 percent. Moreover, put five more random people into the same room, and the probability suddenly jumps to 70 percent! How's that possible? The expert starts to explain, but the solution involves a page full of equations. It's complicated. [9]

Remember, the question asks about *any* two people within a group of twenty-five who celebrate their birthdays on the same day—not about the very different and much simpler question of whether anyone in the room will share *your* birthday. Hence the explanation involves *combinatorics*, a reasonably complicated branch of mathematics. Because there are three hundred combinations of two different people within a group of twenty-five, the probability of finding a match is much larger than one would expect—and it grows more rapidly with the addition of new people than our intuition would suggest.

Similarly, a highly transmissible virus can feel like a regular and seasonal flu in its early stages because it causes a comparable number of cases and casualties. Experts can try to convince the public that exponential growth would cause the eventual impact to be much grimmer. The numbers would soon explode in the absence of any intervention. It may not feel as if the experts' view is right. But that doesn't make it wrong. That's how probability often works with systemic risks and rare disasters. Our personal experience is an unreliable guide to understand their likelihood and potential impact.

Disastrous Lessons We Learn from Experience

Of course, when a disaster happens, we do have the opportunity to learn from it. We absorb the shock. We realize the problem and the extent of its consequences. We analyze it in depth, as we should. As a result, it seems reasonable that we should learn some valuable lessons from disastrous experiences. But to what extent does that really happen?

In *The Ostrich Paradox*, Robert Meyer and Howard Kunreuther of the Wharton Risk Management and Decision Processes Center analyze this question. They recount multiple cases where disaster-struck areas failed to prepare adequately for future risks and consequently suffered deadly consequences when similar disasters recurred.[10]

One example they provide is Hurricane Ike, which devastated Galveston Island in Texas in 2008. But this wasn't unprecedented. A hundred years earlier, the same place was devastated in a similar way by a similar event. Local leaders initially learned from that experience and took many precautions as they rebuilt the city. But evidence suggests that the lessons eroded significantly in time.

In particular, Meyer and Kunreuther observe that, in 2008, the seawalls protecting the city were not up to the task. They were aging and vulnerable. Some newly established communities hadn't even seen the need to build seawalls at all. When the hurricane approached, the early warnings were ignored by many, even when the situation was declared to be potentially deadly. Among the thousands who suffered losses, only 39 percent had adequate insurance, despite being in a disaster-prone zone. All of these mistakes inevitably contributed to the needless loss of lives and property.[11]

Based on such tragic anecdotes, Meyer and Kunreuther identify two mechanisms fueled specifically by experience that work against us.

First, even though we don't factually forget about extreme events—we often erect monuments to commemorate them and invest in safety measures—the trauma they cause to the community gradually dissipates. Although it may never disappear completely, it regresses to a level we can cope with psychologically.

This regression is very useful for small and frequent failures, like falling from a bicycle or losing a tennis match. If we were traumatized by our every failure, we would never try anything again and would not get better at doing things. If the destruction of a city by a hurricane led humans to never build cities again, the advancement of civilization might come to a standstill. But this same mechanism can also render us reckless and therefore leave us vulnerable to terrible future surprises.

Especially if we did not experience the disaster firsthand, memories, numbers, and warnings don't sting as much after a short while. Recent experiences of tranquility and safety quickly win over past shocks. Other more immediate and tangible worries take over. Some risks may even start to seem more like opportunities, given the absence of recent disasters. Over time, that piece of real estate in the middle of the disaster zone can appear to be relatively cheap. There's been no issue for a while, so now it seems like a bargain.

The second mechanism Meyer and Kunreuther discuss concerns the perception of precautionary measures: the less frequent a particular type of disaster is, the less useful or necessary it seems to implement measures against it. While prudent citizens incur the expense of costly precautions, like installing storm shutters against hurricane damage, those who aren't prudent instead enjoy the new TV set they bought with the same money.

On top of that, false alarms can give a false assurance to those who don't take precautions. Authorities may ring these alarms sometimes to be more safe than sorry. After a few false ones, however, some people start to assume that there will be no disaster and that those who believe in their existence are simply losing money by investing in protection. The prudent residents, who struggle to put up shutters after a storm warning only to realize that it was another false alarm, are likely to become frustrated and to be tempted to join their neighbors in relaxing in front of the TV the next time the warnings sound.

Gradually, the community as a whole may decide to forgo certain crucial mitigating policies, such as building regulations and special insurance plans, which once again renders them vulnerable to devastation.[12]

Ultimately, an unthinking reliance on experience increases the likelihood that damages from catastrophes recur, despite having caused much misery in the past. And this issue is not limited to environmental disasters.

Research in finance, for example, suggests that people are inclined to put a relatively higher weight on the recent past when evaluating their investment decisions. That experience is fresh and is assumed to represent reality better. Once again, this tendency serves us well when things only change gradually. It keeps us up to date and improves our performance. Paradoxically, however, it can also lead us to lower our guard too much against unexpected dangers.[13]

For instance, the fact that we suffered a global recession in the past doesn't guarantee that we won't make similar mistakes again. Yet the absence of a recession for some time can make us more willing to repeal precautionary regulations or warning systems that we had set up to protect ourselves from future troubles.

As for keeping world peace, strategic international alliances were established over the last century largely to avert violence and wars among member states. Yet as the lessons of the devastation caused by global conflicts fades, the perceived importance of these safeguards withers as well. As a consequence, if the alliances are gradually eroded or dissolved without much effort to replace or renovate them, the risk of future conflicts may unnecessarily increase.

Similarly, because we have eradicated certain diseases through vaccination, we seem to have forgotten the damage they once caused. Today, there's an ongoing antivaccination movement, gaining traction through social media and celebrity endorsements. But if too many people forgo essential vaccinations, some of these extinct diseases will be needlessly revived.[14]

Hence, given our historical disastrous experiences and the possibility of future catastrophes, one crucial approach in all these domains would be to appreciate the value of timely and effective preventions. Unfortunately, however, the lessons of experience also undermine the importance of such vital protective actions.

Solution Versus Prevention: When a Disaster Gets Averted

Consider an epidemic that is spreading uncontrollably across the globe. It started in a small town in a certain part of the world and was transmitted by people who contracted the disease while traveling. It's caused by a newly evolved strain of a known virus and it's extremely deadly: it has a 50 percent mortality rate.

After tens of thousands of people have died and even more have been infected, Dr. Mark Jillson and his team manage to develop a cure through extensive research and development. It's a miracle treatment that works in almost every case. Dr. Jillson is hailed as a hero. Is he a hero? Yes, he definitely is.

But now imagine an alternative scenario.

In a small town in a certain part of the world, a newly evolved strain of a virus starts spreading. It's deadly and fast. Within a few weeks, it has killed dozens of people in the community and, with people traveling in and out of the town every day, containing it may soon prove impossible.

Luckily, Dr. Jill Markson and her team have been stationed there. Facing the danger of a potential outbreak and risking their own lives, they contain the spread through strategic checks, strict quarantines, and vital precautions. The incident remains localized, and the virus is soon eradicated. Dr. Markson and her team have prevented a pandemic that would have cost tens of thousands of lives across the globe had it spread. Is she a hero? Yes, she definitely is. Will she be hailed as a hero? Unlikely.

There's an asymmetry in how these two events are experienced and subsequently evaluated by the rest of us. Both Dr. Jillson and Dr. Markson took indispensable actions that helped to save many lives. We can argue forever about which is more remarkable. But lessons from experience give only one of them the respect they truly deserve.

The first case involves a *solution* to a deadly disaster after it occurs. The events are widely and easily observable and beyond doubt. Dr. Jillson's actions are rewarded accordingly. People feel the presence of the disaster firsthand, and this leads to properly recognizing the importance of the solution.

The second case, on the other hand, involves the *prevention* of a deadly disaster. It does not lead to an observable event, and it's not experienced by the wider world—which of course is a very good thing. Yet, for that very reason, Dr. Markson's efforts will not be acknowledged or rewarded as in the case of a solution.

More importantly, because the disaster was prevented, the public at large may not recognize its true destructive potential. But the more devastating the disaster, the less we can afford to learn about it from experience, and the more indispensable prevention becomes. Thankfully, the real world includes many people doing the same work as our fictional Dr. Markson.

For example, over the past decades, scientists and health workers have continuously been trying to prevent outbreaks of Ebola, which has had a high mortality rate (WHO reports suggests an average of 50 percent). Their efforts have truly been extraordinary. Some of the remedies, for example, are reportedly being transported and kept at extremely low temperatures in zones with unreliable electricity. Local treatment centers are being built. Ebola patients and their close contacts are being vaccinated. Communities are being informed about the truths and myths of the disease. And all this is sometimes done in the face of security risks.[15]

Fortunately, reports suggest that we may actually be getting near to a reliable cure for Ebola. Great news. But this experience shouldn't cause us to underestimate initiatives that take longer-term views and preventive efforts that precede the cures. The case of COVID-19 shows us how difficult and time consuming it can be to come up with preventive measures during a disaster. It's thus crucial to envision them before catastrophe occurs. [16]

One organization responding to this challenge is the Coalition for Epidemic Preparedness Innovations, which was founded in 2017 to organize cautionary measures and fund vaccines for a wide variety of pandemic diseases *before* they become global threats. We can only hope that the lessons of COVID-19 will eventually boost support for such initiatives.[17]

But preventions are cursed by experience.

First, to prevent a problem, one needs to acknowledge its existence and potential effect. But our experience does not necessarily alert us to the presence of a possible disaster and its likely magnitude. Remember the dinosaurs. Their experience told them nothing about the giant missile from outer space and the destruction it would cause.

Second, if a disaster *is* prevented, we don't experience it. Hence, we don't really learn about its existence or potential impact. In turn, this makes similar future disasters harder to prevent. As a result, preventions can prevent preventions.

Yet another obstacle with rewarding and recognizing preventions is the issue of punishing likely culprits. After all, something had to be prevented probably because somebody made a mistake. However, organizations and communities may be embarrassed to reveal these failings, which may end up keeping preventers hidden from experience.

To complicate things even further, because experience fails to appropriately teach us about preventions, we also don't properly recognize or reward them enough. As a result, we may be actually getting fewer preventions or getting them much later than we need. Who knows? Maybe the efforts of some people actually prevented a major financial crisis a few years back. We cannot be sure how many conflicts and wars have been prevented by diplomatic efforts and trade alliances. There are many books and films about those who benefited or suffered due to crises and disasters, but there aren't many about preventers of disasters, or those who at least tried, even if they eventually failed.

We could call this the Arkhipov-Petrov puzzle.

Vasili Arkhipov was a submarine flotilla commander for the Soviet army in the 1960s. During the Cuban Missile Crisis, he prevented a nuclear war by refusing to give his approval for a nuclear attack, despite the fact that the submarine crew was apparently under the impression that a war had broken out between the United States and the Soviet Union. Sensing this belief could be false, Arkhipov reportedly dissuaded two of his fellow high-ranking officers who were willing to launch a nuclear missile. As a result, he most likely saved millions of lives across the globe. Arkhipov took an action that averted a disaster we could not afford to learn about from experience.[18]

Stanislav Petrov was a colonel in the Soviet Air Defense Forces in 1983, and he also prevented a nuclear apocalypse during a period of high tension in the Cold War. In this case, the early detection system that would alert the Soviet army of a US attack reportedly mixed up some rare weather phenomena with intercontinental ballistic missiles. Rather than sounding the alarm for this "attack," Petrov reported a system malfunction. Had he not recognized the glitch, millions could have died. He averted a disaster we could not afford to learn about from experience.[19]

Some preventers are more fortunate than others. Arkhipov and Petrov were eventually recognized for their acts. Better late than never, perhaps. The story of Paul J. Crutzen, Mario Molina, and Frank Sherwood Rowland is thankfully much better. They were among the scientists who showed the effects of certain man-made chemicals on ozone depletion, catalyzing immediate preventive measures on a global scale. They were awarded the Nobel Prize in 1995 for their efforts.[20]

But the story of Richard Valery Mouzoko Kiboung is very different. An epidemiologist, he joined WHO's efforts to curb the spread of Ebola. In the spring of 2019, he was reportedly killed in an attack while responding to an Ebola outbreak. He probably prevented many deaths and would have prevented many more. But his demise and the fears it might cause among other health professionals and the agencies that employ them might tragically prevent future preventive efforts.[21] Not many people know about Richard Valery Mouzoko Kiboung. And that's a shame.

We could use more specialized prizes, accolades, and recognition for those who strive to stop bad things from happening. As a society, we don't recognize them enough. We could reward efficient efforts, especially those aimed at averting potentially big and irreversible catastrophes. We could establish a new international award honoring viable preventions in relevant domains—transportation, technology, health, economics, environment, and so on. We could call it the Arkhipov-Petrov Prize.

Dodged Bullets:
When a Disaster Almost Happens

A close cousin to preventions are *near misses*—failures masquerading as successes. Something bad almost happens, and we are provided with the ability to have a clear look at the possible disaster, without suffering its consequences.

Near misses are potential information treasures. Unfortunately, learning from them doesn't come naturally to us. When was the last time you sighed in relief because you dodged a bullet? Maybe you were in your car and looked at your phone for a second, only to glance up and avoid a collision at the last moment. Most of us have experienced one, or a few, such incidents. But we don't learn from those near misses nearly as much as we learn from costly mistakes. After all, though these events happened they did not lead to a traumatic experience.

In organizations, near misses tend to get further hidden and downplayed by those who caused them. People don't typically report when they almost made a terrible mistake. Incentives are often not designed to make that happen. As a result, we also end up not learning from events that almost happened to others yet may one day affect us.

Worse, such buried near misses could even increase the chances that the disaster will happen in the future. If there were a hidden blunder that did not cause trouble (or worse, led accidentally to success), it will probably happen at a certain point. Because the result is satisfactory, many people would keep using the same process or system, but the risks would still be there.

For these reasons, ignoring crucial near misses is considered unacceptable in industries like manufacturing, aviation, and health care, where safety is a major concern. In many companies in these sectors, reporting systems are in place that encourage those who are aware of a problem to inform upper management, in some cases anonymously. As a result, necessary precautions can be taken to avoid potential future disasters. Sometimes something goes wrong in an aircraft, but it still manages to land safely. Treating that event as a possible disaster teaches invaluable lessons to prevent an actual one.[22]

Yet learning from near misses is still the exception rather than the rule, even when the likelihood of disaster is high and the potential impact extreme.

In 2004, Hurricane Ivan hit the Gulf of Mexico, the Caribbean, and the southeastern United States, bringing mayhem and destruction. But it also brought a near miss.[23]

Projections initially indicated that the hurricane would hit New Orleans with full force. As a result, one-third of the population of the greater city evacuated their homes. The evacuation itself turned out to be costly and dreadful. People were stuck on poorly designed escape routes for hours. Some simply could not leave even when they tried.

Luckily, however, Ivan missed New Orleans.

At the time of this event, sociologist Shirley Laska was working on the potential effects of natural disasters in the same area. Her home and office were in New Orleans, and she clearly saw that the city could not survive a hurricane. The near miss gave her the opportunity to put her worries into a concrete analysis. Right after the event, she penned an article in *Natural Hazards Observer* titled "What if Hurricane Ivan Had Not Missed New Orleans?" in which she detailed the likely devastation based on the readily available evidence and projections. Her efforts were noted in Congress, where she testified that a similar hurricane would result in hundreds of deaths and tens of thousands of people left behind, most of them underprivileged members of the community.

Later events provided the proof that this scenario wasn't a mere conjecture. Less than a year after Laska's warnings, Hurricane Katrina hit New Orleans, among other cities, at full force. Three days before the destruction, the National Weather Service reportedly contacted Laska for advice on what could be done. But it was too late to learn the lesson. Hundreds perished, and tens of thousands were left behind in miserable conditions, most of them underprivileged members of the community.

In this case, experience wasn't a reliable teacher. There was a history of hurricanes in the region. There was a credible expert report that issued a stern warning based on a specific near miss. But none of these were nearly as powerful as the lessons that came from experience, which rendered us more vulnerable than we should have been. Similarly, given their relatively smaller impact on the lives of the majority of the world population, diseases like SARS and MERS could be considered as near misses that preceded the devastation brought by COVID-19. We now know that we failed to learn appropriately from them.

In 2008, Laska received the American Sociological Association's Public Understanding of Sociology Award, for her efforts before, during, and after Hurricane Katrina. Good news. Yet would we know about her and have awarded her had her warnings succeeded and the destruction from Katrina been minimized? Nobody knows. Still, more people should acknowledge people like her and seek to replicate their approach. Not many people know about Shirley Laska. And that's a shame.[24]

Grasping the Realities of Risk:
Benefits of Statistical Literacy

As we've seen, there are multiple, interconnected problems that make it fiendishly difficult for us to learn useful lessons from experience to help us predict, prepare for, and avoid disasters. There are tools and practices that have the potential to help, but putting them into practice is hampered by many factors. These include the difficulty of connecting our personal experience with the perceptions of statistically informed analysts—what we've called the expert-experience gap—and the mismatch between our experience-based intuition and the realities revealed by probability calculations.

To complicate things even further, experts' motivations and their personal agendas are not immune to challenge. Are the credentials of those who claim to be experts truly legitimate? Do some of them have vested interests that cloud their judgments, analyses, and recommendations? Is it possible that the uncertainty is so high in a given field that there are no real experts? Experts, after all, have been wrong many times in the past: Why shouldn't we feel free to ignore what many of today's experts are claiming?

These are all valid concerns. Yet this attitude can easily go too far. In *The Death of Expertise*, political scientist Tom Nichols warns against an unwavering and sometimes hostile stance against expert opinions, especially when their message conflicts with one's gut feelings. Doubt is a precious commodity. But it wouldn't hurt to direct a fraction of that doubt against one's own experience and the resulting intuition.[25]

If we apply this philosophy in the context of disasters, it then becomes possible to manage the expert-experience gap more skillfully. An example of this is the Montreal Protocol on Substances that Deplete the Ozone Layer, which was universally agreed upon on September 16, 1987. During earlier years, certain manufactured chemicals had been rapidly damaging the ozone layer. Although experience didn't reliably warn us about this unprecedented problem, scientific studies revealed the irreversible adverse effects of ozone erosion on both the environment and our health. Eventually, people decided to solve the problem in innovative ways. As a result, we expect ozone to return to its 1980 levels sometime between 2050 and 2070.[26]

How can we learn from examples like this, increasing the chances that we can identify and then address potential disasters in a timely and effective fashion? An important step is to become more statistically literate.

This is more elaborate than taking a class on probability and statistics in school. Katherine Wallman, chief statistician of the United States between 1992 and 2017, defined statistical literacy as "the ability to understand and critically evaluate statistical results that permeate our daily lives—coupled with the ability to appreciate the contributions that statistical thinking can make in public and private, professional and personal decisions."[27]

One way to acquire such literacy would be to follow and reflect on the works and arguments of certain scientists who have dedicated their professional lives to the problem of how to communicate statistical insights to the general public in a transparent fashion. Essentially, these experts have taken up the task of helping us better understand experts.

One of the most famous members of this tribe is the late Hans Rosling, who contributed a long list of analyses and methods of displaying complex social and economic data in accessible ways. He cowrote *Factfulness* and cofounded Gapminder, a foundation that "produces free teaching resources making the world understandable based on reliable statistics."[28] Over the years we (the authors) have also learned a great deal from the works and discussions of Gerd Gigerenzer, Howard Wainer, Nassim Taleb, David Spiegelhalter, Ben Goldacre, Philip Tetlock, Andrew Gelman, John Allen Paulos, Sam Savage, Edward Tufte, and Spyros Makridakis, among others. They have different specialties, and we refer to their perspectives in various sections of this book (more details and some suggested readings are in the notes).[29]

These and similar experts are often opinionated and don't necessarily agree on every matter. Yet they discuss the language of statistics in a way to render other experts' messages more accessible to the rest of us, so that we can make informed judgments about the realities behind the important decisions we're called upon to make.

In the context of disasters, statistical literacy would not only help make our intuition sophisticated enough to seek what lies beyond our experience but would also help us distinguish between good and bad advice from experts. It would help us recognize the expert-experience gap and avoid discounting (or amplifying) doomsday scenarios based on a simple clash between what we can observe and what we are told. We would be able to track more objectively the progression of disaster-prone processes over longer horizons, discredit inferior or problematic analyses earlier, listen to those who make better arguments, learn appropriate lessons from past traumas, and make wiser decisions regarding subsequent actions or inactions.

Also, by thinking statistically, we not only understand what experience and analyses can enlighten, but we can also better appreciate what they can't. Accordingly, one concept that scientists and policy makers often consider when thinking about potential disasters is the *precautionary principle*. It addresses the question of how we should proceed in making a vital decision when experience is unreliable and scientific knowledge is either unavailable or insufficient. It suggests that we should ask: Could the eventual harms we seek to avoid be so devastating that we should consider these even if they seem improbable based on the available experience and evidence? If there are multiple ways of progressing in a new field, which path would be better designed to ensure that disasters with irreversible effects are less likely to happen?[30]

Genome editing is an example of a context where a precautionary approach is deemed relevant. It's a high-tech field where science is progressing rapidly, with potentially enormous long-term consequences. We know, for instance, that the impacts of a small change in certain genes can affect many generations to come in ways that we cannot reliably predict. When it comes to somatic cells, like those that make up our organs and blood, genetic modifications generally affect only the person who receives the treatment. But the germ-line cells that make up our sperm and eggs pass our genes onto our offspring, which means that editing them can irreversibly interfere with the natural process of evolution. Most scientists currently exercise extreme precaution against such editing, which means that certain procedures may be opposed or banned even if the technology allows for them. This is the precautionary principle at work.[31]

Applying this principle, however, isn't always straightforward. In recent decades, there have been reports of several small-scale experiments that involved germ-line genetic modification in humans. For example, we know of cases where the procedure was performed to increase fertility or provide resistance to certain diseases. There may also be several relevant cases that we don't know about. Such initiatives have raised much debate in the scientific community on both ethical and practical grounds. We are unsure about other long-term effects such mutations may have. So where do we draw the line when it comes to such engineering? How do we draw that line? And where do we go from here?[32]

This is a complex problem that cannot be solved by relying on what we've learned from experience. Inevitably, some practices are bound to open a Pandora's box, which will have crucial consequences that we won't be able to foresee in the short term. So despite our best intentions and precautions, some disasters will end up happening in the long term. There's no escape. But if we wish to improve our ability to mitigate disasters and minimize their damage, we have to counteract the various delusions caused by experience and consider approaches that help us learn the right lessons for the benefit of future generations.

What's Missing? What's Irrelevant?

Experience protects us on a daily basis from many common dangers, teaching us how to manage and avoid them. No doubt about that. Yet when it comes to rare and impactful events, our personal and daily experience offers inadequate guidance to understand yesterday's disasters and prepare for tomorrow's.

Irrelevant daily tranquility. Our experience is rooted in the past and the present, and these don't provide clear signals of unprecedented catastrophes. On the contrary, it can give us an unrealistic sense of safety.

Missing disastrous impact. Experience not only fails to warn us in a timely fashion about rare disasters, it also doesn't reliably inform us about their potential impact.

Missing preventions. Actions taken to resolve disastrous situations are often recognized and rewarded, but actions that prevent disasters are typically unobservable. Preventions also prevent us from experiencing disasters, which can lead us to further underestimate their value.

Missing near misses. Near misses are sources of valuable information about potential disasters that could have happened but didn't. Identifying them and appreciating their lessons would help us better prevent future catastrophes.

Missing statistical literacy. Warnings by experts often clash with our perceptions based on experience. Statistical literacy can help us grasp and accept the significance of scientifically reliable warnings about dangerous trends and future risks.

Ultimately, the decision of how to act—or not to act—in the face of a potential disaster is still ours. To make an informed decision, however, we need to see beyond the lessons of experience.

4

FREE CHOICE THAT ISN'T

When Experience Narrows Options

PLEASE MAKE A DECISION BASED ON THE FOLLOWING INFORMATION.

```
01000001 00111010 00100000 01001100 01101111 01110111 00100000
01110010 01101001 01110011 01101011 00100000 01100001 01101110
01100100 00100000 01101100 01101111 01110111 00100000 01110010
01100101 01110100 01110101 01110010 01101110 00001101 00001010
01000010 00111010 00100000 01001000 01101001 01100111 01101000
00100000 01110010 01101001 01110011 01101011 00100000 01100001
01101110 01100100 00100000 01101000 01101001 01100111 01101000
00100000 01110010 01100101 01110100 01110101 01110010 01101110
```

You can't. Unless you are somehow proficient in reading binary code, you don't have any idea what the decision is about. You need someone to design an interface, allowing you to see the content in a way that enables an informed judgment about the situation.

Here's the same information, presented in a different way:

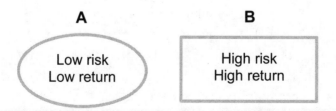

Now you have a much clearer understanding of the situation.

First of all, you recognize that you have access to two kinds of investment options, and you have some idea on how they are different from each other. Of course, there's still much more you'll need to learn to be able to make up your mind. Your choice would undoubtedly depend on the context, and then the specific risks, returns, benefits, and costs. Given all the details, you may even opt for neither A nor B.

But with the information presented through rows of 1s and 0s, you couldn't even see what the issue was. Your experience with the second interface makes a big difference in terms of helping you eventually arrive at an informed choice. Its design translates an incomprehensible situation into one that you can easily understand and engage in an intuitive way.

While perhaps not as obscure and puzzling as binary code, many aspects of modern life can also be hard to decipher accurately and navigate easily.

Rapid changes in technology, globalization, and society have recently given us unprecedented access to all sorts of goods, services, information, connections, and opportunities. Companies, politicians, organizations, causes, and people around us increasingly compete for our time and interest. We often find ourselves paying attention simultaneously to multiple objectives, passions, ideas, duties, responsibilities, and choices. Yet our concentration, time, energy, funds, and abilities are limited. How do we manage our decisions in such a world? This is a vitally important question, one that impacts all the many roles we play in an increasingly complicated society.

Accordingly, there has been a surge of studies into the factors affecting our judgments and decisions in almost every context imaginable. A growing number of investigations offer new insights on how doctors diagnose, judges judge, managers manage, workers work, teachers teach, students study, voters vote, investors invest, sellers sell, and consumers consume. And their findings are increasingly becoming mainstream. Psychologist Daniel Kahneman (2002) and behavioral economist Richard Thaler (2017) have won

Nobel Prizes for their contributions to our understanding of how psychology shapes economic and social decisions.

One of the core findings of this growing field is that making the right choices at the right time for the right reasons is not easy. On the one hand, we cherish our freedom and carefully guard our autonomy over the decisions we make. On the other hand, we need help to quickly access reliable information and make sense of what's going on. This is where *experience design* (XD) comes into play.

XD is a metadiscipline that draws insights from psychology, design, technology, architecture, marketing, management, and communication, among other fields. It primarily focuses on understanding and then shaping the way we experience a wide variety of goods, services, places, processes, and contexts. XD practitioners focus on both our minute-to-minute interactions with particular items or environments and on the longer-term impacts that those interactions have on us.

XD has spawned a host of new professions. There are experts on customer experience (CX) and on user experience (UX), experience architects (XA), design thinkers, and choice architects. Individually or in teams, these people design interfaces that make experiences understandable and decisions manageable. In today's digital world, they're often called upon to translate binary code into visual, verbal, and aural cues we can easily understand and respond to. For example, we wouldn't be able to benefit from the Internet without the necessary tools that allow us to seamlessly surf it and look for relevant information. XD is thus essential for many of today's most powerful innovations to be useful. We simply can't do without it.[1]

Futurist Alvin Toffler anticipated the rise of XD in his 1971 book *Future Shock*. In its tenth chapter, "The Experience Makers," Toffler foresaw the "psychologization of the economy," where producers and providers increasingly need to care about how consumers experience their goods and services, beyond the mere utility that they provide. Thus, a car may primarily be a tool for transportation, but as competition and complexity increase, details of a car's design and the way these details impact the experience of drivers and passengers play a larger and larger role in people's preferences and selections.[2]

That shock is no longer in the future. In their 1999 book *The Experience Economy*, authors Joseph Pine II and James Gilmore argue that the modern economy primarily values and serves people's experiences. Every supplier in this system is continuously trying to achieve designs that improve the consumer and user experience.[3]

The age of XD has created a world in which countless organizations are striving to cater to our needs through meticulously engineered experience designs. As a result, we gain access to extraordinary amounts and types of information and a wide range of new technologies, all crafted to help us enjoy a deeper understanding of the situations we face and the ability to make better informed decisions—whether about the products we buy, the news sources we trust, the investments we make, the charities we support, or the candidates we vote for.

We may not always be able to control or predict the outcomes we ultimately obtain. But thanks to the ever-advancing discipline of experience design, we can enjoy greater freedom over the choices we make.

Great. What can go wrong?

Problems arise when there is a clash of objectives. What happens when our wishes and desires don't match with the goals of those who design our experiences? After all, there can be a lot of money, power, and influence to be gained by designing experiences to guide our choices in particular ways. And the effectiveness of well-crafted XD is only enhanced by its ability to make us think that we, rather than the experience designer, are actually in control. As a result, there can be a substantial difference between how much freedom we *think* we have over our decisions and how much we actually have.

Further aggravating this situation, executives, entrepreneurs, policy makers, and politicians are now able to collect and analyze vast and ever-increasing amounts of data and information on many of our characteristics, choices, connections, and preferences. Coupled with continuing research into the dynamics of decision-making, such big data allow them to estimate what types of experience lead to particular judgments, opinions, beliefs, tendencies, and behavior. With that knowledge, they can design our experiences to support *their* objectives. And the more important the decision, the greater their incentive to bend our will toward theirs, while making us believe that we are actually in control. As a result, blindly relying on our personal experience can lead us to make decisions that outside influencers have meticulously planned.

The notion of undue influence by those who shape our experiences is not entirely new. Psychoanalyst Erich Fromm's 1976 book *To Have or To Be?* is based on a pessimistic perspective about our control over our choices in the Industrial Age. He observed that many people started to feel free to realize their wishes and achieve their potential. And with increasing industrialization, everyone believed that this freedom would eventually be available to all classes of society. But Fromm saw this as an illusion where "we have all become cogs in the bureaucratic machine, with our thoughts, feelings, and tastes manipulated by government and industry and the mass communications that they control."[4]

There's no doubt that, as citizens, consumers, and decision makers, our experience is increasingly enriched by a wide variety of tools, resources, and technologies. This is partly thanks to XD, which makes these easily accessible to us. But as a result, we may also have a deluded sense about the degree of control we have over our judgments and decisions.

There are countless factors that influence our choices, with varying effects that depend on both the person and the situation. For example, while we may tend to rely heavily on doctors' opinions when we make medical decisions, we may not be affected by advice from others when we make vacation choices. Makes sense. Given the implications and risks involved, such behavior would give us a better chance of reaching our desired objectives in each case.

But these and other predictable decision-making tendencies can also be used to design experiences that can encourage us to make decisions that go against our best interests. To understand how, we'll consider in depth three major influencers of our experience as we make decisions: *emotions*, *options*, and *games*.

Once we acknowledge the different ways our intuitions and preferences are affected by various forms of experience design, we can think of mechanisms to reconsider or counter these if and when needed. We can then better draw the lines that determine where our freedom of choice ends and influence starts.

Are You Hot?
Designing Emotional Experience

Édouard Claparède was an influential neurologist in the early 1900s. He once had a patient with a particular form of amnesia that prevented her from forming new memories. She reportedly could not recognize the doctors or nurses she frequently met. When someone read something to her, she not only quickly forgot the content she had listened to but also the fact that someone had read something to her. In essence, her condition was akin to that of the main character in the 2000 film *Memento*, or Dory from the 2003 animation *Finding Nemo*.[5]

It was a tragic situation. But such anomalies often offer scientists a glimpse into the functions and boundaries of the human brain. By analyzing this condition in more detail, Claparède hoped he could better discern the effects of traumatic experiences on a person's mind and behavior. So he devised a small test.

One day, as he met the patient again, he introduced himself as he usually did by shaking her hand. But this time, he used a concealed pin in his palm to stick her hand and startle the fragile woman. In her mind, she was meeting her doctor for the first time. She trusted that he was there to help her, not to hurt her. The trauma of this action was real to her, and she reacted in fear. Yet a short while later, she inevitably forgot about the incident. This was her curse.

Claparède then approached her to meet once again, as if for the first time. He introduced himself and extended his hand. No pin this time: he was there to help her. From her perspective, she had never seen him before, but she refused to shake his hand.

Claparède discerned that her frightful experience had affected her despite the absence of any clear thoughts or recollections about it. In *The Emotional Brain,* neuroscientist Joseph LeDoux uses this anecdote to define "emotional memory" as a mechanism that helps us learn about the threats and opportunities around us without thinking about them. Emotions are useful for our survival and help us navigate a complicated world. Our current and past feelings guide us in predictable ways. They can have consequences for our subsequent beliefs and behavior, even when we are not consciously aware of them.[6]

In *Descartes' Error,* neuroscientist Antonio Damasio describes another way emotions interact with thinking and behavior. Damasio recounts his encounters with patients suffering from a different type of brain damage, one that prevents them from combining emotions with reasoning. It turns out that, in the absence of emotions, normal decision-making is almost impossible.

On one occasion, for example, when Damasio suggested two alternative dates for an upcoming visit, he observed the patient dive into a lengthy cost-benefit analysis that simply failed to converge to a decision. The patient reportedly fretted about "previous engagements, proximity to other engagements, possible meteorological conditions, virtually anything that one could reasonably think about concerning a simple date," without being able to come to a conclusion.[7]

Damasio argues that this case illustrates how we need the help of our emotions to subjectively weigh the costs and benefits involved in any decision and then make a final choice. When we experience a decision, we don't just record the facts associated with it. We also tag it with the emotions we experienced. How we *felt* matters. Later, we use those emotional tags to recall the experience and to make fresh decisions about similar issues.[8]

In the Star Trek universe, Vulcans are a species that can detach their emotions completely from their decisions. We humans can't do that. Given the central role of emotions in storing and summoning experiences, it is important for us to understand their effects on our decisions. And some of these effects are fairly predictable.

When we are angry, for instance, we tend to take more risks than we otherwise would. This can prove useful under certain circumstances. But it may also make us excessively confident in our abilities and ideas, while less likely to admit fault. When arguing, we typically speak louder, listen less, and say things that we don't necessarily mean.[9]

When we are sad, we tend to have a more pessimistic view of the world. When we are happy, we become more accommodating and agreeable than normal.[10]

Fear monopolizes our attention. It propels us to action when we sense a threat and so has been essential for our survival. Fear of a potential loss can affect the way we take risks. Laws often rely on our fear of punishment to deter us from criminal acts. But too much fear can also paralyze. We may be inclined to do anything to get out of a terrifying situation.[11]

The emotion of disgust can play a powerful role in our thinking too. In *The Righteous Mind*, social psychologist Jonathan Haidt explains how it can influence our social perceptions, moral judgments, and political attitudes.[12]

Knowledge of general tendencies like these coupled with personal data on our characteristics and past decisions provides a powerful resource for those who are designing our experiences. So, especially when the stakes are high, XD practitioners make a point of building powerful emotions into our experience. This can be beneficial when the designs render our difficult decisions more attractive and enjoyable. However, it can also get out of hand.

One example is politics, where emotions often run high. Candidates, pundits, and advisers can snow people with a wide variety of messages that contain high doses of emotion. Research suggests that these tend to influence people's perceptions and how they eventually vote.

It's difficult to escape this experience. Because it attracts attention, all types of media can join the frenzy. As the anxiety mounts, the line between fact and fiction can be blurred. Sensational claims can garner undue attention, while thoughtful, fact-based investigations and nuanced messages may frequently be undervalued. The experience can perpetuate from one election to the next. While the issues and people may change, the emotional tags may remain, and the effects deepen with each cycle. After a while, shaking hands across the aisle can become increasingly hard.

As a negative side effect, the voters who swing elections may consistently find themselves making choices to avoid certain outcomes they dread rather than to produce outcomes they desire. In fact, political scientists Alan Abramowitz and Steven Webster argue that "the rise of negative partisanship has had profound consequences for electoral competition, democratic representation and governance." Hence, the resulting political environment could lead to further polarization and dissatisfaction.[13]

Such a setting can also temporarily hijack our intuitions and drive us to embrace illusory solutions to the emotion-fueled specters conjured up by the influencers—solutions that might involve abandoning long-established alliances, making expensive investments, or implementing extensive and irreversible policies without adequately considering their long-term consequences.

Throughout history, messages and campaigns designed around emotions have been applied in diverse contexts and situations. They vividly illustrate how the powerful pull of our emotional experience can trump our cognitive capacities, often regardless of our level of education, and make us needlessly commit and then repeat possible mistakes. To enhance our freedom of choice, we'll have to learn to reevaluate our emotional experiences and the designs behind them under a different light.[14]

But emotions aren't the only experiential factor that can be designed to influence the decisions we make.

Which Do You Like?
Designing Optional Experience

We (the authors) have watched as each of our children and grandchildren reached the age of two and started to have minds of their own. It's been exciting to observe, as they realized they were now able to make some of their own decisions.

But two-year-olds are notorious for their stubbornness—occasionally backing up their choices with screams and tears. At times, it seemed impossible to reason with them:

"Let's get your coat on, honey."

"No!"

"Honey, we all need to wear our coats. It's freezing outside."

"Noooooo!"

"Honey! You *have* to wear your coat."

"Noooooooeeeeaaaaaeeeeee!"

Luckily, some parents before us had come across a partial solution. Experience had taught them that getting stuck in the please-listen-to-reason loop only made things worse. So they cleverly redesigned the situation by offering two options rather than one. Hence, instead of a decision between coat or no coat, the question now became this coat or that coat.

One of us tried this two-coat approach and found that it usually worked. The average duration and intensity of the tantrums diminished, and the whole family usually left the house with their coats on.

This is a simple, practical illustration of the power of *option design* to reshape an experience and thereby influence the way people (in this case, small children) respond to it. Of course, as sophisticated adults, there's no way we could be influenced by such tricks.

Or could we?

Say there are two options of boxes in a store. (They could be boxes of cookies in a grocery store, boxes of tissues in a pharmacy—it doesn't really matter.) One box is gray and the other is black. That's their only difference. Both have a price of five dollars.

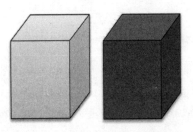

Some customers buy one and some the other. But let's say that a manufacturer would like to convince more people to buy either the gray or the black box, without interfering with the customers' freedom of choice or limiting their options. How could the manufacturer accomplish this?

One possibility would be to increase the available options by adding a third box to the mix, one that is exactly the same as the one they wish to sell more of, except that it's slightly smaller. What if they priced this third box at five dollars too?

It could be gray, as shown here.

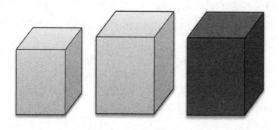

Or it could be black, as shown here.

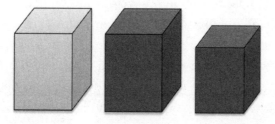

Maybe this sounds absurd. Presumably, not many customers would go for the smaller box under these prices and circumstances. Why pay the same for slightly less product? Yet providing the option may influence the customer experience—and therefore the customer's choice. Do you feel the extra pull that the new option creates toward the similar yet bigger box—the gray one in the first case with three options and the black one in the second? Because that box now appears relatively cheaper, it's more likely to become the number-one seller from among the entire range of three choices. And if, for whatever reason, some people choose to buy the smaller box, all the better.

In both three-option scenarios, the smaller box would be called a decoy. It's priced and offered mainly to influence the decision between the other two options. Of course, this example with simple, unmarked boxes is unrealistically abstract, and it's not a given that decoys work well all the time. But there are several reasons why this sort of option design would be attractive for companies.[15]

First, the choice still belongs to the customer. Additional options would be seen as enriching the customer experience and unlikely to dissuade many from buying altogether. Some people may even be more inclined to buy now that the original five-dollar choice appears "cheaper." So the added choice would have little downside, but some real potential upside.

Second, the decoy option doesn't have to be blatantly undesirable. Companies can determine the existence, the type, the price, and then the number of decoys produced and offered, some of which may prove to be desirable in their own right.

And third, if some people buy certain decoy options, so be it. Evaluations can be subjective. It was their choice.

As a result, various types of option designs are now part of the consumer experience in a variety of sectors. A famous example is the strategy employed by *The Economist* in the recent past, which was analyzed in detail in behavioral economist Dan Ariely's *Predictably Irrational*.[16]

Back in the day, the magazine offered three options to prospective subscribers: digital-only access at $59, print-only at $125, and a package deal for both at $125. But that sounds absurd. Presumably, not many would buy the print-only option under these circumstances. Indeed, experimental data collected by Ariely and his colleagues showed that 84 percent of the participants opted for the package deal, while the remainder went for digital-only access. The print-only option was not selected; it was a decoy.

So next, the researchers got rid of the decoy option to see how this change would impact people's choices. When participants from the same population were given only two options (digital-only and the package deal), 68 percent opted for the digital option, while the remaining 32 percent went for the package deal. Hence, in this particular study, the decoy served to sway 52 percent of the prospective subscribers from one option to another option—one that was presumably preferred also by the publisher.

But wait . . . Maybe this case is a fluke or outdated. We shouldn't generalize based on a single experiment conducted several years ago. Times have changed, and people's taste in periodicals may have evolved. Indeed, while some researchers did replicate this result in similar experiments, some failed to do so. That means such option designs with blatant decoys don't always control our behavior quite so powerfully.[17] Good news.

But let's explore the current situation. While writing this chapter in 2019 and then revisiting it in early 2020, we checked the subscription options *The Economist* was offering. When we visited the publication's website as nonsubscribers, the magazine gave us an introductory offer involving three options. One was called "Digital," another "Print," and a third package deal "Print + Digital," which was prominently displayed in the middle of the other two options, crowned with a tempting "Best Value" banner. And to our surprise, like our imaginary gray and black boxes, they all had exactly the *same* price: each was twenty euros for a period of twelve weeks for the European country sites and twelve dollars for the US site. It felt like, in this case, there were not one but *two* decoys!

Many other option designs can be subtler. They can be designed in ways that help companies legitimize the different prices of their different products, and lure customers to goods and services that the company would primarily like to sell.

For example, how much should a cup of coffee really cost? A price of $4 for a large cup may be difficult to evaluate if it is offered by itself. But if there is a medium cup for $3.50 and a small cup for $3, then all three prices suddenly seem more reasonable. Almost all coffee chains thus feature menu designs with multiple size options.

How much should a laptop really cost? Hard to say, but if the company offers a basic option for $1,500, a slightly better model for $1,800, and the best model for $2,000, then the prices suddenly seem to make more sense. The basic model justifies the prices of other options, and the middle model pushes customers toward buying a better and more expensive model. All tech manufacturers employ these option designs to simultaneously enrich the customer experience and optimize profitability.

In fact, many companies that cater directly to consumers design customer experience in a way that encourages us to anchor on some of the alternatives and then adjust toward others. Otherwise, like our two-year-old children and grandchildren, we may often choose not to "wear our coats" and buy less than (or differently) than companies wish. As consumers, we have a much easier time making up our minds under their well-crafted option designs. The crucial issue, however, is that they get to determine our anchors and adjustments, in many cases by employing fine-tuned decoys.[18]

Such strategies can have dynamic features that change over time as well. Consider the world of fast fashion, in which clothing companies bring new goods rapidly from design tables to clothing stores. The companies are also fast to replace those goods on their shelves, thus playing a role in defining fashion trends: when prospective customers visit a store, they know that what they see may be unavailable during their next visit. Hence, the customer experience involves an added sense of urgency due to worries about scarcity, which can lead to more frequent and impulsive buying behavior.[19] What we are wearing and for how long we'll be wearing it may thus not be fully up to us. It's influenced, if not strictly bounded, by this sort of dynamic option design.

Similarly, technology companies launch new products and upgrades based not just on technological advances but also reflecting careful time lines designed to define the evolution of our experience with their products. Immense amounts of consumer data make it possible to design these time lines and options to meet the companies' business objectives.

Such subtle option designs can also be used in negotiations.

For example, let's go back to the decision between options A and B presented at the beginning of the chapter. This decision reflects a real-world problem that many organizations face when they contemplate making a costly change in their business strategy.

Say that the company has an established low-risk strategy A, which yields low yet consistent returns. It's their current practice, their status quo. Then a manager proposes a promising change that could potentially bring higher returns. However, like any change, this option B would involve certain risks as well. Hence, in crudest terms, the situation looks like a choice between our original two options:

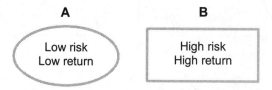

It's a difficult decision. Should the company change its strategy? Should it do that now or maybe at a later time? What may be some of the known and unknown unknowns that need to be considered?

In such a setting, a manager hoping to push his or her colleagues toward selecting the new strategy B might want to introduce to the mix a third option C. This addition could be purposely designed to make the new idea look immediately more reasonable and attractive.

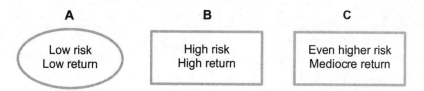

Indeed, depending on the conditions and parameters, option B could now be perceived as being the "best value" and thus become easier to choose. And once the third option is introduced, it's quite tricky to imagine a scenario without it. The experience is difficult to undo. Once it's part of the menu, option C becomes hard to unsee.

Of course, such an option design can be used with good intentions, helping people overcome a frustrating impasse. But it can also be used for more questionable purposes—to gain influence on the outcome and push a personal agenda, even one that may not be best for the company in the long run.

On the whole, having multiple options to choose from is a positive feature of our modern economy. Having a variety of alternatives allows us to make decisions that better fit our individual wishes and needs. We become freer to choose.[20]

However, like emotions, option designs have a major influence on our decisions. Their effects are hard to resist—and because we don't generally participate in the work of designing the options, we usually don't recognize how they impact us. Hence, it becomes difficult to pinpoint where exactly our freedom ends and the influence of others starts.

What's Your Game?
Designing Interactive Experience

We humans enjoy games. We like playing them. We like watching them. They involve goals and achievements, competition and co-operation, rewards and punishments, learning and improvement, uncertainty and creativity—all experiences that people find engrossing and engaging.

Some games have relatively simple structures. Solitaire, for example, is a game that involves no interaction with another player but only with the game's design itself. In peg solitaire, the player moves pegs or marbles around a board; in card solitaire, the player tries to sort the cards in a certain order.

Chess is more complicated. It requires two players who interact based on relatively complex rules. Backgammon adds other factors to the mix by introducing a pair of dice (and, in certain social settings, by allowing trash talking).

In the 1970s, digitalization led to a revolution in gaming. Computer games gradually evolved from 1972's Pong to interactive multiplayer games like Minecraft or World of Warcraft. The underlying principles of gaming, however, remain largely intact. They still involve goals and achievements, competition and cooperation, rewards and punishments, learning and improvement, uncertainty and creativity.

As with games, digitalization also sparked a revolution in human interactions.

The Internet made available an unprecedented degree of connection to the rest of the world. Millions can now instantaneously access a wide variety of goods, services, information, and opinions. The ensuing interactive environment is so complicated that we need user-friendly systems to help us organize, track, navigate, and store these interactions. XD has played a key role at every step of the way.

Designers optimized our user experience by developing graphic interfaces for computers and then adding navigation tools for the ever-growing World Wide Web. Nowadays, they offer us immense platforms where we can build personal profiles, buy products, and engage with one another in various ways. And companies increasingly use various games to interact with us—a phenomenon often referred to as *gamification*. The details of how this customization and gamification is done has profound effects on our choices, which we may not be fully aware of.[21]

Booking.com, for example, is an online supermarket for short-term accommodation that takes advantage of multiple behavioral insights to provide users a game-like environment. In particular, the site provides its users with all sorts of information about their choices in real time, continuously updating their perceptions about their circumstances. What's the current price of a hotel room? What was the price sometime earlier? How many rooms are left at the current rate? How many other people have been considering that same option? What are the conditions and amenities? How does that option compare to other, seemingly similar ones? What would the users prefer based on their previous choices? The company decides which details to provide and how to present them. And the users get immediate feedback. It's an intense experience.

Airbnb is also in the short-term accommodation business, but it belongs to the sharing economy, where users get to share their properties with one another for a fee. Its design features different elements that allow players to interact with one another in multiple ways. Hosts and guests get to review each other, make recommendations, and give feedback both publicly and privately. The system rewards such behavior and teaches users to behave in various ways.

Uber is one of the worldwide pioneers of the sharing economy. It facilitates car rides and has refined its interactive features over several years. It involves gamifications for the end customers and, more importantly, for the drivers as well. Uber would prefer them to drive more during certain hours, in certain places, at certain times. So it reportedly provides real-time feedback and immediate incentives to its drivers to increase the chances that they act in line with the company's preferences and objectives.[22]

Many experience designs make sure that users are still "free" to behave within their parameters. And they generate many previously unavailable consumer benefits and employment opportunities. But drivers are not Uber's employees, nor are homeowners Airbnb's. Hence, this ongoing gamification may be expected, especially in a private and competitive business context, providing a subtle way for these and similar companies to manage the behavior of their diverse sets of users without appearing dictatorial.

However, when does a design become too intrusive? Where to draw the line? For instance, what happens when these approaches start substantially affecting our personal and social lives?[23]

Who Are You?
Designing Social Experience

Experience design in social and organizational life is not really a new phenomenon. For centuries, institutions and organizations have deliberately organized and restricted activities so that their members would acquire certain preferences and beliefs by learning from experience. Think of churches, universities, armies, and corporations. These all provide organizational designs in which their members learn what is and what is not "appropriate," typically by observing and participating rather than by being told.

If this is possible in the offline world, it's even easier online, where information and feedback travels much more quickly and widely. Some level of top-down control in an online social platform is inevitable. All online social platforms—where people interact with one another, share content, and search for information—have to employ certain designs and filters to ensure that our experience is manageable, efficient, rich, and enjoyable, all at the same time. There's really no way around this. But it's important to have some idea about how the system works.

For instance, just as we purify water by running it through filters made of multiple layers of different materials, online social platforms use digital filters to distill and refine information for us, thereby shaping our experience. Users usually build the first set of filters themselves. In online platforms, we usually get to decide on what to search, what to share, with whom to connect, and how to act based on the available features. These actions reduce the whole space of possible interactions to a much smaller, personal subset. Through our own behavior and selections, we declare our interests, fears, tendencies, characteristics, habits, likes, and dislikes. We may still not be in total control, as our strategies in different sites have to abide by their specific rules and functions, but we ultimately end up building an online and platform-specific persona.

The platforms then build a second set of filters. They use our user data and interactions to guide our attention toward content that they think we'd personally like to experience. They recommend and show us the part of the whole picture that is in line with our revealed preferences. All of this filtering is intended to yield an improved user experience and increase the time and energy we spend in these platforms. It's win-win, except for one caveat.

As author and entrepreneur Eli Pariser argues in *The Filter Bubble*, such intricate filtering tends to constrain us within echo chambers—wicked learning environments featuring personalized and systematic censorship. And the more we remain in that bubble, the more we get exposed to a filtered experience and the more our resulting distorted intuition gets reinforced.[24]

Making matters worse, some of what we experience may not only be filtered but also false or fake. In 2018, researchers at MIT investigated all the news stories distributed on Twitter from 2006 to 2017. This involved about 126,000 stories tweeted by some three million people more than 4.5 million times. Some of the stories were verified as true, while others were false. The researchers found that falsehood "diffused significantly farther, faster, deeper, and more broadly than the truth in all categories of information."[25]

Hence, not only is fake news common in online social platforms, but it also seems to have considerable impact on our perceptions. Such content tends to be out of the ordinary, thereby grabbing our attention. In particular, a lot of it inevitably appeals heavily to the emotions. And fakeness can also be a matter of degree; some content may be partially false or exaggerated, further muddying one's experience.

Were you surprised about some of the latest election or referendum results in your country or in other races that you followed? Perhaps you were one of the millions of people who responded to the news with thoughts like, "How did this happen? How could I be so blind? How could *they* be so blind? Where are these people? Who are they? How could they think that way? I cannot recognize my country/city anymore."

Yet we shouldn't be surprised about people being surprised. Whatever our personal beliefs, opinions, and ideals, we each consistently experience only part of the picture. We know best the people in our own circle of family, friends, colleagues, and acquaintances. Now the filters that design our social media diets are further affecting our perceptions. And recent scandals have shown that the short-term benefits of such experience design can hide some significant long-term costs.

In 2018, a small IT consultancy named Cambridge Analytica got into trouble after obtaining vast amounts of Facebook data on people's profiles. One aim of the company was reportedly to design personally tailored posts and ads intended to influence voting behavior. Political campaigns have been designing tailored messages for years—for use in targeted mailings, for example. But what shocked the world was the scope of Cambridge Analytica's operation and the notion that they used "private" information. As computer algorithms become even more extensive and powerful, we should expect to see many similar efforts in the future. Our online experience may be even less under our control than we believe.[26]

How should we tackle these issues so that our social experience can be less narrow, more reliable, and less prone to influence by others with their own agendas? Many scientists, technologists, and politicians have been working on this question. But it would be naïve to expect solutions from the companies that run online social platforms themselves.

First, they may care about us, but they care more about keeping us engaged and longer at their sites. The minute we choose to use those sites, we are automatically facing an environment designed to shape our experience without us being completely aware how.[27]

Second, because they constantly innovate, the companies behind these virtual environments and marketplaces will not always be able to accurately predict the eventual impacts of their designs. No amount of testing can prevent bugs and unexpected side effects. Interest groups will constantly work to find loopholes in the systems to manipulate our experience. And given the sites' popularity, some of these flaws will create problems for millions of people. Facebook may have not envisioned Cambridge Analytica's intrusion, yet such complex systems are inevitably vulnerable to it.

Ultimately, we don't have much control over how others design our online experience. It's safe to assume that they will also design things primarily with their own institutional goals in mind. Hence, we need to find ways to claim more control over our own experience—as consumers, employees, voters, and users of technology.

Reclaiming Experience:
Increasing Our Control Over Our Decisions

Let's first acknowledge the reality. Emotions, options, and game-like interactive interfaces are indispensable parts of our decisions and lives. We can't make decisions without them.

But all these factors can be used to shape our experience and thereby influence our decisions in intricate ways, without us being completely aware. This becomes especially problematic when the objectives of those designing our experiences differ significantly from our own.

In certain circumstances, governments and policy makers use similar methods with the aim of protecting our well-being. In *Nudge*, behavioral economist Richard Thaler and legal scholar Cass Sunstein discuss how choice architects can provide "nudges" that ease decision makers' tasks and guide their choices, while respecting their interests, not limiting their choices, and safeguarding the welfare of the society as a whole.[28]

Nudges are increasingly prevalent in our daily lives. They take different forms. They include, for example, the use of defaults in investment options in pension plans and the manner in which healthy foods are given visual prominence when presenting options in school cafeterias.[29]

Some nudges are also designed to provide a kind learning environment to users through immediate and accurate feedback on their actions. For example, a wide variety of wearable devices show us how many steps we take during the day, thereby prompting us to exercise more. Studies also find that people regulate their energy consumption in their homes if they are provided with regular information on how they fare relative to their neighbors. Depending on the context, such experiential nudges can encourage decisions that lead to socially desirable outcomes.[30]

But nudges have some drawbacks from the perspective of learning from experience. One issue is that each decision or problem requires its own nudge that some benevolent choice architect has to design. As a result, we are once again merely reacting to an experience created for us by a third party, though one that presumably has our own welfare at heart. And because many nudges aren't designed to teach long-term lessons but merely to guide us toward specific behavior in one situation, we may find it easy to revert to old habits once the intervention ceases.[31]

So how can we reclaim our experience without relying on help from a benevolent third party or government?

One way is to develop an internal *design radar*—a sensitivity to designed experience that can help us recognize when our immediate experience is being manipulated and to consciously discount its impact on us.[32]

This isn't easy to do. It takes a degree of mental and emotional discipline. Experience is hard to deny even when it works against us. Fortunately, however, while we may not have much choice about how we immediately feel when we experience a design, we have more control over how we react to it.[33]

When making decisions with long-term consequences—who to vote for, what to invest in, how to shape our habits—we could use the immediate sensation caused by the situation as a trigger to intellectually analyze the situation rather than as a guide. Instead of giving in to emotions, option designs, or gamified interactions, we could remind ourselves that we are experiencing a design intentionally built to make us feel and behave in a certain way.

For example, if a situation or institution consistently instills a strong emotion, positive or negative, we should consider the possibility that this is a premeditated attempt to influence our intuition and preferences though our emotional experience. The more at stake, the more likely it is that strategists have planned to make us feel and then behave in particular ways.

The same goes for organizations and platforms that feature experience designs. In *Influence*, social psychologist Robert Cialdini explains how we are often quick to like people who are good-looking or similar to ourselves and how this automatic reaction leaves us vulnerable to making choices or buying things we might not otherwise choose or purchase. He suggests that we should learn to react with caution when we experience an immediate liking for something or someone. At least as a first step, we could use our initial reaction as a reminder to discount or minimize the impact of first impressions, instead of relying on them as a guide.[34]

When choosing among multiple options, we could similarly be alert to the impact of option design. Why are items priced and presented that way? Does one item seem exceptionally preferable? Are there any alternatives that seem to be relatively inferior? Regardless of the comparisons encouraged by option design, which options would fit our long-term objectives best?

Developing a design radar would be a first step toward reclaiming experience and exerting more personal control over our choices. A next step would involve relying primarily on our personal objectives, instead of our immediate experience with a certain design, as the main anchors for our attention and drivers of important decisions.

To achieve that, however, we may need to stop and think about our objectives more clearly. In particular, to mitigate the influence of designed experience, we could periodically ask ourselves a set of questions about our various aims and answer them sincerely. Borrowing from the toolkit of journalists, researchers, and detectives, these would be called the *5W1H questions*: What? Why? Who? When? Where? How?[35] Let's review them in order.

In the context of personal objectives, the first question would be *what*.

What is the objective? Of course, we may have several objectives, and these may change over time. That's OK. Yet we need to first define them to set a course and make our decisions accordingly. Without a clear initial definition, our attention and decisions will be swayed more easily by experiences designed by others. This first W question makes it less effortful for us to regulate our beliefs, reactions, convictions, and decisions in a way to help us reach our goals.

As an example, consider starting a business as an objective. What type of business will it be? What needs will it address? What goods or services will it offer? What kinds of customers will it serve? These questions would define the initial scope of this particular objective along with its boundaries. Our answers could possibly change during the course of the project, but they'd provide us with a concrete reference that would guide our behavior and constitute a basis for our strategies.

The second question would be *why*.

Why that objective? The more and diverse reasons we have, the better. If we don't have much reason to achieve a certain goal, or worse, have some artificial and externally defined reasons, we face the danger of running out of breath long before we get there. Hence, this second W is the fuel. Without several whys, we would needlessly be susceptible to outside designs and influences.

Going back to the business example: Why launch a business? Why this particular business? Why not another type of business? Why this product, service, and customer base?

The third question would be *who*.

Who will we be as we set out to achieve the objective? We can choose to behave in different ways for different goals. We may choose, for example, to be extremely ambitious, settling for nothing but the very best for some objectives. Alternatively, we may choose to overlook certain imperfections for others, as long as some of our basic preferences are met. The decision is really ours and might change along the way. Yet, unless we deliberately regulate our personal approach to each of our objectives, we would be vulnerable to designs that suggest we always need more, better, improved versions of everything, whatever the cost, for all our objectives.[36]

In the business example: Who will operate the business? Will they need to leave their current work to get started? How ambitious would they be about different aspects of the business? Will workers of specific types be employed?

The fourth question would be *when*.

When to achieve the objective? Determining the timing would help us avoid needless distractions, deferrals, and delays. We could plan things backward and know better what we need to do next. If achieving an objective requires first completing some other tasks, planning and setting deadlines for those tasks would be critical.

In the business example: When would the business be launched? Accordingly, when does a business plan need to be developed?

When will money need to be raised? When will the product or service need to be designed in detail? When do marketing and sales ideas need to be prepared?

The fifth question would be *where*.

Where to engage the objective? This would depend on what the objective is. Some aims could be global, while others would be limited to smaller geographies. There may be diverse legal or bureaucratic constraints to conduct a certain project based on the location. Certain places can provide people with more interactions with others who engage in similar projects, thereby featuring more opportunities for collaboration.

In the business example: Where will the business be housed? Are special spaces needed for producing goods or providing services? Where does the business need to be located for easy access by customers?

And the last question would be *how*.

How to achieve the objective? This is usually one of the first questions people ask themselves. Yet without first knowing the 5Ws, one would not be able to answer it appropriately and may even be swayed to solve the "wrong" problem. To understand the various methods one can use to reach a goal, an ideal way to start would be to research how others have previously attempted and achieved (or failed) similar goals. As we discussed in Chapter 2, originality is usually overrated when we are trying to determine how to solve complicated and important problems.

Going back to the business example: How have other similar businesses been launched? How did the whole process evolve? How to contact the people who previously made it happen? How did they fail? How did they succeed?

Ideally, we would conduct this type of 5W1H analysis for all our main objectives. Some of these could be more personal, while others could focus more on the needs of the collective, like our family, community, or humanity. Such an approach would subsequently help us prioritize among our objectives, improving the chances that we attend to our goals in a structured and timely fashion. And once we have these on record, we would have a much better idea about which decisions we should make and when. We would make adjustments and changes along the way and be able to track our learning and progress.

In this way, clearly defined objectives would provide us with a solid reference on which to base our decisions, rather than being influenced by designs we encounter along the way. 5W1H would first help us question and investigate our goals. And then, with our focus on them, we wouldn't be swayed as easily by emotions, options, interactive games, and other sorts of experiences designed for us by others to help achieve objectives other than our own. We would reclaim some of our freedom.

What's Missing? What's Irrelevant?

The modern world provides many freedoms when we make our political, social, and personal choices. Experience designs provide us intuitive access to information and technology, making sure that we can cope appropriately with complex and important situations.

However, experience designers can also exert substantial control over our decisions, potentially constraining our freedom without our awareness. Especially if their aims clash with our personal objectives, our choices may be affected in ways that don't necessarily match our interests and preferences.

Irrelevant emotions. Given the fundamental role emotions play in our decisions, it's important to recognize how and when they can be designed to influence our choices. If we sense that the emotions we're feeling might be detrimental for our objectives, it would be wise to defer and reconsider decisions when emotions are no longer "hot."

Irrelevant options. Choice options can have various compositions and be presented in different ways, allowing people to compare alternatives. But option designs can also be shaped to steer us in specific directions, including some that may be irrelevant to our own long-term objectives.

Irrelevant games. User-friendly designs are essential for us to be able to interact with complex systems and platforms, especially in the digital space. However, some of the games, social networking platforms, and other forms of interaction we encounter are designed to shape our learning, our decisions, and our habits, which may not necessarily be in line with our personal objectives.

Irrelevant designs. Experience designs primarily reflect the concerns of the designers, which may be irrelevant to us. When we sense the impact of XD, rather than taking their suggestions at face value, we can try to understand their possible detrimental effects on our decisions and objectives.

Missing objectives. Our important political, social, and personal choices should be mainly guided by our own long-term objectives rather than by any particular design we experience. The 5W1H framework provides a tool to clarify one's objectives, personalize them, and take them as a reference when learning and making decisions.

It's important to recognize the limits of our freedom in our choices and the various roles that XD plays in our decisions. Once we achieve that awareness, we can reclaim our own experience, learning useful lessons from it while refusing to be swayed by it in ways that conflict with what we really want to achieve.

5

IF IT FEELS GOOD, DO IT

When Experience Erodes Integrity

YOU ARE OFFERED AN AMAZING DEAL.

You'll get to eat anything, whenever and as much as you'd like. And you won't get fat!

What's more, you'll actually get healthier the more you eat. You'll be able to enjoy all the food you want and experience only the pleasures of self-indulgence. Nothing is off limits: steak, pizza, pasta, cheese, chocolate, ice cream. And especially junk food: chips, fries, hotdogs, candy bars, sodas. You name it. Anything goes. For those of us who've struggled with dietary temptations, this is a dream come true.

But there's a catch.

While you get happier and healthier as you eat whatever you wish, some other people somewhere else have to get correspondingly fatter and unhealthier. The more you enjoy yourself, the more they're going to suffer. You don't need to personally know who those other people are and where they live. And you won't feel their misery at all while you revel in your limitless, painless gluttony.

That's the deal. It's amazing for you—and terrible for someone else.

How would you respond if offered such a deal? What questions would you ask? Is there anything you could learn that would change your response to this offer?

Of course, this scenario is pure fantasy. We'd lose our health if we consistently and excessively adhered to an unhealthy diet, so it may seem pointless to ponder these questions. But what if we could actually get this type of deal for many other things we enjoy in life?

Our personal experience matters to us. We aspire to improve it. We often seek pleasures that will make us happy, while we try to avoid pain and suffering. And in the advanced world we live in, many of the good things that we wish to use and experience, including but not limited to transportation, technology, connectivity, clothing, information, infrastructure, and health care, are becoming simultaneously more useful, affordable, and accessible. Hence, we can increasingly hope to get more of these while spending less.

Great. What can go wrong?

The problem arises when our positive experience imposes significant costs on others, without impacting our own experience. And when we scratch the surface of today's economy, we see that this type of "amazing" deal actually takes place far more often than we might realize.

Whenever we buy and consume a product or service, we experience the final outcome of an intricate process. Many important aspects of this outcome are readily observable—its price, its perception within the community, its usefulness to us, its quality. But the details of the process that produced it and delivered it to us typically remain hidden from our experience. If there were any ethical issues along the way, we don't really have to be aware of these as we enjoy the outcome.

As a result, we may find it easy to "eat" more, without adequately considering that some unknown others keep getting "unhealthier"—that is, they suffer commensurately as a result of our behavior. We may even fail to realize that those who bear some of the costs of our actions may not be strangers but our fellow citizens, people we know, or even our own children, grandchildren, or more distant future descendants. By hiding the burdens inflicted on those we care about, our personal experience may render us unwittingly more selfish.

Profit-seeking corporations can further exacerbate this problem. They know that consumers primarily value their experience with the final goods and services they buy, so they build their processes and incentivize their employees accordingly. In such an outcome-driven competitive marketplace, however, organizations can be tempted to obtain desired results by stretching the boundaries of the law and even by breaking it. And these transgressions typically remain hidden from consumers' experience. Even when such behavior is eventually revealed, it's often too late—the damage is done.

And over time, we can get used to "overeating" without paying any apparent consequences. It can easily become our status quo, our daily experience, our reality, and thus hard to change. With better access to information, we might start to sense that some outcomes and situations we experience are simply too good to be true. We might realize that the underlying processes led to costs that we would never want to impose on others, let alone incur ourselves. Such awareness may be crucial for our considerations of fairness. But our experience might also teach us that we are unlikely to ever bear those costs ourselves.

Oscar Wilde famously defined a cynic as "a man who knows the price of everything and the value of nothing."[1] By this definition, how cynical can our experience make us?

We can only find out by going beyond what our experience readily offers. We can then decide for ourselves how much we really value the "amazing" deals we are offered and how we want to behave in the light of that new wisdom.

Meet Joe's Experience: Conveniently External

Joe works in a corporation. He deals with daily struggles and problems with the help of his colleagues, friends, and family. His life could be improved, of course, but there's not much to complain about. When he gets his next promotion, things will get better.

Joe enjoys many products, services, and conveniences that technology and society offer him at affordable prices. He has a mobile phone and a personal computer, both constantly connected to the Internet. He uses them to conduct many of his daily duties, check his messages, watch videos, manage his schedule, follow the news, look for information, and interact with colleagues, friends, and family. The productivity of these devices has increased a lot over recent years, while their prices have steadily declined. He switches to newer models every few years.

Joe selected and organized his wardrobe over time. On work-days, he prefers to wear a comfortable gray or dark-blue suit with a white shirt. For other times he owns a selection of T-shirts, pants, sneakers, and accessories that go well together. He changes part of his wardrobe every year, as some items get worn out. This also ensures that he loosely keeps up with fast-changing fashion trends.

Joe drives to work every day. Good mileage was a must when he chose his car. He was pleased to see that new engine technologies made it affordable for him to travel efficiently while harming the environment less.

Joe's job can be intense. He oversees several operations and needs to meet his quotas to qualify for his annual bonus and then ultimately get the promotion he desires. He has been working ex-ceptionally hard over the last few months, yet he is astonished to observe that some of his colleagues in other comparable depart-ments are obtaining better outcomes with similar or less input. This situation recently led the management of the company to scrutinize Joe's department to see what may be going wrong. This adds signifi-cantly to Joe's daily stress.

Joe has various investments. In the past, he had bet that the housing market would keep soaring, and as a result he lost a con-siderable sum during the 2008 financial crisis. He is trying to be an informed investor, but investing is not his job. Hence, he often listens to the advice of financial analysts.

Joe's daily experience features ups and downs. But he leads a decent life. He usually falls into a deep, comfortable sleep at night, knowing that he has another hard day ahead of him. For the most part, this is how Joe goes through life.

Joe's level of wealth is significantly higher than the global average, and he rightfully deserves part of his riches. He has worked hard, sacrificed, and compromised to attain his possessions and his relatively lofty status. No doubt about that.

Yet part of Joe's situation is inevitably due to luck. For instance, he did not choose where, when, and into which family he was born, all of which have a big impact on his current well-being. Good luck may not be sufficient, but it is necessary for a comfortable life.

And part of what Joe has involves what economists call *externalities*. These occur "when the effect of production or consumption of goods and services imposes costs or benefits on others which are not reflected in the prices" set by market forces.[2]

Some externalities are positive. For instance, Joe and his spouse benefit their children by providing them with a good education. In doing so, they also add to the overall productivity and well-being of their community. Similarly, Joe's company improves its own bottom line when it engages in research and development activities, but the discoveries thus generated also add to the knowledge base of society. Hence, the benefits these individual and group investments generate in the long term may be considerably higher than those they produce in the short term.

But Joe's life also involves many negative externalities. The global systems Joe operates in allow him to have good experiences. For this to happen, however, other parties may have to endure bad ones for quite some time. And these parties tend to be among those who had little luck on their side to begin with.

If Joe had a detailed understanding of the existence and extent of positive and negative externalities in his life, it would impact how he behaves and what he consumes. This understanding is thus essential for making informed decisions. Sadly, however, information about most of the externalities in Joe's life is missing from his experience. As a result, Joe gets to enjoy some "amazing" deals.

For example, the United Nations and the International Labor Organization report that some workers who build parts of the technological devices that Joe uses every day have to leave their homes and families during most of the year to work for subsistence wages. Their contracts tend to be temporary ones that provide minimal safeguards for human rights. They work excruciatingly long hours under strict rules that disrupt their lives in and outside of work. Of course, they work such jobs because they lack alternatives. If these jobs didn't exist, they might be worse off.[3]

The majority of Joe's electronic devices also contain materials that need to be mined in different locations in the world. One such material is coltan, a metallic ore that is used to produce batteries and capacitors in many everyday electronic products. The mining practices, however, have reportedly resulted in environmental hazards, civil unrests, conflicts, and misery for different populations.

This is not an isolated case. Millions of people around the world have suffered so that natural resources can be extracted at minimum cost to corporations and end users. Various minerals, oil, gold, and other valuable elements are sometimes exploited for readily observable economic benefit, while leading to local social problems that remain hidden from Joe's experience.[4]

Plastics contained in vast numbers of items Joe uses every day pose a wide variety of potential long-term environmental problems. Country-sized accumulations of plastic debris have collected in the oceans. A large amount of such waste invades wildlife and threatens to poison food chains. But unless this plastic ultimately ends up contaminating his food, Joe will remain the benefactor of the "amazing" deal offered to him.[5]

Similarly, to bring many goods to Joe at affordable prices, companies in many sectors pollute and waste at unsustainable rates. Food safety is a concern in many countries, where irresponsible mining, industrial production, and irrigation practices have reportedly been contaminating farmland soils.[6]

As for Joe's clothes, the global fashion industry also aims to reduce costs of production and ultimately the price of their final goods. As a result, many of Joe's favorite items were produced by processes with safety issues. There are reports of buildings collapsing with garment workers still inside and of some subcontractors using child labor.[7]

Many food items at Joe's house involve hidden negative externalities as well. The American Society for the Prevention of Cruelty to Animals reports that industrialized farming has long been putting efficiency before animal welfare. Millions of animals are kept indoors in small stalls or cages, bred for fast growth or yields, and treated roughly, guaranteeing a lifetime of suffering. A high demand for animal products also damages the environment by producing greenhouse gases and depleting essential water supplies. Family farms often struggle to keep up with large-scale industrial producers that are better able to take advantage of these negative externalities.[8]

What Joe gets to observe, however, are displays of conveniently packaged products on easily accessible shelves. In many industries, the experience of buying and consuming the final product is radically removed from the way it was produced. Many chains, department stores, and online sites that deliver goods and services to Joe also employ processes that are missing from his personal experience. They cut costs by pressuring their workers and contractors as much as they legally can.

Many of these procedures and systems are not necessarily illegal. But to lessen the restrictions from regulations designed to protect workers' rights and the environment, organizations can use part of their proceeds to lobby for more favorable laws. This is another aspect of the process to which Joe is normally oblivious.

As a result, while consuming most goods and services, Joe has little or no sense of the depression of the workers, the misery of the animals, the desolation of clear-cut forests, and the debris accumulating in the oceans—or the potential suffering of his own children's children due to the long-term problems that current practices may be causing. On the contrary, Joe's daily experience is basically quite delightful. He can afford many luxuries at low prices, his comfort level is high and rising, and he has made a habit of replacing many of his possessions frequently.

Similarly, Joe doesn't experience the positive externalities of many practices either. He thus fails to appreciate appropriately all the benefits generated by certain products and services, such as the hundreds of millions of people lifted out of poverty by the spread of industrial production into the countries of the developing world. Many global corporations have helped communities around the globe by creating opportunities for employment. Many also support charitable foundations that provide funds for a wide variety of vital causes.

Ultimately, Joe's experience filters out all sorts of externalities involved in the processes, making it difficult for him to judge the true cost and the real value of the goods and services he consumes. He has a partial view of the situation, which has important implications on how he, corporations, and governments ultimately behave.

Meet Joe's Experience: Comfortably Numb

Joe's car emits low levels of pollutants while not compromising on performance. It was reasonably priced, it's reliable, and it looks good too. The whole deal seems almost too good to be true.

It is. Unbeknownst to Joe, the car has a "defeat device." It's programmed to behave cleanly only when authorities are testing it. Because test conditions are known, the car's operating system was rigged to make the appropriate emissions when the car is put in exactly those conditions. The company needed to achieve a certain outcome under specific conditions. It made that happen. And as a result, it could advertise the final product as "clean"—despite the fact that, under normal driving conditions, it emits pollutants at a rate exceeding those permitted by law.[9]

Joe couldn't learn about this problem from his experience. The test results he observed were good, so he assumed that the underlying processes must also be good. Why check things if they don't seem broken? But this attitude can ensure that, like externalities, *deceptions* also remain below the radar for a long time. Meanwhile, our daily experience is unaffected or even improved by such misbehavior. We get to enjoy a seemingly amazing outcome at an affordable price.

This kind of outcome bias definitely played a role in the 2008 financial crisis. House prices and the stock market were going up for a long time. Investments had amazing returns. Joe (and millions of others) pleasantly rode that boom until it suddenly and unexpectedly collapsed. Joe realized that the whole period before the burst had actually been too good to be true.

Joe had invested in financial instruments that reputable banks had created, rating agencies had vetted, and large insurance companies had insured. By the time he felt the negative consequences of the scheme, it was too late. Within days, a huge fraction of his savings went down the drain. He blamed himself afterward. What was he thinking?

He wasn't. He was mainly guided by his experience and by experts, who were also guided by their own experience. The resulting lessons did a good job of hiding the underlying elaborate deception.

We sometimes witness impressive, seemingly miraculous performances by countries, companies, and individuals, month after month or year after year, only to realize later that to achieve these outcomes, books were cooked, laws were broken, bribes were paid, bodies were doped, and strings were pulled behind doors that hid these events from sight. Experience often fails to provide the right clues at the right time to recognize and stop fraudulent activities. The desirable outcomes we witness once again mask the hard-to-decipher underlying processes.

Once we realize that a deception was involved, however, the irreversible damage is usually already done. As one small Enron investor put it after the company went bankrupt and its misconducts were exposed, "I did not lose billions . . . but what I did lose seems like a billion to me."[10]

Joe is now experiencing a similar situation at his own job. For a number of years, several departments have been generating results that are simply too good to be true. It's possible, of course, that they have found some radically more efficient ways of doing business. Yet, knowing the intricate details of the process, Joe suspects foul play. He has also come across some evidence that supports his doubts.

Management at Joe's company, however, chooses to scrutinize Joe's processes instead of those of others, precisely because his outcomes are not as good in the short run. This frustrates Joe. And he gets further irritated when he ponders that by working in the company he is helping to perpetuate the same conspiracy. But what can he really do?

Joe feels stuck. If somebody else were in his place, Joe reasons, he or she would probably behave in the same way. Moreover, through effort, luck, and externalities, he has reached a level of comfort that he and his family cannot afford to disturb. His current pleasant and stable experience is limiting his options. He finds himself in a comfortable ethical trap.

Joe is not cruel, selfish, or immoral. He cares about fairness, integrity, and the welfare of others. He's not naïve either. He suspects that part of his level of comfort is thanks to certain externalities and possible deceptions. But he's comfortable. His personal positive experience stands to be affected by changes in the status quo. Thus, there's a constant conflict between Joe's knowledge and his experience.

When he speaks, his knowledge tends to prevail. He is astonished and angry about the ethical issues he sees playing out in the world of economics and business. He knows that these don't take place exclusively in remote places and underdeveloped economies. He observes and reads about injustices that many of the victims don't deserve. He sometimes talks about these with his friends and family. He occasionally rants about such problems in online networks and forums to complete strangers.

But when he acts, his experience gets priority. He feels like a small cog in a large globalized system where he does not really feel responsible for what's going on. He is merely doing his part. His personal impact is minimal. Owners, managers, regulators, and politicians should know better, and they should "do something" about the unfairness of the system. Joe is just trying to get by and provide the best for himself and his family. He has also learned from experience that acting like this has served him well in the past.

Management scholars Max Bazerman and Ann Tenbrunsel have studied the kind of ethical dilemma to which people like Joe can easily fall prey. In *Blind Spots*, they describe how the lessons of experience can normalize unethical and fraudulent behavior.[11]

First, many ethical problems develop slowly. Contrary to widespread belief, a frog in a pot of gradually warming water will actually jump out as the temperature rises. But humans in a comparable ethical quandary may not respond as alertly. Bazerman and Tenbrunsel argue, for example, that the fraudulent investment scheme run by the notorious Bernard Madoff might never have reached its ultimate size had it grown faster. Because the fund grew slowly over many years, investors felt increasingly comfortable and got used to their circumstances.

Second, some misbehavior doesn't lead to a catastrophe. People and organizations may act irresponsibly and risk irreversible damage, but the results may not be disastrous. Like most people, Joe tends to judge his experience based on the outcomes it produces. He starts questioning decisions and practices only after they lead to unexpected and unwanted consequences. But that may already be too late.

Ultimately, Joe's experience creates a blind spot concerning externalities, deceptions, unfair practices, and other ethical issues. But this isn't true only for him. There are many people like Joe. And the cumulative impact of such partial understanding of the actual situation can quickly become unsustainable.

Going Beyond Outcomes to Reveal Hidden Processes

Joe tries his best to behave ethically. If he hears about the misconduct of a manufacturer or a service provider in the shape of a negative externality or deception, he considers not purchasing from them. It helps him keep a clear conscience.

However, such situations can also be more nuanced than they seem. The ethics of an issue are rarely clear-cut and easy to decipher. Companies change over time and have complex relationships with employees, subcontractors, and collaborators. They may be acting harmfully in one place while helping in another, producing all sorts of negative and positive effects at once.

So are there any methods that could help Joe—and the rest of us—consider the implications of our actions beyond the lessons provided by our experience?

One relatively straightforward method is the so-called *sleep test*. This idea is based on the notion that our gut feelings are a reliable guide to the ethical status of a situation. If people are able to sleep well at night while living with a particular ethical challenge, then it's safe to assume that all is well. Good sentiment. But bliss may be due to ignorance. Having a serene gut feeling and sleeping well may induce a sense of relief, but it doesn't prove that crucial issues aren't hidden from experience.

Entrepreneur and author Margaret Heffernan explores in *Willful Blindness* our capacity to deliberately ignore information that makes us uncomfortable and problems that are hard to solve. Especially when our current experience is pleasant, we can find it easy to pretend that ethical issues don't exist, even those that are seemingly obvious. For example, Joe finds it easy to walk past homeless people as he roams the city. He is at least vaguely aware that some of the animals that he routinely eats are being mistreated. But not ignoring these experiences would paralyze him. Being numb to them makes it easier for him to function as a citizen.[12]

Hence the sleep test may not be adequate to objectively judge the ethics of a given situation. The main issue here is that the underlying processes can still remain largely hidden from experience. To enjoy the wide variety of goods and services we use every day, we don't really have to know at all about their histories, makings, and consequences. These details are easy to ignore.

To be able to better evaluate the ethical realities behind certain "amazing" deals we're offered, we need at least some knowledge about what's going on behind the scenes. Accordingly, we can take a close look at some of the outcomes we enjoy and, as a first step, inquire more frequently about their processes. How were they conceived? How are they made today? Who works in their production and under what conditions? What types of materials are used?

How are these obtained? Is anybody cheating? What are the effects of the whole process on the welfare of others and the environment?

And overall, what are some of the potentially "amazing" deals we currently have? What type of externalities do they involve? Is anything illegal, unfair, or immoral involved? To what degree are we comfortably numb to the uncomfortable realities behind the good things we enjoy? These questions are not about assumptions or ideals. They are about the facts that underlie the goods, services, and other benefits that shape our lives. And these facts are more widely available today than ever.

If we were part of a process and were being treated unfairly, we would want others to know about it. We would be annoyed by consumers focusing solely on their experience with the final outcomes, while conveniently ignoring the problems in the process that led to their enjoyment. We could thus extend the same courtesy to others by finding answers to such questions at least for certain products and services we regularly enjoy.

Our willingness to dig sincerely into such processes would inform us about the value of many things beyond their price. Then it would be still up to us to evaluate these details and decide on whether or not to revise our judgments and behavior. At the very least, such a process-revealing exercise may lead us to appreciate more aptly what we have and can afford. It can improve our own cost-benefit analyses. In some cases, it may convince us to change the way we do and consume things before a catastrophe or scandal occurs. It may also lead us to acknowledge appropriately some of the positive externalities and honest practices around us.

In a few cases, it may even act as a deterrent against misconduct and lead to more ethical long-term business strategies. When it's harder for companies to hide negative externalities and dodgy practices from us, managers considering such methods might not engage in them in the first place. Considering the added approval they will receive for their positive contributions and fair practices, they may opt for these more often.

Accordingly, in Joe's company, management should take a good look into some of its key processes regardless of their outcomes. If managers wish to keep track of externalities and deceptions that may result in long-term problems, they shouldn't take results at their face value. Otherwise, they could be rewarding luck, unethical practices, or even illegal behavior and sending the wrong message to the whole company.

Going Beyond Empathy
Through Informed Compassion

The 2005 science-fiction film *The Hitchhiker's Guide to the Galaxy* features an unusual weapon called the point-of-view gun. It makes the person who is shot feel things exactly the way the shooter does. The gun was created at the request of the Intergalactic Consortium of Angry Housewives to make sure that for once their husbands would understand their point of view.[13]

Such a weapon, if it really existed, would be a way of automatically producing empathy—the act of experiencing in our minds what others experience. Empathy is often regarded as a powerful inducement to fair and ethical behavior. When we share the feelings of another person, it becomes harder to treat them in ways that cause suffering. Empathy can indeed be helpful in counteracting ethical problems intensified by the way we learn from experience. But it isn't flawless.

We recently came across a training session for teenagers whose main aim was to encourage empathy, in particular for the problems of people who live with a disability. Each participant was randomly assigned to experience a disability during part of a day. Some were blindfolded, some had their arms tied to their bodies, preventing their use, and so on. They were asked to continue with their usual tasks: eat, drink, use the toilet, and engage in other daily chores. As expected, participants struggled. No doubt this exercise left an impression on them.

Such an experiential activity could indeed lead people to identify flaws in the design of environments we experience on a daily basis. For example, people might realize that there aren't enough ramps for wheelchairs in a given environment or that existing ones are inadequate. Or certain details can be designed better to ease the lives of those who are blind, deaf, missing a limb, or living with another disability. Having to experience a disability for a short time can enable people to notice a variety of obstacles that could be addressed and be motivated to rectify these. By producing a degree of empathy, the exercise could help people without disabilities find ways to change their attitudes and behaviors in the interest of greater fairness.

But the exercise is also inadequate. These teenagers don't actually live with a disability during their usual lives. They just happen to experience one, in an artificial fashion, for a few hours. They are merely inconvenienced. They can afford to consider the difficulties they faced more as a challenge than as a way of life. It's impossible for them to truly empathize with those who have to live with a disability for most of their lives. To expect that degree of empathy is unfair both to the teenagers and to people who actually live with a disability.

Accordingly, in *Against Empathy*, psychologist Paul Bloom sets out to convince us that we shouldn't reliably count on empathy when making judgments about others. The point-of-view gun is sadly fictional. Precise and unbiased empathy cannot really exist, especially when the people on either side of the equation have widely diverging conditions, situations, and backgrounds. Two siblings or neighbors who have lived in close proximity for some time may indeed have a high capacity for empathy toward one another. But it will be hard if not impossible for someone healthy and wealthy to truly empathize with someone from an underprivileged community, halfway around the world, who continuously has to face multiple threats to health, safety, livelihood, and freedom.[14]

Moreover, when we attempt to empathize, specific, visible events and individual tragedies usually capture our attention, while general facts and broader information get undervalued. This notion is often dubbed the *identifiable victim effect*.

In 2015, the image of Aylan, the Syrian refugee boy lying dead on a beach hundreds of kilometers away from his home, had worldwide impact. It brought overwhelming sorrow to many news viewers, and it caused immediate outrage, as it should. But the lesson remained only on the surface and didn't last long. And thousands of other lives claimed by the Syrian conflict (and similar wars around the globe) didn't have much force on public understanding, opinion, or action.

As the scope of a disaster increases, our ability to face and deal with its consequences diminishes. What we learn from experience doesn't necessarily reflect the objective measures of what has occurred. Psychologist Paul Slovic and his colleagues argue that *compassion fade* occurs especially when we move from considering just one to multiple victims. Their findings echo an observation often attributed to Joseph Stalin: "One man's death is a tragedy, a million deaths is a statistic."[15]

A strategy that could help improve our learning in these circumstances would be to use the immediate emotional experience caused by identifiable victims and events as a trigger to look for more facts and figures about the broader situation.

When our empathy is stirred by the image or story of a particular identifiable victim, we can attempt to go beyond that observation: How many other victims are there—children, people, animals, and other creatures we care about? How were they affected? What was the cause? What is the underlying process that led to their harm? What illegal and/or unethical actions produced the damage? Is there anything we'd like to do to alleviate their suffering or that of future victims? Who else is knowledgeable and cares about the situation? What are they doing?

Going beyond anecdotes about identifiable victims and overwhelming experience with which we can't truly empathize can help us achieve the potentially more effective state of *informed compassion*. This can help us make more ethical decisions and subsequently reduce societal problems.[16]

Fortunately, we live in a world where gathering information about the ethical realities behind our experience is increasingly possible. As individuals, our decisions are getting steadily more transparent and traceable. With the digitization of data, greater access to the Internet, and the faster spread of information through social networks, it will be more and more difficult to hide ethically questionable conduct. The rise of transparency increases the chances that a person will experience the consequences of his or her behavior at some point, be it positive or negative. Hence, potentially, it could push us to scrutinize our decisions and look beyond their observable and immediate outcomes.[17]

But like all the other tools we've considered, transparency has its weaknesses too. First, it doesn't necessarily guarantee fair judgments. The rewards or punishments meted out by society may not be based on the benefits and costs of people's behavior but on who they are, their positions and power in society, and how much others care about their actions. A single indiscretion may cause one individual to lose his job forever, while another may be excused for many acts of misconduct.

Second, transparency in one domain does not guarantee transparency in others. Sexual misconduct and victimization of others by prominent figures in Hollywood and the mainstream media have been exposed in the #MeToo movement. Does this suggest that other sectors are doing much better? Not necessarily.

Many Internet companies and social networks have recently run into trouble due to data usage and breaches. Does this mean that other industry giants are doing a better job on that front? Not really.

The lack of transparency in the private sector, coupled with a steady stream of fresh scandals, often from unexpected sources, suggests that we should not interpret absence of evidence as evidence of absence when it comes to fair and ethical conduct.

And finally, for transparency to affect behavior, people need to care about and strive to achieve a just outcome for all parties. If one does not really care about externalities or deceptions, then no degree of transparency will deter unethical behavior, induce compassion, or guarantee decency.

What's Missing? What's Irrelevant?

When we focus on long-standing, complicated ethical and moral problems embedded in our social system, it can be tempting to give in to despair. But there's a lot of positive news as well. Recent decades have seen vast improvements in worldwide levels of poverty and health. Data suggest that in 1981, 42 percent of the world's population lived below the poverty line established by the World Bank. By 2015, this figure had fallen to 10 percent. And according to WHO, life expectancy has been steadily rising across the globe. These are examples of positive developments that reflect genuine accomplishments of the world's economic, political, and social structures.[18]

But the ways we learn from experience can provide a serious obstacle to things getting better quicker. Experience shows us results while hiding underlying processes, thereby masking ethical dilemmas.

Missing externalities. Although outcomes are readily available, many processes remain hidden from experience. As a result, most consumers can simply remain blissfully unaware of the positive and negative externalities behind the goods and services that shape their lives.

Missing deceptions. Some positive outcomes and "amazing" deals can, in fact, be too good to be true. They may depend on dishonest behavior, which is generally hidden from experience and therefore may go uncorrected for a long time.

Irrelevant comfort. For those of us who live with the privileges found in affluent societies, our enjoyable experience with outcomes can eventually render us comfortably numb, unequipped to make choices that are consistent with our ethical values.

Missing compassion. Empathy is hard to achieve, especially when the experiences of people on either side of the equation are vastly different. Also, our concern for a single identifiable victim of tragedy can easily fade when confronted with multiple victims. Informed compassion can be a more useful and effective replacement for empathy in these situations.

Missing transparency. Rising levels of transparency can improve the chances that people will experience the consequences of their behavior, be it positive or negative. But transparency is not guaranteed in many sectors and domains. And the effectiveness of transparency as an ethical spur will depend on how we consider and act upon what it teaches us.

To learn more about how our world *really* works, we can strive to go beyond the lessons of our experience. We can then more accurately perceive the values of things we care about beyond their prices and draw the ethical lines where we truly wish.

6

———

MAGIC BULLETS

When Experience Feeds Illusory Secrets of Success

WAKE UP EARLY.

Drink water before breakfast.

Put first things first.

Say no to almost everything.

Avoid meetings.

Exercise.

Have grit.

Know when to stay and when to leave.

Network.

Think win-win.

Fail.

Ignore others.

Would you like to be successful in life? If you do, you'd better follow these suggestions. They are a selection of principles based on analyses of what successful people have in common. They have been tried and confirmed by the best of the best. Learn from their experience.[1]

Great. What can go wrong?

As we work to achieve our goals, we may seek to learn from those who have already been successful. And while one particular case may be a coincidence, it would be useful to know what multiple achievements have in common. Sounds reasonable.

Yet focusing only on successes can distract us with irrelevant details, while hiding important facts. The resulting lessons can be useless and sometimes even work against our goals. Success, by itself, is not a reliable teacher.

Should we instead stick to learning from failures? Perhaps we can avoid future mistakes through a deep dive into what went wrong. And while one particular case may be an accident, it would be useful to know what multiple mishaps have in common. Sounds reasonable.

Yet focusing only on failures can also distract us with irrelevant details, while hiding important facts. The resulting lessons can be useless and sometimes even work against our goals. Failure, by itself, is not a reliable teacher either.

Experience can be surprisingly misleading if we attempt to learn from *either* success *or* failure. A better strategy is to consider *both* successes and failures, cautiously exploring what may be causing their difference. Yet this approach is not straightforward, it may not feel natural, and we may not like what we end up learning.

Deceptive Lessons from Others' Successes

The stream of seminars, books, articles, blogs, and tweets on success is endless. Many attempt to synthesize the habits and behaviors of the successful, often reinforcing their advice with striking anecdotes and first-person accounts. The list of things that successful people do, featured at the beginning of this chapter, is based on several prominent publications in the genre. Such advice based on stories of success offers us a useful means to pinpoint the problems with learning from successes. It will also allow us to recognize parallel problems related to learning from failures.

There is indeed some value in examining the practices of successful people and organizations. For instance, they can show us what is possible to achieve. They can inspire us and push us to action. Success stories motivate.

And most of the suggestions derived from the experiences of the successful feel real and reasonable. They grab attention and are difficult to deny. Hence, they provide us with a sense of control, making us feel we can drive our own success.

But let's be story skeptics. Instead of trying to confirm that the lessons from successes are reliable, let's consider how they can be deceptive.

The first issue is *accuracy*. What if some lessons from success are not actually real to begin with? Winners usually get to write the stories of how they achieved what they did, or to narrate their experience to others who eagerly report what they say. This raises the possibility that some stories get embellished along the way.

The stories of many successful organizations, for example, often involve conflicting accounts with widely varying interpretations of events offered by different stakeholders, including cofounders who built the company together. Even when certain prominent cases are explored in detail through blockbusters like *The Social Network*, the end results may still contain dramatizations, subjective evaluations, and editorial liberties.[2]

Worse, there are problems even if the stories of success we hear are accurate. Scan the literature on success, and you'll quickly encounter much advice that is based on multiple common aspects of successful people or organizations: 14 things successful people have in common, 10 common traits of effective leaders, 8 characteristics successful entrepreneurs share. When contemplating these lessons, we assume that everyone in these analyses diligently followed every strategy featured in the advice. After all, "common" means shared by all.

But did all of these winners really engage in *all* those listed strategies? Always?

Look closely, and you'll discover that, in many cases, the protagonists of these stories actually followed only a subset of the supposedly common strategies. Many applied *some* of them while avoiding the rest, yet still became successful. Such inaccuracies can undermine the generalizability of the lessons we derive from others' successes.[3]

Then there's the problem of *causality*. What if some of the characteristics of the successful are a consequence of success rather than its cause? As we saw in Chapter 1, identifying the causal links between actions and outcomes is much trickier than it feels.

Consider, for example, such advice as ignoring others, saying no to almost anything, avoiding meetings, or putting first things first. These all sound great, but in reality, they may be luxuries that only the successful can truly enjoy and afford to practice most of the time. Hence, some common characteristics of the successful may actually be the consequences of their success, not the other way around. As a result, we may feel hopeless when we realize that we are not able to adopt some of the lessons from others' successes before actually reaching a certain level of success ourselves.

Next, there's the issue of *time*. Hindsight is 20/20, and it's easy to define success once it has happened. But the lessons derived in retrospect are not necessarily helpful for future decisions. The feeling of "I knew it all along" may in fact fill us with unwarranted confidence in our ability to predict future achievements.[4]

In a 2015 presentation made at the MIT Sloan School of Management, Uber's cofounder and former CEO Travis Kalanick named the essential elements that great entrepreneurs commonly possess. One ingredient he reportedly listed was "magic," by which he meant "that feeling you have that something is truly special." Yet this feeling is something one can only interpret and evaluate after the fact, while the opportunities we seek only exist in the uncertain future. That's why abilities like recognizing opportunities or knowing when to stay and when to leave seem so "magical."[5]

Time complicates our learning from experience also because the world continuously changes. As a result, strategies that were formerly effective can eventually become obsolete.

Merely a few decades ago, in many parts of the world, a college degree could almost guarantee lucrative job prospects and a good career. Today, the degree may still be necessary, but for most people it's far from sufficient to produce such predictable results. Similarly, business activities like marketing, production, and innovation are continually evolving. What worked a few years ago may quickly become irrelevant with shifts in competition, technological advances, emerging social and economic trends, and other unexpected changes.

In *Think Twice*, investment strategist Michael Mauboussin discusses the perishable nature of secrets of success in the world of investing. In finance, analysts inevitably base their advice on historical data and past trends. But "because the statistical properties of markets shift over time, an investor can end up with the wrong mix of assets." Yesterday's lessons need to be continually updated in wicked learning environments, since time tends to reduce their relevance.[6]

Another detail to consider when learning from success is the issue of *selection*. What if failures get systematically filtered out of experience, leading to what statisticians call a selection bias?

Think back to the case of bloodletting from our introduction. Those who died after excessive treatments with bloodletting are not around to make a compelling case against the practice. Those who survive, on the other hand, would have reason to believe it saved them, and they may not be shy about sharing their wisdom. As a result, the collective experience, as captured in the testimony of those who are around to deliver it, would reinforce overconfidence about the procedure's effectiveness.[7]

In *Success and Luck*, economist Robert H. Frank observes how high achievers in a wide variety of domains tend to be talented and hardworking. These "survivors" give observers—including themselves—a sense of meritocracy in action. Unfortunately, however, while talent and hard work are often necessary for success, they may not be sufficient. After all, many of those who don't succeed in many settings may also be talented and hardworking.[8]

The selection filter leads to the so-called survivorship bias. Operating outside our control, it creates a false sense regarding the guaranteed effectiveness of specific actions when trying to achieve success. What was it that the less successful did or failed to do? Did they not wake up early? Did they not drink water at the right time? Did they not exercise? Are these indicators of some underlying incompetence? Maybe ... but it's more likely that scores of people also did the "right" things yet failed anyway.[9]

Especially in domains where failures greatly outnumber successes, it is unlikely that those who failed did not think of taking advantage of solutions available to them. Hence, the more simplistic a lesson from success, the more it assumes that those who didn't succeed are either naïve or unintelligent. This is disrespectful to many who strive to do their best but fail for all sorts of unforeseeable and circumstantial reasons.

Next, let's consider the issue of *complexity*. The lessons based on successes don't generalize into broadly applicable principles as much as we hope, especially if they are based on anecdotes and small samples of observations.

The real world is filled with countless individual variations and differences. Hence, systematic analyses based on richer evidence are needed to have a better understanding of the different factors simultaneously affecting outcomes in various contexts.

Accordingly, to deal with complexities and make better generalizations, some advisers rely on statistical analyses based on data collected through surveys and observations. They subsequently make claims like "following strategy X significantly increases the chances of obtaining that desirable outcome."

Unfortunately, however, even when the underlying studies are statistically sound, the resulting lessons are valid only for the average populations and professions represented by the data. Individual differences and nuances preclude the effectiveness of any one-size-fits-all solution. As with virtually all complex problems in life, the value of any strategy for success depends on context and circumstances.[10]

Here's an extreme example: given its adverse effects on health, it makes sense to advise someone to quit smoking. In most cases, avoiding cigarettes is likely to help a person extend his or her healthy life span. But what if that someone is a soldier on his or her way to active duty on the front lines in a raging war? For this individual, cigarettes may be a nonissue despite still being unhealthy on average.[11]

In less extreme form, the same problem arises with practically all the simplistic lessons based on successes. Take the case of grit—relentless perseverance in a consuming passion—as a major determinant of success. Research on the subject is scientific and relevant. Grit and persistence may indeed be essential for success given the right methods and circumstances.

But the different ways in which people exhibit grit often remain hidden from our experience. We tend to see the successful end products but not the intricate personal processes that led to them. We can thus fail to observe how blindly soldiering on toward the wrong goal in constantly evolving settings can actually prove to be wasteful.

Depending on the situation, a better approach may instead involve frequent updates in plans, seeking chance encounters, and developing skills within a wider domain, rather than refusing to adapt to changing conditions. Grit is thus a nuanced notion, which often gets conveniently oversimplified. Accordingly, in *Grit*, psychologist Angela Duckworth dedicates a whole book to the subject, striving to discuss all its relevant aspects. One needs to consider the same kind of complexity-revealing scrutiny for other bits of advice that are much more nuanced than they sound, like "exercise," "fail," and "think win-win."[12]

Last but not least, our quest to learn about success from the experience of the successful downplays costly *trade-offs*.

Success is personal, something internal and variable in time, despite the fact that it often gets treated as if it's external and constant. Bob Dylan is credited with a remark that aptly captures its personal nature: "A man is a success if he gets up in the morning and gets to bed at night, and in between he does what he wants to do."[13]

The *Oxford English Dictionary* defines success more bluntly as "the accomplishment of an aim or purpose." But what is *our* aim or purpose?[14]

For lessons from success to be valid for us personally, the starting points, abilities, preferences, and desires of those who are considered successful should be similar to ours. Yet we often don't know about these details. Our careers, families, social lives, priorities, abilities, and visions may differ significantly from those who are hailed as successful. We might not want to trade places with them, given what they had to give up to be where they are. Yet when considering others' achievements, the personal compromises they may have chosen to make often get strategically overlooked.

Pursuing success often involves costly trade-offs. Waking up early and doing a bunch of things in the morning may mean that we have neither the will nor the energy to do the things we are meant to do late at night. Accumulating wealth in a relatively short time through persistent hard work may mean sacrificing quality time with loved ones. Depending on our individual desires, such costs can be unbearable. It's thus important to consider what one has to forgo to reach any type of success.

Worse, as we discussed in Chapter 5, the road to success for some people and organizations may involve unfairness, deceptions, or other unethical behaviors. These costs are also often overlooked when people experience, analyze, aspire to, and glorify the resulting achievements. Yet we may personally find that successful ends can't be justified by immoral means.

For all these reasons, even if they may sound convincing and commanding, lessons of experience based exclusively on others' success are unreliable. They're likely to leave us with a belief that success is more objective and predictable than it really is.

Deceptive Lessons from Our Own Successes

So what about our own achievements? Unfortunately, they are not much better teachers, as they are not immune to the flaws of learning from others' successes.

Just as others can embellish their stories of personal success, we can too. We often find it easy to interpret our personal outcomes in a self-serving fashion, which primarily fits our own agenda and preferences rather than the more complex underlying realities. For instance, even though luck may have played a large role in a good result, we may prefer to attribute our success mostly to our skills.[15]

We may also remember things in ways that exaggerate our contribution to projects in which we were involved. And happy endings allow us to downplay the things that went wrong, or could have gone wrong, during the process.[16]

In addition, cause and effect often get muddled when we try to learn lessons from our own success. Some of our habits and attributes that we see as causes of our success may actually be results of it. For example, our proficiency in networking with influential and powerful businesspeople may be the consequence of our professional achievements rather than a skill we had all along.

Lessons from our own achievements can also oversimplify the determinants of success due to tempting but flawed generalizations. The vividness of the paths we took and the decisions we made can prevent us from accurately imagining how another person taking similar paths and making similar decisions in a slightly different context might experience wildly different outcomes. Hence, our own memorable and vivid past achievements can make us underestimate the obscure failures of others that, despite having acted much as we did, did not reach the same results due to factors that were unforeseeable and uncontrollable. Their failure may even give us undue confidence about our relative abilities. We could be tempted to interpret the outcomes of complex processes as having been caused by our own brilliant and timely strategies.[17]

And finally, in all that excitement, we may fail to recognize and acknowledge what we had to give up to reach our achievements.

Ultimately, regardless of how we may personally define success, if we're interested in learning more about its causes, merely considering successful experiences—including our own—would not yield the reliable insights we seek.

Deceptive Lessons from Others' Failures

What about flipping to the opposite side of the coin and seeking to learn from failures?

One disadvantage of this approach is that failure is much less fun than success. Nobody likes to fail. So to make learning from failures less painful, it would make sense for us to strive to draw lessons from others' mishaps. Why suffer when others have already been there, done that, and endured the unwanted consequences? Unfortunately, this turns out to be much easier said than done.

Consider, for example, the field of entrepreneurship—an arena in which failure is relatively common and acceptable. In startup culture, failure is typically respected as a natural element of any risk-taker's life and a good teacher that can pave the way to future success. And learning from others' mistakes is especially endorsed.

Over the last couple of decades, one of us (the authors) has taken on different roles in the establishment, management, and observation of various startups. While creating, developing, producing, and marketing new ideas, it always seemed reasonable to first learn from others' failed attempts, strategies, or decisions, especially before making a costly move. Yet this approach often proved to be difficult and sometimes surprisingly misleading, as it actually suffers from the same problems involved in learning from successes.

For starters, accuracy can be in doubt. The story of a failure often changes depending on who tells it, making it difficult to determine objectively what actually took place. We typically don't have much access to details on what happened behind the scenes of a failed decision or project. In extraordinary cases where we do get such access, each founder, manager, or decision maker is inclined to remember and tell a self-serving account of the events. It's like trying to learn about why a marriage failed by listening to the separate stories of each spouse: any lessons one might derive are likely to be unclear and biased.

Causality can also be blurry. There may be many causes that lead to a particular failure. Some of these are beyond people's control. Some may lead to failure only some of the time. And sometimes, people may behave in a certain way *because* they are failing and not the other way around. For example, one of the founders of a business may change his or her leadership style, which might later be seen as a reason for the project's failure. Yet the change may have been driven by emerging problems with the business. Our human tendency to make up plausible cause-and-effect claims doesn't guarantee that our stories are accurate.

Time also complicates any effort to learn from failures. Many failures can be understood and explained only after the fact. But a poor outcome, seen with hindsight, doesn't necessarily mean that a strategy was poorly chosen given the information available at the time. Furthermore, causes of failure can change over time. An idea or project may fail simply because it was either too late or too early.

We (the authors) know of one entrepreneur who entered the drip irrigation business in a developing country decades ago with high hopes. He failed. After the fact, his failure was attributed to particular flaws in his business plan and its implementation. Yet almost the same plan and implementation was successful only a few years later in the same market. It turns out that timing was a bigger determinant of the entrepreneur's failure than any other factor. If anything, he was actually one step ahead of those who subsequently succeeded. He had seen the need and developed the idea before they did—but he was too early.

Selection is a serious issue, too. Unlike others' successes, which are often trumpeted to the skies, others' failures are usually un-available and invisible—missing from experience. Even when failed ideas, projects, and companies ultimately become successful, most observers remain oblivious to the battles the entrepreneurs lost before their final triumph. The imperceptible censoring caused by the selection process can render us blind to the real causes of failure.

Complexities and trade-offs distort the lessons of failure as well. We are not the same as the people and organizations that failed before us. Our conditions and objectives may be significantly dif-ferent. Definitions and degrees of failure can also change from per-son to person and from organization to organization. We may learn different lessons from similar mistakes, and determining which les-sons are "right" is thus a more complicated task than it seems.

All these issues with learning exclusively from others' failures are valid beyond the entrepreneurship domain. They suggest that focusing on them offers no magic bullet that guarantees our own future success.

Deceptive Lessons from Our Own Failures

What about the painful possibility of revealing the secrets of success by learning from one's own personal failures? Is this source of knowledge free from the distortions and errors that plagued the other sources we've examined? Sadly, no.

In *Black Box Thinking*, author Matthew Syed discusses how learning from one's own failures is not necessarily automatic or accurate. He observes that we are often very proficient in pointing the finger at others when something goes wrong but reluctant to acknowledge our own mistakes. We may be tempted to cover up our mishaps or even to preemptively define our goals vaguely so that we can save face when things don't go as well as expected.[18]

There are other distortions we have to face as we try to avoid grappling with the hard truths about our failures. For instance, a particular strategy might be reasonably sound given the information available at the moment of the decision, only to be declared a mistake in hindsight, when the uncertainty gives way to clarity. Conversely, an action can be considered a mistake in the short run despite generating long-term benefits. These complications make the lessons from our own mishaps difficult to define.

To make things even more complicated, it's not a given that we'll learn the right lessons from our own failures even when we correctly and sincerely acknowledge their existence. In particular, we still wouldn't be able to reliably reveal what differentiates them from successes.

Here's an example.

Say you have recently been scrutinizing your past investments. The recipients of your funds were all medium-size companies in a particular business sector that you've spent time studying. A few of these performed exceptionally well, some did fine, some fared subpar, and several performed extremely badly.

You obviously feel good about your successes. But making good investments is essentially your job. Your failures, on the other hand, were unexpected and particularly hurt you. You knew the sector and the companies well, or you thought you did. Now you wish to learn from your experience and improve your performance.

To do this, it seems indispensable to examine specifically the instances where things went wrong in an attempt to learn from them and avoid similar mistakes in the future. What do your failures have in common and how can you eliminate or, at least, reduce them?

As you dig deeper, you stumble upon a striking detail. You realize that 70 percent of your worst past investments were in companies that have outsourced several key functions, such as accounting, security, and IT maintenance. You hadn't noticed this trend before, but this common pattern among your failures is now as clear as day. You conclude that the outside contractors and consultants that the companies hired must have done a bad job. In this sector, it seems, this level of outsourcing is bad news.

You learned your lesson. Accordingly, in your future investments, you consider the proportion of the budget allocated to such outsourcing as a crucial variable. Specifically, a high proportion is bad news. That knowledge should increase your future success rate, right? Not necessarily. Not only may this lesson be worthless, it could even hurt your future investment performance.

What about your investment successes? What if the companies that performed much better employed the same strategy? What would your perception be if you learned, for instance, that 80 percent of the best cases in your portfolio also allocated a similar proportion of their budgets to outside contractors and consultants? By focusing on your failures, you have just identified a simple causal story that sounds reasonable but doesn't actually exist. This lesson could lead to a costly future practice.

But wait . . . There's more. While attempting to learn from your mistakes, what if you also miss a valuable causal story that actually exists?

As you dug deeper into your bad investments, another variable you checked across different companies was the proportion of the budget they spent on fringe benefits, such as training, health care, travel allowances, and other types of special perks. You used to think that, if done badly, these expenditures could be wasteful. However, data show that some bad performers spend a large percentage of their budgets on these benefits, while others are more frugal. Your experience thus indicates that there's no correlation between such spending and poor performance.

You learned your lesson. As a result, you update your belief and dismiss this variable as a major cause of failure. That knowledge should save you some time and energy in your future investments, right? Not necessarily. There may still be a useful lesson here, hidden from experience.

What about your successes? What if the companies that performed much better systematically employed a different strategy? What would your perception be if you learned, for instance, that 90 percent of the best cases in your portfolio allocated a considerable proportion of their budgets to such benefits? This crucial difference between your successes and failures suggests that you should start thinking differently about the impact of this variable on performance in this particular sector.

As these examples illustrate, analyses that focus *only* on failures—both others' and our own—run the risk of misleading us about their causes. We may see a pattern that doesn't exist or fail to see one that actually does. Worse, the process may make us feel as if we've learned a valuable lesson.

Magic Cures: Unhealthy Lessons from Alternative Remedies

The search for the secrets of success in fields like business, investing, and careers can lead to disappointing results when the advice based on experience proves illusory. But in other fields, similar misapprehensions can actually be unhealthy. In particular, experience can make certain self-help movements and alternative therapies seem more effective than they really are, making it harder to distinguish between which remedies are and aren't really helpful.

For example, according to author Rhonda Byrne's *The Secret*, the secret to a wealthy, healthy, and happy life is the so-called law of attraction. Byrne claims that we have the power to summon the things that happen to us. If we believe that we'll be successful, we eventually will.[19]

There are reasons why this and other analogous concepts attract acclaim and followers. They can lead to a mindset that has some short-term and self-fulfilling benefits. For instance, they may make people momentarily happier by giving them hope about the existence of a solution to life's dilemmas and an easy one at that. They may assure that people have control over their fate and are not helpless.

But they also present long-term dangers. Such concepts imply, for instance, that people create their own problems and illnesses through their outlook on life. If something bad happens to them, it's primarily their fault. Consequently, these approaches advise people to avoid negative thoughts and hurdles, which can prevent them from learning useful lessons that may be contained in adversity. And, as discussed in Chapter 1, while regression effects, spontaneous improvements, placebo effects, self-fulfilling prophecies, and coincidences may occasionally seem to confirm such "laws," life's outcomes are generally not as easily controllable or predictable.

To gain further insight into alternative therapies, one of us (the authors) has attended various sessions.

One meeting was attended by people who had recently been fighting grave diseases and endured heavy medical procedures that had inflicted tremendous physical and psychological tolls. At that lowest point, they were recommended an alternative healer, whom they subsequently viewed as a savior. The resulting experience-based beliefs of the patients in turn boosted the confidence of the healer, which led to a larger practice, attracting even more followers with even deeper convictions. We observed that such a cycle can, in fact, fuel cult-like movements.

In a different case, we were surprised to see the healer confidently claim supernatural powers, such as telepathy. We were even more astonished when we heard some of his ardent followers categorically confirm this claim. It was, in fact, the patients who gradually convinced the healer about his mystical powers over the years.

Overall, from the perspective of learning from experience, the story of such self-help movements and alternative therapies is complicated.

We (the authors) are open to the possibility that some nonintrusive and complementary treatments may potentially have positive effects. Fortunately, scientists are conducting evidence-based analyses to see whether any of these alternative approaches can hold up to their claims. These investigations could reliably signal which treatments indeed deserve some credit.[20]

We also observed that being part of a community seems to help people with their struggles. It's encouraging to see that there are others who have been experiencing and tackling similar troubles. Some of these meetings provide an opportunity for sharing. So, they deserve some credit for these features too.

But there are many good reasons to question the experience-based evidence these practices rely upon.

There are regression effects. Many patients seek alternative interventions when they feel at their worst. But as they get better, the healers get most of the credit.

There are time lags. Healing is a lengthy process in any severe situation. The visit to the healer sometimes happens to coincide with a period when the body starts to heal, which leads to a faulty story that gives undue weight to the intervention.

Some alternative therapists argue that modern medicine can be harmful due to debilitating side effects and occasionally fatal medical errors. Although both charges can sometimes be accurate, many alternative therapies are far from innocent. For example, bloodletting would be considered an alternative therapy today and could exacerbate problems if applied excessively, sometimes in a dangerous way. Not to mention that we may not even be aware of many side effects and issues caused by various alternative therapies, as they are not being properly evaluated.

Another argument is that the pharmaceutical industry harms the environment and mistreats animals. There may indeed be a need for improvement along these lines. Yet alternative medicine is once again far from innocent. A wide variety of alternative procedures reportedly involve exotic ingredients like pulverized rhino horns, powdered tiger bones, jellies made of seawater turtle shells, and bear bile. Excessive and cruel poaching for these items has been driving many species to suffering and even to extinction.[21]

Finally, a strict reliance on healing stories based on alternative medicine derived from personal experience can lead some people to gradually lose their confidence in modern medicine, substitute alternative therapies for scientifically based remedies, and elevate untested practices to a status they don't deserve. At this point, the quest for the secrets of success drawn from individual experience becomes unhealthy.

Thinking Clearly About Success and Failure

Without our realizing it, learning from successes *or* failures is bound to distort our intuition rather than explain what may actually be going on. Learning the right lessons from experience should ideally involve both successes *and* failures.[22]

A crucial initial step is to personally define them. What does success entail? What does failure mean?

Without such *working definitions*, we don't know what to take from experience and what to ignore. We may also be unable to recognize when a success or failure happens and hence lose opportunities to learn from them. Worse, if we let external factors define success or failure for us, we may needlessly seek achievements that we don't truly care about and fail to reach the ones we do. We may stress about possible failures that don't necessarily matter and neglect to consider potential failures that actually do.

Once we have some working definitions, we can then choose our strategies accordingly and begin thinking about the lessons we can derive from the outcomes we experience.

Say, for instance, we decide to apply for a certain position or make a request for resources for a project. What if the response we get is positive? What should we learn from this experience? And what if the response we get is negative? What should we learn from that experience?

The answers to these questions hinge on the underlying *success rate*. What's the prevalence of a certain desired outcome in the general population of relevant, similar examples? What's the proportion of those who succeeded relative to all those who tried to succeed? The lower this rate, the less likely we will be to find an easily identifiable difference between successes and failures.[23]

For example, thousands, even millions of people want to be famous actors, sports stars, best-selling authors, CEOs, or multimillionaires, while only a handful reach that particular dream. This means it's unlikely that there's a specific magic solution for achieving those outcomes. Luck and hard-to-identify, seemingly random factors probably play a major role. We will not only have to work hard and continuously hone our skills, but we will also need to be in the right place at the right time.

In many contexts, unfortunately, information on success rates will be hidden and require effort to uncover. Countless rejected ideas, failed projects, bad decisions, and bankrupt enterprises are usually not readily available to our experience. Recognizing this fact should not render us helpless but instead push us to rethink the lessons of experience.

On the one hand, if we achieve success in a setting with a low success rate, we could congratulate ourselves, as it takes effort and courage to compete in a crowded field. But it would be wise not to attribute this outcome to a simple strategy and not to dismiss the role of chance.

On the other hand, if we stumble or fail in a setting with a low success rate, we shouldn't conclude that the strategy behind our failure is necessarily bad. We should welcome any feedback and give special care to comments that are common across many rejections. Yet we should also acknowledge that the lower the success rate, the less straightforward the path to success. Failure is rampant in such an environment and thus should not be a main concern. Once again, it is unlikely that a specific and simple strategy will guarantee the desired outcome.[24]

In fact, in such circumstances, rejection itself ought to be a part of one's strategy. This doesn't mean that we should purposefully produce flawed ideas so that we get rejected. It means that we should plan to knock on many doors in various ways to increase the chance that we will find ourselves in the right place, at the right time, with the right idea.

Unfortunately, the settings and systems we operate in don't always facilitate a strategy based on multiple trials, errors, and rejections. As we discussed in Chapter 2, the schools we attend and the institutions we work for don't usually provide us with the necessary time and space to engage in such explorations, which is essential for mitigating low success rates. Instead, they opt for standardizing the definition and methods of success for everyone involved. Hobby hacking, escape to passion, and senate of managers are mechanisms we have offered to counter that practice.

Acknowledging the realities behind the success rate also empowers us to give credit where it's due. Suppose you are preparing to launch an important venture in your chosen field—a new business startup, for example. A consultant approaches you, bragging that he has helped ten similar projects achieve what you would consider great success. He asks for a hefty fee to help you do the same. You check and confirm his claim: he was involved in those ten projects, which indeed became huge success stories.

You may be tempted to hire the consultant. But there are important questions to consider first. Were these earlier projects truly similar to yours? If so, how many such projects was the consultant involved with overall? If he took on two hundred projects like yours in the past ten years and achieved success ten times, he has a success rate of only 5 percent. This detail would be important when judging a consultant's effectiveness and price.[25]

In *Reckoning with Risk,* psychologist Gerd Gigerenzer warns us to be particularly careful about statements on *relative* risks while considering advice regarding success and failure: Doing Y will increase your chances of success! Doing Z will reduce your risk of failure! These claims may be accurate and based on reliable data, but they aren't useful without taking into account the underlying success rate.

What were my chances to begin with? If they were low, say 1 in 1,000, a strategy that doubles the chances would lead to a success rate of 2 in 1,000. Nothing to really celebrate. If the success rate was 4 in 10, on the other hand, we could really consider following the advice, as a strategy that would double it would now make it 80 percent.[26]

Of course, how the success rate in a given field is evolving over time is also crucial. If it was high in the past, there may once have been some specific determinant of success or failure. But if it has gotten lower and lower over time, it may mean that those factors have fallen in importance. For example, they may have been identified and widely applied by other decision makers, making them less valuable as differentiating factors for future entrants to the field.

Success Versus Failure: What Causes the Difference?

Coming up with working definitions of success and failure and then researching, revealing, and tracking success rates based on those definitions are fundamental steps. Next, we would need to consider becoming more of a story scientist to understand the crucial differences between successes and failures.

In a post on his blog *You Are Not So Smart,* journalist and author David McRaney tells a curious story about damaged World War II planes. Every day, US Air Force personnel got to observe plane after plane, landing on an airfield with bullet holes in their bodies after having been exposed to enemy fire. What should the American engineers on the ground do with the information they derived from these observations?

A seemingly obvious answer would be to repair the damaged parts before sending the planes back into battle. A further action could be to let the plant that produces the planes know about the weak parts that consistently get damaged by flying bullets and request that these be better reinforced during production. That seems like the right thing to do, based on experience.

But wait . . . The damage inflicted by the bullets was actually immaterial to the aims of the military. Their ultimate objective was to prevent aircraft from crashing and falling in battle. The planes that the engineers experienced had all returned safely despite being hit. The parts that were damaged did not cause them to crash. Thus, the bullet holes were not as relevant as they seemed to be.

This insight led statistician Abraham Wald to warn the US Air Force that fixing and reinforcing particular damaged aircraft parts would actually be counterproductive. He argued that one should look beyond the planes that returned successfully and attempt to gauge what really made the difference between life and death in battles up in the sky. While the fallen planes were unavailable for close inspection, he proposed looking at where the returning planes were in fact *not* hit.

Wald reasoned that, if planes received damage in certain places and still survived, those that fell must have received damage in other places. Hence, some of the cleanest, scratch-free parts of the surviving planes must be the culprits. Those were the areas in need of special reinforcement. Wald's approach required an analysis that went beyond the available experience to reveal the difference between successes and failures. What's remarkable is that he managed to do it when most of the failures were missing from observation, shot down in battle.[27]

The popularity and prevalence of lists of things successful people do, however, suggest that we typically don't look for such systematic differences. We tend to learn from survivors and their readily available experience—the more striking and obvious, the better. Instead, to better understand the determinants of success or failure, we need more initiatives that uncover whatever is missing from our experience so that we can recognize and analyze the difference.

For example, FailCon, Fail Festival, and similar events can help us do that. These are conferences where decision makers take the stage to talk about their screwups, which would normally stay hidden, much like the fallen planes. Thanks to these encounters, the audience has a better idea about the sheer number of failures in comparison to successes (the success rate). They also learn more about the obscure details in decision processes that are associated with mistakes. This allows them to better contrast effective processes with those that were fruitless and identify differences between successes and failures.[28]

Princeton University scientist Johannes Haushofer recently offered another unique view on experiences that tend to remain hidden. He has an enviable profile: faculty member in a world-renowned institution, publications in prestigious scholarly journals, awards and fellowships, and an impressive list of ongoing and upcoming projects. Yet his CV offers little clue as to how other academics might achieve similar accomplishments. What are some of the nuances, trade-offs, or success rates?

Now we know more, thanks to Haushofer's "CV of failures." On the advice of fellow scientist Melanie Stefan, he decided to publish a document that lists and summarizes his misadventures. The reader quickly notices the various institutions, journals, and programs that rejected Haushofer and his ideas over many years, thereby gaining a better understanding of his success rate. We also get a glimpse of how many ideas he produced during a given period and how those evolved over time. Overall, examining the difference between a regular CV and a CV of failures would help us recognize how much of the iceberg gets buried under the cold, dark ocean of failure and rejection.[29]

But let's be cautious: there are a few hidden caveats about studying the difference between successes and failures.

First, this approach doesn't always guarantee understanding the direction of the causality. Successes may indeed be different from failures, yet this difference may not be the cause behind success but a consequence of it. In the case of WWII planes, the causality is clear: bullet holes cause the crashes. But in more complex domains like business and social life, the relationship between actions and outcomes can be more complex and harder to decipher. A person may be able to afford particular strategies only *after* becoming successful, yet these can be falsely interpreted as causes of their achievements.

Second, remember that when success rates are small, randomness may be playing a key role in the outcomes. If the population is large enough, we will observe all sorts of performances that we can then dissect, nitpick, and "explain" after the fact, with the help of 20/20 hindsight. But that doesn't guarantee that these differences can be successfully controlled and managed—let alone that they were really crucial in determining the outcome.

Third, the differences between success and failure may change over time. Not tracking that evolution could lead to misconceptions. As the world changes, so inevitably will any secrets for success, and most advice for success is thus bound to become obsolete. Hence, analyses of the differences between successes and failures need to be periodically reviewed, repeated, and replaced.

Ultimately, learning about success and failure from experience is more nuanced and complicated than it seems. If we are not careful, issues with accuracy, causality, time, selections, complexity, and trade-offs are bound to induce errors in our evaluations that are hard to detect. Once we think we have learned our lesson, the simple and alluring stories that emerge can be more illusory than real.

Deep down, we may all know there are no magic solutions to many challenging problems in life, but experience can suggest otherwise. We may be tempted to simply stick to the plans we made in advance, without checking their validity for ourselves. Our first instinct during a crisis can easily be to repeat a habitual practice rather than to question it. A better strategy would be to promptly become a story scientist and test ideas early to refute bad hunches.

In *The Lean Startup*, entrepreneur Eric Ries argues that businesses, especially startups, should adopt a scientific approach to learning. Experience can endow entrepreneurial decision makers with undue confidence in their ability to predict which products or services will be successful. But they should supplement the lessons of experience by building experiments to receive quick feedback on their ideas and "to see which parts are brilliant and which are crazy."[30]

This is the philosophy behind the Marshmallow Challenge, invented by Peter Skillman and popularized further by Tom Wujec, both design thinkers. The challenge involves placing a marshmallow on top of a tower that is made from dry spaghetti, tape, and string. The aim is to build the highest structure within a limited time frame.

Both Skillman and Wujec report that many competent adults perform worse at this task than kindergarten children and the worst performers, on average, are business school students. The reason: they don't test their ideas as quickly and effectively. Skillman has observed that "multiple iterations almost always beat the single-minded commitment to building your first idea." Although children tend to try their various theories almost immediately, the adults devise an elaborate and elegant plan, work on it tirelessly, and wait for the last moment to put the candy on top. Wujec thus says that the "ta-da!" moment they expect in many cases instead ends up becoming a disappointing "uh-oh!" feeling.[31]

This insight, then, suggests a general overall strategy for pursuing success in any given field. Once we know our working definitions of success and failure and have some notion of the associated success rates, we can decide which advice or strategy for success to test to see whether it makes a difference at an acceptable cost. We can add or subtract potentially relevant features to our routines, ideas, products, and services and then check the results over time.

During the next couple of weeks, for example, we can choose to drink water right after waking up, exercise, ignore others, or employ any other specific strategy in a certain aspect of our lives and see whether the additional benefits the strategy brings is worth the trouble. If yes, that's great news. If not, we can consider another approach, test its efficacy, and keep tracking the difference as objectively as possible.

What's Missing? What's Irrelevant?

There are essentially four main sources of lessons from experience we typically consider as we try to avoid failure and reach success: others' successes, our own successes, others' failures, and our own failures. Learning from any one of these exclusively would be misleading.

Missing accuracy, causality, time, complexity, and trade-offs; irrelevant selections. Learning only from successes or failures could render us blind to what made the actual difference between what went right and what went wrong.

Missing working definitions. If we don't define what success or failure means for us in a given context, we cannot evaluate the outcomes we experience accurately. Worse, if we let others define them for us, we might eventually regret the outcomes we obtain and the effort we expended.

Missing success rates. If the proportion of successes is small within all outcomes, then it's unlikely that there's an easy and guaranteed way that would lead to success. Thus, determining the average success rate in our chosen field of endeavor is an essential step in deciding whether there are really any specific secrets of success to be learned.

Missing differences. It's not intuitive to analyze carefully what differentiates the cases where things went right versus those where things went wrong, but such an approach could give us a better idea of what leads to success and failure. We should, however, still be careful about issues regarding causality, uncertainty, and changes brought by time.

Missing tests. Once a theory about specific differentiating factors between success and failure is formed, it's important to put that theory to test. Ideas that may seem reasonable at first sight may lead to disappointments that prior experimentation can help us avoid.

In our success-hungry contemporary society, we'd all love to believe that there are magic bullets to be found—secrets of success we can apply to guarantee the results we want. And when experience is examined uncritically and carelessly, it may seem to yield such secrets. But all too often, they prove illusory. Fortunately, though guarantees are nowhere to be found, a more scientific approach to experience can provide insights that can make our personal success measurably more likely.

7

HAPPINESS FOILED

When Experience Impedes Satisfaction

YOU ARE ON TOP OF A MOUNTAIN.

As of a few weeks ago, you weren't looking forward to visiting this remote place, which has recently become a popular skiing destination. You've gotten progressively less enthusiastic about ski trips in recent years, finding them expensive, long, cold, and crowded, as well as all too likely to end in injury. But when your friends proposed this latest trip, you found you couldn't say no. Over the years, you've invested considerable time and effort to develop your skiing skills, accumulating quite a bit of experience that you didn't want to waste. Many of your ski-loving friends, coworkers, and acquaintances have been to this mountain. Even your boss recently posted captivating pictures from that location on her social media. This trip would be a unique opportunity to catch up with all of them.

So you signed on. And now here you are, on the first morning, after an exhausting and extended journey, wearing several layers of clothing, standing near a dangerous ridge, inhaling the freezing air, wondering if your feet have ever felt less comfortable in your whole life.

But wait ... There's a silver lining.

As you look around, you cannot help but gasp in awe. The scenery before you is breathtaking. The endless sky features a brightness that you have never seen before. You can clearly make out every contour of the massive clouds that are leisurely drifting by in the distance. The mountains and valleys that surround you are so majestic that you feel both exalted and insignificant at the same time. The only sound you hear is the wind's high-pitched whistle. Several people around you are witnessing the same scene and all seem to be hypnotized. Some are overwhelmed, one or two actually silently weeping. Your knees feel loose and your limbs start shivering but not entirely from the cold. It becomes impossible to move or to think clearly. You cannot help but sigh.

At that very moment, you feel truly and undeniably happy. You suddenly judge the trip as one of the best in your life. Had you not come to this mountaintop, you would have missed this once-in-a-lifetime experience—this miracle.

To make things even better, the forecast suggests that the weather will be great throughout the rest of your trip. So you'll be enjoying yourself all week, away from your daily worries in a snow-filled paradise. You promise yourself to cherish it and be happy as long as you know that this place exists, whether you are there to experience it firsthand or not.

Great. What can go wrong?

It turns out, it wasn't easy to keep that promise. With each day that follows, your intense initial pleasure slowly subsides. You return to the same mountaintop and face the same mesmerizing view many times, but after a while, it no longer affects you in the same way. In the meantime, the pain in your feet refuses to go away, which has started to make it hard to focus on anything else.

Finally, there you are, on the last day, on the same mountaintop, about to start your final descent. You have been pleased with your performance during the trip, and you've had a good time with your friends. You enjoyed tasty meals throughout the week and slept well at nights. You've started to feel physically tired from your week of rigorous exercise, which adds to your sense of accomplishment.

Given that you practiced and advanced your skiing skills during the past week, you decide to take a harder but faster off-piste route, looking for one final burst of excitement. On your way down, you start thinking about the upcoming journey back and the tasks that await you when you return to your usual life.

But wait . . . Something's terribly wrong.

A large chunk of ice has suddenly derailed you. One of your skis has detached. You are going fast but no longer in control. Attempting to slow down, you throw yourself to the ground, but you keep sliding uncontrollably toward the side of the slope. It doesn't help that you were tired to begin with. Terrified, you realize there's no way you can stop. You fall off a small cliff and fly toward a large rock and an even larger tree stump with sharp edges. You close your eyes and scream as loud as you can.

You land with a jarring thud.

Moments go by in semiconsciousness. Gradually, you try to assess the situation, but you find it hard to concentrate. Having heard your screams, other skiers have spotted you and are coming to your aid. They are shouting questions:

"Are you OK?"

"Do you need help?"

"Can you hear me?"

You can hear them. And all seems to be fine. Your arm, back, and legs hurt, but you can move them without a problem. You are completely covered in snow. You look around and realize that you just missed the rock and the tree, falling on a spongy pile of snow between them. The bystanders help you recover your equipment, and you slowly head down the hill, shaken but in one piece.

But wait . . . It's not over.

Upon arriving in your room, you realize that you have lost your wallet. During your fall, it must have slipped out from a pocket that you had failed to zip shut. Your cash, credit cards, and ID were in it. There's no way of recovering it, as you and your friends are planning to leave the ski resort within the next hour. You're upset. You'll have to cancel your cards, borrow some money from your friends, and deal with some tedious bureaucracy back home as you rebuild the contents of your wallet. You growl and shout at yourself in anguish.

So now, look back on the week you've just experienced. Was this a good trip? How would you evaluate it? Would you be happy?

Satisfied? Distraught? Which parts of this experience are you likely to remember more vividly in the distant future? Which parts are you likely to forget?

This mountaintop adventure is based on a true story. We'll return to it to offer different perspectives on the role of experience in our happiness. Acknowledging the existence of various filters and their effects on our experience would enable us to assess our happiness from a wider perspective, regardless of our personal dispositions.

Experience over Time: Adaptations and Conventions

Time can have a significant effect on how we feel about our experience.

For instance, *adaptation* ensures that the effect of past experiences gets diluted over time or loses its strength due to repetition. This process involves an emotional adjustment to our present situation, which ensures that our ultimate happiness remains relatively unaffected by the different events we live through, both good and bad.[1]

Sadly, life sometimes can be full of horrible experiences. Thousands of people die every day, many in an untimely and unexpected fashion, leaving shocked loved ones to grieve. Many more face disability, serious diseases, violence, war, famine, painful accidents, long-term unemployment, miserable work conditions, or poverty.

As a civilization, we seem to be getting better at preventing and mitigating many of these problems. That's definitely good news. But these unwelcome experiences have always existed, still exist, and will continue to exist for the foreseeable future.

Luckily, we have the capacity to adapt. When we live through certain negative events, we tend to gradually revert to a more moderate level of happiness after an initial shock. The speed and degree of adaptation depend on the nature and intensity of the event and also on one's personality and circumstances. Adaptation is not guaranteed in every case, but time can help cope with bad experiences.[2]

Some scholars have likened adaptation to running on a treadmill. When it comes to happiness, no matter where we go, we have some ability to adapt to the new situation and return near to where we were before.[3]

One process behind adaptation is desensitization. Continuous exposure to an unwanted experience usually leads to familiarity, which reduces its adverse effects on our happiness. This is akin to getting accustomed to an initial foul smell. After a short while, the smell might still be there, as foul as before, but our noses desensitize remarkably fast. Similarly, for example, seeking a new job can be frustrating and difficult. The first couple of applications and interviews can be really stressful. After a while, however, many applicants manage to adapt to some degree to the anxiety that comes with the situation.

Another process underlying adaptation is the effect of recency. If a bad experience took place a long time ago, newer and better experiences can dilute its impact on one's current mood. This prevents people from being perpetually traumatized by a single calamity in the distant past, allowing them to keep on living, improving, and learning.[4]

So the way we evaluate and learn from experience can help us bounce back and prevent a one-time misfortune or even a prolonged bad situation from ruining our lives forever. Through the process of adaptation, experience helps us to be happier.

Unfortunately, the same process operates just as well, if not even more strongly, in the opposite direction too.

After all, life is also full of delightful experiences. Thousands of babies are born every day, usually to the delight of their parents. People enjoy delicious meals, buy things they covet, make new friends, spend time with their loved ones, make love, get married, learn new things, travel to distant lands, heal from diseases, help each other, come up with new ideas, and work toward their goals.

We feel happy as we live through these experiences. But the capacity for adaptation means that their positive effects may not last as long as we wish.

Going back to the mountaintop, we may have felt ecstatic when we first glimpsed the spectacular view, but its initial effect can diminish substantially after a few similar episodes. We may also quickly become desensitized to our past pleasures and consequently find ourselves looking for further thrills, opting, perhaps, to take the more dangerous path down the mountain on our final descent.

Similarly, as we gain more possessions and higher status in life, time can normalize our initial extreme joy to a more familiar level. Worse, the taste of that original jolt of excitement can push us to perpetually seek even more possessions and even higher status, failing to appreciate what we already have as much and as long as we'd like. No mountain peak may feel high enough; no descent may be sufficiently thrilling.

To make things more complicated, negative experiences can have a bigger impact on our ultimate happiness compared to positive ones—losses tend to loom larger than gains. Hence, we can be particularly proficient at taking our achievements for granted but remain persistently upset about our failures.[5]

At work, we could struggle for a promotion for months and years and become overjoyed upon getting it. Yet how long does it take before we get back to our old selves, stressing for the next one? A few months? A few weeks?

On the one hand, running on a treadmill that limits our happiness is healthy for our continuous development and inventiveness. It prevents us from stopping when we are ahead and drives us to keep improving.

On the other hand, the treadmill often makes us overestimate how much happier we would be if we had more possessions, achieved more, or rose in status. We can easily find ourselves believing that the grass on the other side of the fence is greener. But if we were to hop the fence, we would quickly adapt and begin to yearn for even greener fields.

In short, adaptation has a considerable impact on our happiness. Accumulating more experience can indeed help us bounce back up from sadness over time, but it's also at least as effective in pulling us down from peak ecstasy.

In time, more experience also leads us to form *conventions*—habits and customs that are hard to break, regardless of their effect on our happiness. Conventions themselves give rise to further experience, which in turn helps solidify those conventions, in cyclical fashion. In this way, certain experiences become part of our lives, defining our status quo.

Luckily, conventions can sometimes make us happy. It's possible to like something more as we gain more and more experience with it. Listening to a piece of music in a genre that one likes often has such an effect. The more one listens, the more it becomes familiar and gratifying. As a result, one can enjoy listening to a song more for the fifteenth time than for the second. This process is called sensitization.[6]

Sensitization, unfortunately, can also work to decrease happiness in various contexts. Research suggests, for example, that negative feelings caused by noise and commuting can intensify with time. Similarly, tensions with a colleague or a family member may flare up with repeated contact rather than cooling down.[7]

A particularly powerful unhappiness trap gets forged when several underlying processes work together. This happens when our initial experience is positive but then slowly gets replaced by indifference and eventually by discontent. Yet, due to our accumulated experience until that point, it may become a convention that is hard to change in a way that would make us happier.

For example, we may go on a ski trip not because we really want to but partly because we have gained experience and knowledge by investing in skiing in the past. Unwilling to lose that investment, we might end up deciding to add even more to it, thereby increasing our investment and making our fear of wasting it in the future even more compelling.

This dynamic is perhaps most evident in certain types of online games, where people's hard-earned progress gets erased if they stop playing regularly. One famous example is FarmVille, where players plant virtual fruits and vegetables that need to be harvested periodically. If they fail to do so, their virtual produce dies. The game counts on people's aversion to the trauma of that loss. The more one plays the game and progresses, the bigger the potential loss, and the more unbearable the trauma of losing it all becomes. Of course, such games typically offer alternative monetary solutions: players can progress faster or avoid losses if they make in-game purchases. After a while, such offers can become harder and harder to resist.[8]

Economists argue that irrecoverable investments we made in the past should be considered sunk costs, irrelevant to our decisions about the future. Especially in the case of pixelated entities that only live in a website, we ought to be able to snap our fingers and simply quit, if we want, without feeling remorse. Failing to do that, we'd only be planting further lifeless plants that stand to affect our happiness in the future.[9]

Unfortunately, that's not how experience works. As we gain experience, we essentially dig ourselves into a hole. If we manage to enjoy that hole and even get happier as we dig ourselves in deeper, that's great. But if we start to resent the hole, our happiness diminishing the further we dig, we become trapped by our experience.

Relationships and careers are two kinds of long-term missions that are susceptible to these effects. They generally start with positive feelings and good intentions, which have the capacity to make us truly happy in the long term. But if the experience is not carefully curated and cultivated, people can gradually adapt to their initial excitement and grow weary of the situation and yet feel stuck because of their accumulated experience. They may respond by deciding to invest further into those missions, which may leave them feeling even more stuck.

As a result, more experience can trap people in a state of unhappiness. It becomes possible to feel constant regret for staying on the same path, yet find it increasingly difficult to divert due to the anticipated regret of losing the entire past journey.

Remembered Experience:
The Clash of the Two Selves

Like time, memory plays a major role in the way we feel about our experience. Different people may experience and remember the same situation differently, producing different levels of happiness.[10]

At the beginning of this book, we defined experience as encompassing both our momentary interactions with our environment (a process) and the resulting lessons that ultimately remain with us (a product). When it comes to happiness, these two dimensions need to be considered separately. In *Thinking, Fast and Slow*, Daniel Kahneman calls the first "the experiencing self," the second "the remembering self."[11]

The experiencing self deals exclusively with how we feel at each and every moment. It's about the instant when we enjoy a melody, a bite, or the view on top of a mountain.

The remembering self regulates what we subsequently remember from the broader episodes that are made up by such moments. It chronicles and composes a story based on what happened, which subsequently determines the long-term satisfaction we derive from listening to a song, eating a meal, or going on a trip.

Crucially, the remembering self takes many editorial liberties when writing the story that the experiencing self actually lived. For example, how does the loss of a wallet at the end of a ski trip affect our satisfaction with the whole journey? Can it outweigh the many hours of joy that preceded it, brought on by conversations and meals we had with friends during the very same trip? And how would that peak moment of happiness at the mountaintop factor into the remembered experience? We inevitably recall some aspects of the trip more vividly than others.

In particular, research suggests that we tend to compress a specific sequence of events so that the beginnings, peaks, and endings get special treatment. This is often dubbed the *peak-end rule*. Our feelings attached to these moments are heavily weighed as we contemplate our satisfaction about the whole experience. Meanwhile, the length of time that other moments last are discounted in our considerations, a tendency known as *duration neglect*.[12]

In fact, this is the basic process we follow when we write stories. The account of the ski trip presented at the beginning of this chapter focused mainly on the two peak moments: a pleasurable one toward the beginning and a miserable one toward the end. But consider an alternative account based on the same trip. If we were to be more respectful of the actual duration of the events, the introduction to this chapter would have been much different. It would also have been weird and totally unreadable:

> For the ski trip, you had to take a plane to reach the city nearby. In the airport, you waited for seventeen minutes at the gate before boarding. It wasn't too bad. You drank some water while standing in line. You also heard two people in front of you chat in a foreign language and listened to them curiously for three minutes.
>
> As you were boarding the plane, you noticed how cold it was in the corridor that you had to pass through. You wore your sweater while slowly approaching the plane. It felt better.
>
> It took you two minutes to get to your seat. After stowing your carry-on luggage, you sat down and started reading the newspaper you had brought with you.
>
> The first article you read was about a new invention. It took you four minutes to read it. You wondered about the idea's potential. You realized how impatient you are for that technology to become mainstream. Your life would become easier when that happens.
>
> The second article also took four minutes to read. It was about . . . [Approximately fifty pages of details follow before you finally find yourself on the mountaintop.]

In life, our memory selects what to consider from our experience when we think about the satisfaction we derived from an event. This tendency helps us retain the essence of an experience, ensuring that long, relatively meaningless episodes don't flood our final evaluation of what took place.

As a result, the selective nature of memory can enhance our happiness by minimizing the mental space dedicated to relatively dull episodes, like reading a random newspaper article while waiting for the plane to depart. Yet it can also undermine our appreciation of good moments that don't happen to fit the peak-end rule. In a story like the ski trip, for example, dozens of hours of quality sleep, pleasant conversations, and joyful instances can get squished into a general label of "having a good time," while the good and bad extremes end up stealing the show.

Of course, there are also individual differences beyond such common tendencies. Each of us will remember the same experience differently because of the filters imposed by our disposition, attention, personality, previous experiences, mood, expectations, and objectives. The same trip with the same sequence of events would make some people happier than others. As long as there's a subjective dimension to memory, these variations are inevitable.[13]

That's one reason why many of us cannot resist taking photos or videos of a wide range of experiences. We are trying to capture, as objectively as possible, all the moments that might be relevant. We especially want to retain any positive parts and spectacular peaks. We would like the remembering self to have a permanent record of the events that determine our satisfaction. We may even choose our future experiences based on the immortal moments we believe they'd produce. And we also want to have the ability to share these with others and make the same memory a collective one.

Makes sense. But when it comes to happiness, moderation is key. Excessively striving to capture every moment of a given experience can have adverse effects on our experiencing selves. We may reduce the immediate joy those moments provide. We may also start doing things not because they make us genuinely happy but primarily because they produce moments that we can easily capture and share with others.

Until a decade or so ago, we couldn't afford to do any of that. The process of capturing moments (through photography, for example) was relatively slow and expensive. And for a very long time, before the camera was invented, it was simply impossible. Technology is increasingly allowing us to take an infinite number of high-quality photos and endless videos with a mere touch of a finger. It's hard to resist. But the more moments we capture, the less time and opportunity we'll have to revisit each at a later time.

In short, finding a good personal balance between feeding the experiencing self and the remembering self has become a tricky and important life challenge. And recognizing the operating principles that govern these two selves can help us improve our ultimate satisfaction.

Relative Experience: Keeping Up with Others

Comparing our own experiences to those of other people has consequences for our happiness as well.

Try searching online for images of "disappointed medalists." You'll uncover a collection of photos of some of the best athletes in the world, all looking unhappy because they failed to win the gold medal in their favored event. A famous example is the gymnast McKayla Maroney, whose scowl when she won the silver medal at the 2012 Olympics in London was covered widely by the media.[14]

Intrigued by this phenomenon, social psychologist Victoria Medvec and her colleagues investigated the levels of happiness exhibited by medal-winning Olympic athletes. As expected, gold medalists showed the greatest satisfaction. However, bronze medalists were found to look happier on average than the better-placed silver medalists.[15]

Medvec and colleagues concluded that, although the silver medalists were happy with their achievements, they couldn't help thinking about the gold medals they'd almost won. Their feelings of happiness were thus tainted by what they had failed to achieve. The bronze medalists, in contrast, compared themselves to non-medalists and thus could celebrate wholeheartedly.

We often respond to events in a way that's similar to Olympic medalists. We tend to judge our experiences in relation to specific reference points, such as prior expectations or the behavior of others. Hence, the same experience can have different effects depending on one's benchmark. Such relative evaluations, however, render us vulnerable to anxiety-inducing schemes created by external forces.

For example, organizations typically feature hierarchical career paths that encourage comparisons among coworkers. In *Luxury Fever*, economist Robert H. Frank argues that self-evaluations based on one's possessions and status relative to others lead to an endless arms race that ultimately leaves people unsatisfied, despite their abundant possessions.

An extreme depiction of this race is the famous meeting scene in the 2000 film *American Psycho*, where the main character, Patrick Bateman, is absolutely mortified when his business card design is judged as inferior in terms of texture, color, and font style to those of his colleagues.[16]

Social media and online platforms also make a wide variety of reference points increasingly more accessible and therefore easier to rely upon when judging the outcomes we experience. They allow us to expose our own lives and explore others'. Our online profiles and histories are becoming increasingly important in our lives. Thanks to these, we learn new insights, receive our news, share our stories with others, and make connections, among other valuable activities. This experience has the potential to make us happier. But these platforms can quickly become wicked learning environments, constantly supplying us with unreliable benchmarks and biased feedback.

For example, suppose our friends went on a ski trip without us some time in the past. When they posted images and stories about the trip on social media, they probably did not share the whole story, including how expensive, long, cold, crowded, and injury prone it was. Our boss may have posted on her social media the moments that were the most pleasant and beautiful but neglected to feature the moment on the third day of the trip when a freak accident dislocated her spouse's shoulder.

Platforms that feature such selective sharing inevitably lead us to have a biased experience of others' experience. And the more selectively people tailor what they post, the more wicked the learning environment becomes. This situation is akin to a Hollywood movie, where many takes are filmed and only the best ones end up on the screen, perhaps even artificially enhanced to improve viewers' pleasure.

When such a film pretends to be real life, we may not be able to make the necessary corrections in our minds. As a result, we may end up feeling that our life is more boring and unfulfilled in comparison to others than it actually is. The reference we use to judge our happiness would be misleading. In fact, recent studies suggest that passively consuming other people's life highlights can negatively impact perceptions about our own lives. We may also feel worse afterward because we have just spent hours online, not achieving anything.[17]

What happens when we instead become more active users and posters of content? We may feel happy when others interact with our posts, like them, and share them with others. But there are darker sides to such active behavior as well.[18]

For example, some users might end up continuously checking their posts and profiles to track their likes, shares, and status. They would also get real-time notifications that constantly inform them about the posts and profiles of other people. If their own posts have drawn heavy engagement from others, this can bring the posters happiness—but it also drives a compulsion to keep being connected and to tracking more and more content. A lack of engagement by others, on the other hand, can make posters depressed.[19]

To make things even more complicated, in popular platforms where many users are either anonymous or use pseudonyms, trolling tends to be widespread. Countless people are being harassed online through abusive and sometimes threatening responses to their posts. A 2017 Pew Research Center survey reports, for example, that 41 percent of Americans have experienced online harassment and 66 percent have seen others being mistreated. Moreover, in 18 percent of the cases, the situation involved some extreme elements, such as "physical threats, harassment over a sustained period, sexual harassment or stalking."[20]

Hence, our organizational and online social experience includes a range of benchmarks and elements that interferes with our happiness. Luckily, being aware of the various experience-based factors that can adversely affect our happiness—time, memory, comparisons—enables us to consider ways of improving our learning and satisfaction.

Variable Experience: Making Joyful Investments

In a 2017 commencement speech given at his son's high school, John G. Roberts Jr., chief justice of the US Supreme Court, offered some memorable advice regarding the audience's future experience. In particular, he encouraged students to learn from certain misfortunes they may face in time to understand the value of important things in life. For instance, encountering bad luck should make them realize that success and failure may not always be deserved. Similarly, the occasional unfairness, betrayal, loneliness, and pain they experience could help them better appreciate justice, loyalty, friendship, and compassion.[21]

It seems logical to believe that we will be happiest if our experience exclusively includes happy events, successes, and positive emotions. On the other hand, unhappy events, failures, and negative emotions should be kept as far away from our personal experience as possible. But, as the chief justice suggests, we would actually benefit from a healthy degree of variance in our experience, which can lessen the adverse effects of adaptation and help us better appreciate our existing conventions.

Let's consider some of the reasons why this is so.

First, regardless of who we are, it's quite unrealistic to desire a life without any problems. Bad things are bound to happen to all of us. For this reason, in *The Antidote*, journalist Oliver Burkeman emphasizes that constantly chasing after happiness can paradoxically make people unsatisfied. If they expect to achieve and sustain happiness relatively easily, they will remain endlessly disappointed.[22]

Second, some adverse events may not cause as much unhappiness as we'd expect, especially in the long term. In *Stumbling on Happiness*, psychologist Daniel Gilbert argues that we have a "psychological immune system" that fights against unhappiness by striking "a balance that allows us to feel good enough to cope with our situation but bad enough to do something about it." As a result, we may believe that we would be deeply and perpetually affected when we experience an unexpected negative event. But there can be a significant difference between that imagined feeling and our actual feeling some time after the fact.[23]

Third, some events that make us temporarily unhappy actually make us happier in the long run. In *The Myths of Happiness*, psychologist Sonja Lyubomirsky explains that some adversity is actually necessary for people to foster resilience, define who they are, and cultivate optimism. Thus, experiencing anger, worry, and grief can render people better able to manage future situations that involve these emotions.[24]

In short, a healthy dose of variance in our experience—including some negative ingredients—has a positive effect on our long-term happiness. Perhaps we'd understand the value of the mountaintop view better if it were hidden by a thick fog for a day in the middle of the ski trip.

Accordingly, one way to maintain happiness and avoid downward adaptation and dull conventions would be to consider investing time and energy in things that don't quickly dilute with more experience. For example, consider the purchase of an expensive car (rather than a relatively modest one). Would this decision make a person happier in the long run?[25]

The answer may depend on the particulars of the situation, like the traffic conditions one usually experiences and the level of one's interest in cars. But, as an investment in happiness, the car purchase has several drawbacks. First, one could soon get used to having that particular model. Second, having a fancy car can stimulate new expectations based in part on comparisons to others' cars so that one soon comes to desire an even better car. Third, driving a more expensive car may cause one to be worried about possible damage to it and therefore sadder if something actually does happen to it.

Experiences, on the other hand, work quite differently. They become part of one's identity. We are free to remember them in ways that we like and that can't be challenged by others. In Chapter 2, we discussed the importance of dedicating time and space to activities that help us sample pleasant and creative experiences. Especially featuring some exciting periods of flow in our daily lives is likely to render us happier in both the short and long run.

It's no coincidence, in fact, that advertisements by automobile manufacturers often emphasize excitement as a main feature of their products. Rather than explaining the technical properties or other specific features of their cars, their commercials try to appeal to the emotions that people would experience while driving them—the exhilaration of racing around hairpin bends on a mountain road overlooking a spectacular scenic view. They want their customers to feel that, when they buy a new car, they are buying an experience that will add some healthy variance to their lives, rather than merely adding to their possessions. It's a psychologically sound way of appealing to what makes people happy in the long run.

Unavailable Experience:
The Don't-Want-Don't-Haves

Our experience of the world relies heavily on what's promptly available and observable. What one sees can easily feel like all there is, even though there can be more than meets the eye. Experience doesn't take into account reference points that are not readily accessible and plausible events that didn't happen, discounting their effects on our happiness.[26]

For example, what if, during our fall in the last descent of the ski trip, we had hit our head on the giant rock or the spiky tree stump instead of the mushy pile of snow between them? How much misery would that terrible experience have caused us had it happened? Unfortunately, the relief from having avoided such a mishap can be rather brief and fleeting. It's possible that the misery we felt losing our wallet would trump the joy we felt over *not* being in a coma.

While we are quite skillful at regretting lost opportunities and feeling unhappy about these, we can be very quick to normalize situations where we somehow managed to avoid experiencing problems that would have made us unhappy. We are also easily charmed by delightful experiences that others selectively share with us and feel down in comparison. As a result, we can often end up considering ourselves as "silver medalists," perpetually longing for some "gold medals," defined by ourselves, or worse, by others. And we may not appreciate our triumphs appropriately and be happy when we are "medalists" with a solid place on the podium.

In 1986, months before he died prematurely from cancer and years before massively popular online social networks became available, cognitive psychologist Hillel Einhorn gave a rare interview. He recounted how, one night after dinner in a Chinese restaurant, he discovered unexpected wisdom in a fortune cookie. The advice he received said, "Think about the things that you don't want and you don't have." At first, Einhorn shook his head, puzzled. But then he began to ponder the implications of considering happiness to be a function of the relationship between our *wants* and *haves*.[27]

He realized these could be grouped into four categories.

The first involves the things that we *want and have*. Most of our current relationships and possessions fall into this group. These make us happy.

The second involves the things that we *don't want but have*. Health problems, extra weight, and financial difficulties would fall in this group. These typically make us unhappy.

The third involves the things that we *want but don't have*. More money or a better job would fall in this group. These things don't make us happy, although we may become happy when we achieve them and transfer them into the first category.

These three categories are all readily accessible to us and make up most of our reference points as we contemplate our happiness. They constitute almost all of our experience. We can observe them, feel their presence, think about them clearly, and talk about them to others with ease.

Yet there's a fourth category that is typically missing from our experience: The things that we *don't want and don't have*. These include a wide range of plausible health, financial, and social problems that we are fortunate enough not to have, at least at this very moment. In fact, the more developed the society we live in and more affluent our family and the surrounding community, the bigger this quadrant becomes.

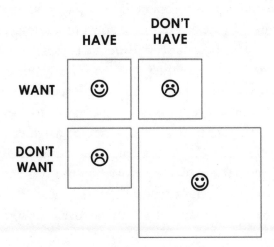

These are the non-occurrences that, should they occur, would make us unhappy. But because we don't experience them, they cease to exist. Their absence doesn't normally make us much happier—but perhaps it should, at least to a certain degree. Einhorn argued that, as a result, we are actually happier than our experience suggests.

What's Missing? What's Irrelevant?

Happiness is deeply personal. It's also not totally in our control. But it pays to understand how experience can impact our happiness.

The ski trip anecdote illustrates some of the ways our experience affects our happiness. We may make a decision—wisely or not—mainly based on conventions and comparisons fueled by our experience. We may gradually adapt to an initially happy episode, and we may risk unhappiness by trying to reach newer heights. Our perception of a situation can be tainted by our selected memories, others' selected experiences, and our inability to adequately consider undesirable non-occurrences.

Missing adaptations. Humans have a remarkable capacity to adapt to their circumstances. After experiencing positive or negative events, happiness levels tend to revert to their prior states. When considering changes or investments in the hopes of becoming happier in the future, it's crucial to take into consideration the pace and amount of adaptation that could take place.

Irrelevant conventions. Experience can lead to routines and habits that are hard to break, leading to unhappiness traps. Hence, it is important for us to base our cost-benefit analyses mainly on our expected future experience rather than worrying about the perceived loss involved in changing an established convention. This will allow us to be more proactive in seeking experiences that challenge our conventions, creating fresh opportunities for happiness.

Missing durations. When contemplating our feelings about past events, our memory is typically driven by the two ends and peak moments, while durations tend to get neglected. Hence, lengthy positive experiences may not affect our overall happiness as we might expect.

Irrelevant comparisons. Feelings of happiness are often relative. A positive experience can have a negative impact if it falls short of one's expectations and reference points. On the other hand, negative outcomes that are not as bad as feared can lead to positive emotions. Hence, it becomes crucial to set appropriate references when evaluating experiences.

Missing variance. The happiness we experience by gaining possessions tends to be compromised by adaptation and conventions. By contrast, the happiness induced by varying experiences can have a larger, longer impact, in part because we have more control on how we remember those happy experiences and don't need to convince others about what they mean to us.

Irrelevant availability. Our experience depends heavily on what is available to observation—even though what's *not* available might be equally important to our happiness. For instance, the things that we don't want and don't have usually fail to register vividly in our minds, even though these may offer powerful reasons for us to be happy. Such counterfactual thinking should help reduce the negative effects of comparative and selected experience on perceptions. It would show us that, statistically, we are happier than we view ourselves.

Understanding how experience shapes our happiness—for good or ill—helps us make more satisfying choices.

CONCLUSION

The Wisdom of the Experience Coach

IS THE EARTH FLAT?

Is it turning?

Is it circling around the sun?

Is it traveling through space?

The 2018 documentary *Behind the Curve* starts with a prominent believer in the so-called flat earth theory answering these questions. He implies that, because we don't *feel* it, it's not really possible that we are on a globe within a solar system within a galaxy, each moving at extremely high speeds within a vast universe. And because he can see the buildings that are miles away from where he is standing, he refutes the existence of earth's curvature. "Science just throws math at us," he says, "whereas we go: Hey by the way, there's Seattle."[1]

The flat earther is right—based on his experience.

Like all the members of the animal kingdom, we humans have a high capacity to gain information and insights through observation and participation. We develop a wide variety of physical and conceptual skills through repetition and practice. We can also reflect on what we've witnessed and make predictions about the future.

Acquiring reliable knowledge as a result, however, is not guaranteed. It's a myth that experience is always a great teacher.

If life were like riding a bicycle or playing tennis, the lessons of experience would be largely reliable. These and similar activities can feature many complexities and uncertainties, especially at competitive levels, but they involve kind learning environments. The feedback is immediate, abundant, and accurate. Even if people make mistakes or sometimes behave in a way that is not optimal, repetition and trial and error provide them with frequent opportunities to gain valid insights and skills. Because the rules of the game don't change suddenly and dramatically, the resulting lessons are also durable. To improve learning even further, professionals hire coaches to judge their skills objectively from outside and provide constructive criticism.

Unfortunately, many situations in life are not like cycling or tennis. In a complex and changing world, the lessons of experience may not be as reliable as we assume. Many learning environments can be utterly wicked, and our resulting intuitions can differ significantly from the realities. They may not only fail to represent a given situation accurately but also constantly feed us a convincing illusion. The rules can change suddenly and dramatically, rendering our intuitions obsolete.

But because the lessons of experience keep being personal, automatic, quick, encouraging, and durable, we still find it easy to trust them and rely on them as we make judgments and decisions.

Denying or going beyond experience can be difficult, especially when the explanations that contradict our experience-based beliefs are abstract and opaque. People may even choose to hold on to their resulting perceptions despite concrete evidence to the contrary. And more experience can make things worse, producing thought leaders with unshakeable yet misleading convictions.

In *Range*, author and journalist David Epstein writes about the benefits of "thinking outside experience" under these circumstances. This approach, supplemented with mathematical methods and technological advances, ultimately allowed scientists to develop a better understanding of the shape and movements of the planet we live on and constantly experience. The view from inside may be clear, but it may not coincide with the view from outside, unexpectedly causing and then reinforcing misperceptions. This is why learning to think outside experience is such an important skill.[2]

But the issue goes even deeper than being right or wrong. We develop many of our tastes and tendencies in life through interactions with our environment. People's preferences can differ simply because they have been exposed to different experiences. And what we subsequently learn can depend on our prior beliefs, preferences, and knowledge. Our personal experience has an enormous influence on who we are, what we want, and how we behave.[3]

Hence, the ability to scrutinize experience critically is of paramount importance. But given the wide variety of learning environments across different domains, analyzing the implications of its lessons becomes a tricky task. To make things even more complicated, some amount of experience—kind or wicked—is often needed even to acknowledge these problems and to recognize valid solutions when they present themselves.

Luckily, unlike most members of the animal kingdom, we don't need to be passive recipients of experience. We can take charge of and actively shape our learning. We have the cognitive resources to look beyond experience and further enrich our understanding of the world we live in. By recognizing how our experience molds our minds, we can learn appropriately from its lessons and unlearn, relearn, improve, or even ignore them, depending on our personal and collective objectives. We can also design methods and mechanisms that render our learning environments kinder and our experience more reliable.

A first step in this quest is to acknowledge that experience is often systematically filtered. It can simultaneously feature missing details and irrelevant information, without our noticing. Sometimes these filters are beyond our control. For example, many failures within a given process may simply be unobservable, while one can readily observe successes and survivors. But some distortions are due to how we gather, consider, and remember information. For example, we may be tempted to overgeneralize from our limited personal experience.

Especially when the stakes are high, it becomes important to ask two questions about our experience: What's missing? What's irrelevant? The answers to these questions can then gradually help us develop a radar that reminds us to take the lessons of experience as signals to reflect on and test further rather than as definitive verdicts.

While this approach is designed to enrich the personal lessons from experience, there's no doubt that applying it to one's own decisions can be counterintuitive and difficult. Here is where the perspective of an outsider can be valuable.[4]

We are usually much better advisers to others than to ourselves. We can quickly and easily see problems in people that we observe and propose ways to solve them. But we can struggle to recognize and manage the same issues when we ourselves suffer from them.[5] Unlike professional athletes, however, most of us don't have coaches to view us from outside, providing constant and reliable feedback about our objectives, perceptions, judgments, and important decisions. Our parents, teachers, friends, and partners may end up spontaneously playing that role. But, like most people, they may simply be unaware of the various illusions of experience.

Instead, is it possible to specifically envision an *experience coach*, who acknowledges and warns us about the potential flaws in its lessons? What would be the main signals that such an adviser would consider when providing feedback about the way one learns from experience and the resulting lessons?

There are three major observable symptoms that suggest when experience is being deceptive instead of providing reliable knowledge. Looking out for these red flags can help to quickly locate the possible learning problems. Once correctly diagnosed, they become easier to mitigate.

Availability Bias

People tend to assess the importance and likelihood of events based on their availability in experience. The more frequently people observe something, the more prominent it becomes in their intuition. This tendency works well in kind learning environments. It saves decision makers a great deal of time and effort as they learn their lessons and make their choices.[6] However, in wicked learning environments, what's readily available to experience is rarely all there is. The following questions should help uncover what's missing.

- *Is experience mainly based on outcomes?* If so, processes are missing from its lessons, along with all their complicated and relevant features.

- *Is experience mainly based on a selection of outcomes?* If so, specific types of outcomes (for example, successes or failures) may be missing from its lessons, along with their own distinct characteristics.

- *Is experience mainly based on personal observations?* If so, counterfactuals and insights from others may be missing from its lessons, along with a more representative and creative view of the situation.

In short, the experience coach would raise a red flag if the lessons of experience are primarily based on what's readily and easily available to observation. Going beyond available experience would lead to a better perception of a given context.

Inappropriate Anchors

When making judgments, predictions, and decisions, people tend to anchor on particular points of reference, then base their judgments and decision on these. This tendency works well in kind learning environments. Comparisons and associations provide a clearer sense of the situation.[7] However, in wicked learning environments, people can easily focus and anchor on details that are irrelevant, or worse, against their best interests. The following questions should help discover what's inappropriate.

- *Does experience lead to a simple causal story, on which decisions are based?* The more complex and uncertain the learning environment, the less reliable this story would be.

- *Does experience involve alluring comforts, emotions, options, and/or games?* These can hide unethical practices or distract people from their personal objectives.

- *Does experience lead to a rigid focus on a selected subset of issues?* If so, changes in the situation would lead experience to become quickly obsolete. Even if the situations remain unchanged, opportunities and happy occasions may exist outside that focus.

In short, the experience coach would identify the primary anchors in a given situation and then raise a red flag if these contradict one's preferences or best interests. Going beyond these inappropriate anchors would improve personal strategies and decisions.

Flawed Convictions

People can gain expertise from experience. As a result, they don't have to think deliberately about many of the details. This tendency works well in kind learning environments. As people increase their knowledge and improve their skills, they can act with greater confidence and competence.[8] However, in wicked learning environments, more experience can lead to unreliable convictions that get in the way of reviewing, unlearning, relearning, and improving the lessons of experience.

There are two sets of questions to consider here. The first set is about the learning environment:

- *In what ways is experience filtered and distorted?*

- *What's the degree of complexity and uncertainty?*

- *Does the future resemble the past?*

- *How much does experience play a role in one's learning and intuition, compared to more formal methods of obtaining knowledge?*

- *What's available, missing, or irrelevant?*

The second set of questions is about the decision maker:

- *How convinced is the decision maker about a certain lesson?*

- *How much of that conviction is fueled by personal experience?*

- *To what degree is this belief self-fulfilling?*

- *What's the decision maker's level of statistical literacy?*

- *Has the decision maker ever tested any experience-based convictions?*

In short, the more wicked the learning environment, the less reliable are the lessons of experience and the less valid are the convictions that these produce. The experience coach would raise a red flag upon noticing convictions based on wicked experience and then attempt to install a healthy dose of skepticism by asking the two sets of questions above. Going beyond flawed convictions would lead to a better and faster adaptation to one's environment.

ooooo

EXPERIENCE CAN INDEED be a reliable teacher, a dear friend, and a crucial ally. It's a major source of information. Its lessons help us form our preferences and perceptions. That's why it's vital to look at it and the environment in which it's obtained with a critical eye.

At an organizational level, one could envision experience coaches working to identify problems with learning environments across different functions and then devising better mechanisms for learning and decision-making accordingly. Viewing the issues from outside would make it easier to identify possible symptoms without falling prey to possible deceptions. In this book, we have attempted to fill the role of such coaches, offering as many solutions as possible to the problems we've diagnosed and analyzed.

At a personal level, one may need to become one's own experience coach. That can feel quite uncomfortable. With this book, we hope to provide the necessary motivation and means to look at the lessons of experience from the outside, and then to offer some practical ideas for dealing with the implications.

That way, some of the wicked environments we often inhabit may become a little kinder.

ACKNOWLEDGMENTS

The idea of writing a book on the myth of experience arose during a retreat at Robin's 450-year-old country house in Avinyonet de Puigventós, a small village in the northeast corner of Spain. Every day, we went on long walks in the morning and sat comfortably near the fireplace at night, jotting down thoughts and planting the seeds.

Between the two of us, we had the advantage of having accumulated a wide range of insights and experiences over many years. Hence, we had a pretty good idea about *what* we would write. That part was relatively easy. *How* to write things, however, is another matter. Luckily, we had help from a diverse group of people as we shaped, reviewed, and reshaped the content. They criticized, verified, refuted, and ultimately improved our examples and arguments.

Among them are prominent scholars in decision science. We are grateful, in particular, for comments received from Irina Cojuharenco, Harry Davis, Linda Ginzel, Reid Hastie, Natalia Karelaia, Spyros Makridakis, Johannes Müller-Trede, and Paul Schoemaker.

We also sought advice and feedback from many readers and decision makers with different backgrounds and specialties. Mehmet U. Soyer expertly and passionately advised and guided us through thick and thin. For their comments, we'd like to thank Hale Soyer, Ipek Aktar, Neelum Khalsa, Emily Mathews, Çiğdem Doğruoğlu, Sasnuhi Muşlıyan, Tahir Öztürk, Eray Yücel, Utku Özmen, Soner

Beyhan, Bora Gökbora, Megan Ford, Mahmut Gökbora, Saadet Öznal Gökbora, Savaş Özdemir, Zübeyir Kurt, Angelica Minaya Akyıldız, and Seha İşmen Özgür.

Our agent Jane Dystel and her team supported us admirably through the whole process. Our editor Clive Priddle and assistant editor Anupama Roy-Chaudhury steered our efforts, skillfully uncovering our blind spots and helping us demonstrate our strengths. They also introduced us to Karl Weber, whose invaluable and inventive inputs lifted the book to its final shape prior to the gloss provided by Kate Mueller´s fine copy-editing skills.

Finally, we are greatly indebted to our families. Without their emotional, intellectual, and physical support, we wouldn't even be able to imagine writing this book. Thank you so much!

NOTES

Introduction

1. There are numerous sources that describe in detail the last days and hours of George Washington, based on the statements and reports by those who witnessed it. For example: V. V. Vadakan, "The asphyxiating and exsanguinating death of President George Washington," *The Permanente Journal* 8 no. 2 (2004): 76–79; H. Merkel, "Dec. 14, 1799: The Excruciating Final Hours of President George Washington," PBS News Hour, December 14, 2014, www.pbs.org/newshour/health/dec-14-1799-excruciating -final-hours-president-george-washington; P. E. Tetlock and D. Gardner, *Superforecasting: The Art and Science of Prediction* (New York: Random House, 2016), 26–27; and D. M. Morens, "Death of a president," *New England Journal of Medicine* 341 (1999): 1845–1850, www.nejm.org/doi/pdf/10.1056 /NEJM199912093412413.

2. There are speculations about Washington's underlying disease. In a PBS interview, University of Michigan historian Howard Markel stated that regardless of the cause of the condition, today a patient in a similar situation would be intubated and provided with more fluids. J. Woodward, "Bloodletting, Blisters and the Mystery of Washington's Death," PBS NewsHour, YouTube, 4:45, December 15, 2014, www.youtube.com /watch?v=6mm9p606Hn0.

3. T. M. Bell, "A brief history of bloodletting," *Journal of Lancaster General Hospital* 11, no. 4 (2016), www.jlgh.org/Past-Issues/Volume-11---Issue -4/Brief-History-of-Bloodletting.aspx; and A. C. Celsus, *De Medicina* (Strasbourg, Germany: Societas Bipontina, 1806).

4. I. H. Kerridge and M. Lowe, "Bloodletting: The story of a therapeutic technique," *Medical Journal of Australia* 163, no. 11–12 (1995): 631–633; R. G. DePalma, V. W. Hayes, and L. R. Zacharski, "Bloodletting: Past and present," *Journal of the American College of Surgeons* 205, no. 1 (2007): 132–144; G. Greenstone, "The history of bloodletting," *BC Medical Journal* 52, no. 1 (2010): 12–14; A. Davis and T. Appel, "Bloodletting instruments in the National Museum of History and Technology," *Smithsonian Studies in History and Technology* (1979): 1–103; T. M. Bell, "A brief history of bloodletting," *Journal of Lancaster General Hospital* 11, no. 4 (2016); and D. Burch, *Taking the Medicine: A Short History of Medicine's Beautiful Idea and Our Difficulty Swallowing It* (New York: Random House, 2009).

5. S. Fried, *Rush: Revolution, Madness, and the Visionary Doctor Who Became a Founding Father* (New York: Crown, 2018).

6. Rush's and other physicians' behavior and approaches should be considered in the context in which they took place. We found the following accounts on the matter to be objective and well researched. See P. E. Kopperman, "Venerate the lancet: Benjamin Rush's yellow fever therapy in context," *Bulletin of the History of Medicine* 78, no. 3 (2004): 539–574; and M. D. Shuman et al., "Bleeding by the numbers: Rush versus Corbett," *The Pharos*, 2014, alphaomegaalpha.org/pharos/PDFs/2014/4/Complete .pdf#page=12. For a detailed account of the 1793 Philadelphia yellow fever epidemic, see J. H. Powell, *Bring Out Your Dead: The Great Plague of Yellow Fever in Philadelphia in 1793* (Philadelphia: University of Pennsylvania Press, 1993). Intensifying treatments is also in line with Hippocrates's sixth aphorism: "For extreme diseases, extreme methods of cure, as to restriction, are most suitable." See Hippocrates, *The Genuine Works of Hippocrates,* trans. F. Adams (Baltimore, MD: William and Wilkins Company, 1939; originally published in 1886 by William Wood and Company, New York), classics.mit.edu/Hippocrates/aphorisms.1.i.html. Rush detailed the extent of his beliefs in bloodletting in "A defense of blood-letting, as a remedy for certain diseases," *Medical Inquiries and Observations*, vol. 4 (Philadelphia: J. Conrad, 1805), 276–361, nlm.nih.gov/2569003RX4.

7. Quote from E. Crahan, *Letters of Benjamin Rush: Volume II: 1793–1813*, vol. 5597 (Princeton, NJ: Princeton University Press, 2019), 665. Letter dated September 15, 1793. Also mentioned in Powell, *Bring Out Your Dead*, 118.

8. A. R. Mills, "The last illness of Lord Byron," *Proceedings of the Royal College of Physicians of Edinburgh* 28, no. 1 (1998): 73–80; and A. Maurois, *Byron* (Paris: Bernard Grasset, 1930), archive.org/stream/in.ernet.dli .2015.98342/2015.98342.Byron_djvu.txt.

9. There are several translations of Hippocrates's aphorisms with similar meanings. We took Francis Adams's translation but used *fallacious* instead of *perilous* because some prominent historians of that era (such as W. Mitchell Clarke) used that specific adjective. Hippocrates, "Aphorisms," in *The Genuine Works of Hippocrates*.

10. K. C. Carter, *The Decline of Therapeutic Bloodletting and the Collapse of Traditional Medicine* (London: Routledge, 2017); D. Gillies, "Why did bloodletting decline?" *Studies in History and Philosophy of Biology and Biomedical Science* 3, no. 44 (2013): 433–434; A. Hróbjartsson and P. C. Gøtzsche, "Placebo interventions for all clinical conditions," *Cochrane Database of Systematic Reviews* 1 (2010); and B. Goldacre, *Bad Science: Quacks, Hacks, and Big Pharma Flacks* (New York: Faber and Faber, 2010).

11. Dr. Elisha Cullen Dick had been Rush's student, but while participating in Washington's bloodletting, he reportedly was doubtful about exceeding a certain amount: D. M. Morens, "Death of a president," *New England Journal of Medicine* 341 (1999): 1845–1849; and D. P. Thomas, "The demise of bloodletting," *Journal of the Royal College of Physicians of Edinburgh* 44 (2014): 72–77.

12. W. M. Clarke, "On the history of bleeding, and its disuse in modern practice," *British Medical Journal* 2, no. 759 (1875): 67; and H. Miton, N. Claidière, and H. Mercier, "Universal cognitive mechanisms explain the cultural success of bloodletting," *Evolution and Human Behavior* 36, no. 4 (2015): 303–312.

13. Different cultures used different methods of bloodletting over many centuries. Cupping and leeching were methods that drew minimal amounts of blood. Today, we use bloodletting in a controlled fashion as a cure for certain rare diseases: R. G. DePalma, V. W. Hayes, and L. R. Zacharski, "Bloodletting: past and present," *Journal of the American College of Surgeons* 205, no. 1 (2007): 132–144.

14. "experience," *Merriam-Webster's Collegiate Dictionary*, 11th ed., www.merriam-webster.com/dictionary/experience; D. A. Kolb, *Experiential Learning: Experience as the Source of Learning and Development* (Upper Saddle River, NJ: FT Press, 2014); and J. P. Wilson and C. Beard, *Experiential Learning: A Handbook for Education, Training and Coaching* (Chicago: Kogan Page, 2013).

15. R. B. Zajonc, "Mere exposure: A gateway to the subliminal," *Current Directions in Psychological Science* 10, no. 6 (2001): 224–228; V. De Cosmi, S. Scaglioni, and C. Agostoni, "Early taste experiences and later food choices," *Nutrients* 9, no. 2 (2017): 107; and E. H. Margulis, *On Repeat: How Music Plays the Mind* (New York: Oxford University Press, 2014).

16. L. Hasher and R. T. Zacks, "Automatic and effortful processes in memory," *Journal of Experimental Psychology: General* 108, no. 3 (1979): 356–388; and R. T. Zacks and L. Hasher, "Frequency processing: A twenty-five year perspective," in *ETC. Frequency Processing and Cognition*, ed. P. Sedlmeier and T. Bestch (New York: Oxford University Press, 2002), 21–36.

17. J. Willis and A. Todorov, "First impressions: Making up your mind after a 100-ms exposure to a face," *Psychological Science* 17, no. 7 (2006): 592–598; A. Tversky and D. Kahneman, "Belief in the law of small numbers," *Psychological Bulletin* 76, no. 2 (1971): 105–110; and M. Rabin, "Inference by believers in the law of small numbers," *Quarterly Journal of Economics* 117, no. 3 (2002): 775–816.

18. R. Hertwig, R. M. Hogarth, and T. Lejarraga, "Experience and description: Exploring two paths to knowledge," *Current Directions in Psychological Science* 27, no. 2 (2018): 123–128.

19. K. A. Ericsson, R. T. Krampe, and C. Tesch-Römer, "The role of deliberate practice in the acquisition of expert performance," *Psychological Review* 100, no. 3 (1993): 363–406; and K. A. Ericsson, "Deliberate practice and acquisition of expert performance: a general overview," *Academic Emergency Medicine* 15, no. 11 (2008): 988–994.

20. The technology for smart rackets is still in its early stages. For one example, see A. Diallo, "Can Babolat's Smart Racket Improve Your Tennis Game?," *Forbes*, August 28, 2014, www.forbes.com/sites/amadoudiallo/2014/08/28/can-babolats-smart-racket-improve-your-tennis-game/.

21. J. Dewey, *Experience and Education* (New York: Kappa Delta, 1938); and Kolb, *Experiential Learning*. For more detailed and recent discussions on learning research, see also P. Honey and A. Mumford, *The Manual of Learning Styles* (Berkshire, UK: Honey, Ardingly House, 1992); and H. Pashler et al., "Learning styles: Concepts and evidence," *Psychological Science in the Public Interest* 9, no. 3 (2008): 105–119.

22. F. Heider and M. Simmel, "An experimental study of apparent behavior," *American Journal of Psychology* 57, no. 2 (1944): 243–259; A. Michotte, *The Perception of Causality* (London: Routledge, 1963); and H. E. Gruber, C. D. Fink, and V. Damm, "Effects of experience on perception of causality," *Journal of Experimental Psychology* 53, no. 2 (1957): 89–93.

23. S. M. Barnett and S. J. Ceci, "When and where do we apply what we learn?: A taxonomy for far transfer," *Psychological Bulletin* 128, no. 4 (2002): 612–637; and L. Argote and P. Ingram, "Knowledge transfer: A basis for competitive advantage in firms," *Organizational Behavior and Human Decision Processes* 82, no. 1 (2000): 150–169.

24. L. Argote et al., "Knowledge transfer in organizations: Learning from the experience of others," *Organizational Behavior and Human Decision Processes* 82, no. 1 (2000): 1–8; B. Levitt and J. G. March, "Organizational learning," *Annual Review of Sociology* 14, no. 1 (1988): 319–338; and T. A. Scandura, "Mentorship and career mobility: An empirical investigation," *Journal of Organizational Behavior* 13, no. 2 (1992): 169–174.

25. D. Kahneman, *Thinking, Fast and Slow* (New York: Farrar, Straus and Giroux, 2011).

26. R. M. Hogarth, *Educating Intuition* (Chicago: University of Chicago Press, 2001).

27. T. Gilovich, *How We Know What Isn't So* (New York: Free Press, 1993), 3.

28. Plato, "The Allegory of the Cave," in *Republic*, VII, trans. Thomas Sheehan (Stanford, CA: Stanford University), 514 a, 2–517 a, 7, web .stanford.edu/class/ihum40/cave.pdf.

29. J. G. March, *The Ambiguities of Experience* (Ithaca, NY: Cornell University Press, 2010); R. M. Hogarth, T. Lejarraga, and E. Soyer, "The two settings of kind and wicked learning environments," *Current Directions in Psychological Science* 24, no. 5 (2015): 379–385; B. Brehmer, "In one word: Not from experience," *Acta Psychologica* 45, no. 1–3 (1980): 223–241; and P. J. H. Schoemaker, *Brilliant Mistakes: Finding Success on the Far Side of Failure* (Philadelphia: Wharton Digital Press, 2011).

30. D. Brown, "Derren Brown's The System," YouTube, 46:57, February 3, 2018, www.youtube.com/watch?v=zv-3EfC17Rc.

31. J. Baron and J. C. Hershey, "Outcome bias in decision evaluation," *Journal of Personality and Social Psychology* 54, no. 4 (1988): 569–579; and J. Denrell, C. Fang, and C. Liu, "Perspective: Chance explanations in the management sciences," *Organization Science* 26, no. 3 (2014): 923–940.

32. S. J. Brown et al., "Survivorship bias in performance studies," *Review of Financial Studies* 5, no. 4 (1992): 553–580; and M. Shermer, "Surviving statistics," *Scientific American* 311, no. 3 (2014): 94.

33. A. Tversky and D. Kahneman, "Availability: A heuristic for judging frequency and probability," *Cognitive Psychology* 5, no. 2 (1973): 207–232; and T. Bock, "What Is Selection Bias?," Displayr Blog, April 13, 2018, www.displayr.com/what-is-selection-bias/.

34. Once again experience led us to confirm a faulty belief about underlying causes. We observed cars rolling uphill, so we thought that the hill must be magnetic.

35. K. Sengupta, T. K. Abdel-Hamid, and L. N. Van Wassenhove, "The experience trap," *Harvard Business Review* 86, no. 2 (2008): 94–101; and

M. Hamori and B. Koyuncu, "Experience matters? The impact of prior CEO experience on firm performance," *Human Resource Management* 54, no. 1 (2015): 23–44.

36. D. Sandlin, "The Backwards Brain Bicycle: Smarter Every Day 133," Smarter Every Day, YouTube, 7:57, April 24, 2015, www.youtube.com/watch?v=MFzDaBzBlL0.

37. Image taken from J. Cole, "Swype Right" (blog post), Almost Looks Like Work, June 4, 2017, jasmcole.com/2017/06/04/swype-right/.

38. Economists refer to this phenomenon as "path dependence." S. J. Liebowitz and S. E. Margolis, "Path dependence, lock-in, and history," *Journal of Law, Economics, & Organization* 11, no. 1 (1995): 205–226.

39. A. Toffler, *Future Shock* (New York: Bantam, 1971).

40. A. Zimmerman Jones, "Copernican Principle," ThoughtCo., July 3, 2019, www.thoughtco.com/copernican-principle-2699117; and S. Arbesman, "The Copernican Principle," in *This Will Make You Smarter*, ed. J. Brockman (London: Penguin, 2012), www.edge.org/response-detail/10277.

41. H. J. Einhorn and R. M. Hogarth, "Confidence in judgment: Persistence of the illusion of validity," *Psychological Review* 85, no. 5 (1978): 395–416.

42. C. Heath, R. P. Larrick, and J. Klayman, "Cognitive repairs: How organizational practices can compensate for individual shortcomings," *Review of Organizational Behavior* 20 (1998): 1–37; A. M. Helmenstine, "What Is a Testable Hypothesis?," ThoughtCo., January 13, 2019, www.thoughtco.com/testable-hypothesis-explanation-and-examples-609100; and L. B. Christensen, B. Johnson, and L. A. Turner, *Research Methods, Design, and Analysis*, 12th ed. (New York: Pearson, 2014).

43. C. R. Rogers, *On Becoming a Person: A Therapist's View of Psychotherapy* (Boston: Houghton Mifflin Harcourt, 1995), 23–24.

Chapter 1: Stories That Lie

1. F. Heider and M. Simmel, "An experimental study of apparent behavior," *American Journal of Psychology* 57, no. 2 (1944): 243–259. View their animation at: Kenjirou, "Heider and Simmel (1944) Animation," YouTube, 1:32, July 26, 2010, www.youtube.com/watch?v=VTNmLt7QX8E; A. Michotte, *The Perception of Causality* (London: Routledge, 1963); B. J. Scholl and P. D. Tremoulet, "Perceptual causality and animacy," *Trends in Cognitive Sciences* 4, no. 8 (2000): 299–309; and L. J. Rips, "Causation from perception," *Perspectives on Psychological Science* 6, no. 1 (2011): 77–97.

2. G. H. Bower and M. C. Clark, "Narrative stories as mediators for serial learning," *Psychonomic Science* 14, no. 4 (1969): 181–182; J. Gottschall, *The Storytelling Animal: How Stories Make Us Human* (New York: Houghton Mifflin Harcourt, 2012); R. D. Hill, C. Allen, and P. McWhorter, "Stories as a mnemonic aid for older learners," *Psychology and Aging* 6, no. 3 (1991): 484; and E. Cooke, "How Narratives Can Aid Memory," *Guardian* (Manchester, UK), January 15, 2012, www.theguardian.com/lifeandstyle/2012/jan/15/story-lines-facts.

3. Y. N. Harari, *Sapiens: A Brief History of Humankind* (New York: HarperCollins, 2014).

4. F. W. Nietzsche and G. Handwerk, *Human, All Too Human, I*, vol. 3 (Palo Alto, CA: Stanford University Press, 2000), 279. The quote is also featured in J. G. March, *The Ambiguities of Experience* (Ithaca, NY: Cornell University Press, 2010), 48.

5. D. J. Watts, *Everything Is Obvious: Once You Know the Answer* (New York: Crown/Random House, 2011), 155.

6. M. Shermer, "Patternicity: Finding meaningful patterns in meaningless noise," *Scientific American* 299, no. 6 (2008): 48; A. L. Mishara, "Klaus Conrad (1905–1961): Delusional mood, psychosis, and beginning schizophrenia," *Schizophrenia Bulletin* 36, no. 1 (2009): 9–13; N. N. Taleb, *The Black Swan: The Impact of the Highly Improbable* (New York: Random House, 2007); and "Avoiding Falling Victim to the Narrative Fallacy" (blog post), Farnam Street, fs.blog/2016/04/narrative-fallacy/.

7. F. Blanco, "Positive and negative implications of the causal illusion," *Consciousness and Cognition* 50 (2017): 56–68.

8. SI staff, "Recent SI Cover Jinx," *Sports Illustrated*, March 7, 2016, www.si.com/sports-illustrated/photo/2016/03/07/recent-si-cover-jinx.

9. "*Sports Illustrated* Cover Jinx," Wikipedia, en.wikipedia.org/wiki/Sports_Illustrated_cover_jinx; and T. Smith, "That old black magic millions of superstitious readers—and many athletes—believe that an appearance on *Sports Illustrated*'s cover is the kiss of death. But is there really such a thing as the SI jinx?," Vault archives, *Sports Illustrated*, January 21, 2001, www.si.com/vault/2002/01/21/8107599/that-old-black-magic-millions-of-superstitious-readersand-many-athletesbelieve-that-an-appearance-on-sports-illustrateds-cover-is-the-kiss-of-death-but-is-there-really-such-a-thing-as-the-si-jinx.

10. "Regression Toward the Mean: An Introduction with Examples" (blog post), Farnam Street, fs.blog/2015/07/regression-to-the-mean/.

11. S. Vyse, "Where Do Superstitions Come From?," TEDEd: Lessons Worth Sharing, YouTube, 5:10, March 9, 2017, www.youtube.com/watch?v=quOdF1CAPXs.

12. J. M. Bland and D. G. Altman, "Regression towards the mean," *British Medical Journal* 308, no. 6942 (1994): 1499; A. G. Barnett, J. C. Van Der Pols, and A. J. Dobson, "Regression to the mean: What it is and how to deal with it," *International Journal of Epidemiology* 34, no. 1 (2004): 215–220; and C. E. Davis, "The effect of regression to the mean in epidemiologic and clinical studies," *American Journal of Epidemiology* 104, no. 5 (1976): 493–498.

13. D. Kahneman and A. Tversky, "On the psychology of prediction," *Psychological Review* 80, no. 4 (1973): 237–251.

14. E. P. Lazear, "The Peter principle: A theory of decline," *Journal of Political Economy* 112, no. S1 (2004): S141–S163; and L. J. Peter and R. Hull, *The Peter Principle* (London: Souvenir Press, 1969).

15. B. Bruinshoofd and B. Ter Weel, "Manager to go? Performance dips reconsidered with evidence from Dutch football," *European Journal of Operational Research* 148, no. 2 (2003): 233–246; and J. C. van Ours and M. A. van Tuijl, "In-season head-coach dismissals and the performance of professional football teams," *Economic Inquiry* 54, no. 1 (2016): 591–604.

16. L. Mlodinow, *The Drunkard's Walk: How Randomness Rules Our Lives* (New York: Vintage Books, 2009).

17. S. Basuroy and S. Chatterjee, "Fast and frequent: Investigating box office revenues of motion picture sequels," *Journal of Business Research* 61, no. 7 (2008): 798–803; S. Lilienfeld, "Beware the Regression Fallacy," The Skeptical Psychologist (blog), *Psychology Today*, January 4, 2014, www.psychologytoday.com/us/blog/the-skeptical-psychologist/201401/beware-the-regression-fallacy; and Z. Crockett, "Why Hollywood Keeps Making Terrible Sequels," Vox, YouTube, 4:39, July 6, 2016, www.youtube.com/watch?v=OYirwDFKEX0.

18. N. P. Repenning and J. D. Sterman, "Capability traps and self-confirming attribution errors in the dynamics of process improvement," *Administrative Science Quarterly* 47, no. 2 (2002): 265–295.

19. J. L. Hilton and W. Von Hippel, "Stereotypes," *Annual Review of Psychology* 47, no. 1 (1996): 237–271.

20. L. Jussim, *Social Perception and Social Reality: Why Accuracy Dominates Bias and Self-Fulfilling Prophecy* (Oxford, UK: Oxford University Press, 2012).

21. K. Fiedler, "Beware of samples! A cognitive-ecological sampling approach to judgment biases," *Psychological Review* 107, no. 4 (2000): 659.

22. M. Gladwell, *Blink: The Power of Thinking Without Thinking* (New York: Little, Brown, 2005); and C. Goldin and C. Rouse, "Orchestrating impartiality: The impact of 'blind' auditions on female musicians," *American Economic Review* 90, no. 4 (2000): 715–741.

23. R. B. Cialdini, *Influence: Science and Practice,* 5th ed. (Boston: Allyn and Bacon, 2009); and P. Rosenzweig, *The Halo Effect . . . and the Eight Other Business Delusions That Deceive Managers* (New York: Simon and Schuster, 2014).

24. M. Lewis, *Moneyball: The Art of Winning an Unfair Game* (New York: W. W. Norton, 2004), 18.

25. L. Wachowski and L. Wachowski, directors, *The Matrix,* film (produced by Joel Silver, Warner Bros, Village Roadshow Pictures, Groucho II Film Partnership, Silver Pictures, 1999).

26. "Oedipus," Greek Mythology, www.greekmythology.com/Myths /Mortals/Oedipus/oedipus.html.

27. "Why did Voldemort want to kill the Potters in the first place?," Science Fiction & Fantasy, StackExchange, February 20, 2014, scifi .stackexchange.com/questions/50467/why-did-voldemort-want-to-kill-the -potters-in-the-first-place; and "Would Voldemort have succeeded if he simply ignored the prophecy?," Science Fiction & Fantasy, StackExchange, December 1, 2016, scifi.stackexchange.com/questions/146330/would-volde mort-have-succeeded-if-he-simply-ignored-the-prophecy/146331.

28. L. Thomas, *The Youngest Science: Notes of a Medicine-Watcher* (New York: Penguin Books, 1983), 22; and R. K. Merton, "The self-fulfilling prophecy," *Antioch Review* 8 (1948): 193–210.

29. H. J. Einhorn and R. M. Hogarth, "Confidence in judgment: Persistence of the illusion of validity," *Psychological Review* 85, no. 5 (1978): 395–416.

30. D. Glover, A. Pallais, and W. Pariente, "Discrimination as a self -fulfilling prophecy: Evidence from French grocery stores," *Quarterly Journal of Economics* 132, no. 3 (2017): 1219–1260.

31. P. Smith, *Lead with a Story: A Guide to Crafting Business Narratives That Captivate, Convince, and Inspire* (New York: Amacom, 2012); P. J. Zak, "Why Your Brain Loves Good Storytelling," *Harvard Business Review,* October 28, 2014, hbr.org/2014/10/why-your-brain-loves-good-storytelling; and D. Schawbel, "How to Use Storytelling as a Leadership Tool," *Forbes,* August 12, 2012, www.forbes.com/sites/danschawbel/2012/08/13/how-to -use-storytelling-as-a-leadership-tool.

32. K. Schulz, "The Pessimistic Meta-induction from the History of Science," in *This Will Make You Smarter,* ed. J. Brockman (New York: Random House, 2012), www.edge.org/response-detail/11135.

33. K. Schulz, *Being Wrong: Adventures in the Margin of Error* (New York: HarperCollins, 2010).

34. U. Gneezy and J. List, *The Why Axis: Hidden Motives and the Undiscovered Economics of Everyday Life* (New York: Random House, 2014).

35. N. J. Roese, "Counterfactual thinking," *Psychological Bulletin* 121, no. 1 (1997): 133–148.

36. S. Johnson, *Farsighted: How We Make the Decisions That Matter the Most* (London: Penguin, 2018).

37. J. Pearl and D. Mackenzie, *The Book of Why: The New Science of Cause and Effect* (New York: Basic Books, 2018); K. Hartnett, "To Build Truly Intelligent Machines, Teach Them Cause and Effect," Quanta Magazine, May 15, 2018, www.quantamagazine.org/to-build-truly -intelligent-machines-teach-them-cause-and-effect-20180515/.

Chapter 2: Lost Insights

1. "List of Google Products," Wikipedia, en.wikipedia.org/wiki/List_of _Google_products.

2. Successful ideas being rejected is indeed a ubiquitous phenomenon. For example: S. H. Aronson, "Bell's Electrical Toy: What's the Use? The Sociology of Early Telephone Usage," in *The Social Impact of the Telephone*, ed. I. de Sola Pool (Cambridge, MA: MIT Press, 1977), 15–39; and P. David, "The Hero and the Herd in Technological History: Reflections on Thomas Edison and the Battle of the Systems," in *Favorites of Fortune: Technology, Growth, and Development in the Industrial Revolution*, ed. P. Higonnet, D. Landes, and H. Rosovsky (Cambridge, MA: Harvard University Press, 1991), 72–119.

3. J. Norah, "Where JK Rowling Wrote Harry Potter in Edinburgh" (blog post), Independent Travel Cats, April 7, 2019, independenttravelcats .com/cafes-where-jk-rowling-wrote-harry-potter-in-edinburgh/; A. Flood, "JK Rowling Says She Received 'Loads' of Rejections Before Harry Potter Success," *Guardian* (Manchester, UK), March 24, 2015, www.theguardian .com/books/2015/mar/24/jk-rowling-tells-fans-twitter-loads-rejections -before-harry-potter-success; "Revealed: The Eight-Year-Old Girl Who Saved Harry Potter," *Independent* (London), July 3, 2005, www.independent .co.uk/arts-entertainment/books/news/revealed-the-eight-year-old -girl-who-saved-harry-potter-296456.html; Keli, "Harry Potter Rejected" (blog post), January 29, 2010, harrypotterrejected.blogspot.com; and J. Shamsian, "How J.K. Rowling Went from Struggling Single Mom to the

World's Most Successful Author," Insider, July 31, 2018, www.insider.com /jk-rowling-harry-potter-author-biography-2017-7.

4. V. Khosla, "Fireside chat with Google cofounders, Larry Page and Sergey Brin," Khosla Ventures, YouTube, 41:55, July 3, 2017, www .youtube.com/watch?v=Wdnp_7atZ0M; and S. Makridakis, R. Hogarth, and A. Gaba, *Dance with Chance: Making Luck Work for You* (Oxford, UK: Oneworld Publications, 2009).

5. R. X. Cringely, *Triumph of the Nerds: An Irreverent History of the PC Industry*, actors: R. X. Cringely, D. Adams, S. Albert, P. G. Allen, and B. Atkinson, DVD (New York: Ambrose Video, August 29, 2002); and R. Pebam, "How Steve Jobs got the idea for GUI from Xerox," YouTube, 9:40, January 4, 2014, www.youtube.com/watch?v=J33pVRdxWbw.

6. J. S. Brown, "Changing the Game of Corporate Research: Learning to Thrive in the Fog of Reality," in *Technological Innovation: Oversights and Foresights*, ed. R. Garud, P. R. Nayyar, and Z. B. Shapira (Cambridge, UK: Cambridge University Press, 1997), 95–110.

7. See J. Schumpeter, "Creative destruction," *Capitalism, Socialism and Democracy* 825 (1942): 82–85; and C. M. Christensen, M. E. Raynor, and R. McDonald, "What is disruptive innovation?," *Harvard Business Review* 93, no. 12 (2015): 44–53. This issue is also related to the concept of "the black swan," discussed and popularized by statistician and author Nassim Taleb. Accordingly, while the concept is often used to refer to risks and negative disruptions, many disruptive innovations could be categorized as black swan events as well. The past includes many white swan ideas, which can lead a forecaster to erroneously declare an upcoming black swan idea as also white. We will not apply this concept in detail in this chapter and focus more on other experience-fueled problems in the context of creativity. But we will apply the concept in detail to issues with predicting and assessing disasters in Chapter 3.

8. B. Chesky, "7 Rejections," Venture Capital, Medium, July 12, 2015, medium.com/@bchesky/7-rejections-7d894cbaa084.

9. "The Anti-Portfolio" (web page), Bessemer Venture Partners, www .bvp.com/portfolio/anti-portfolio.

10. J. M. Berg, "When silver is gold: Forecasting the potential creativity of initial ideas. Forthcoming," *Organizational Behavior and Human Decision Processes* 154 (2019): 96–117.

11. IMDbPRO, Box Office Mojo, www.boxofficemojo.com/franchises /chart/?id=pixar.htm.

12. Of course, we don't know if these were the initial forms of ideas when the discussions about those animations began; in fact, that's our point.

13. Pixar and Khan Academy, "Welcome to Pixar in a Box," Khan Academy, YouTube, 5:19, August 27, 2015, www.youtube.com/watch?v=3Iu1 Z0h1i1Y.

14. E. Catmull, "How Pixar fosters collective creativity," *Harvard Business Review* 86, no. 9 (September 2008): 65–72.

15. R. A. Posner, *The Little Book of Plagiarism* (New York: Pantheon, 2007).

16. A. M. Grant, *Originals: How Non-conformists Move the World* (London: Penguin, 2007), 3.

17. K. Ferguson, filmmaker, *Everything Is a Remix*, video series (Portland, OR: 2015–2020), www.everythingisaremix.info/; K. Ferguson, "Embrace the Remix," TED Talks, 9:27, June 2012, https://www.ted .com/talks/kirby_ferguson_embrace_the_remix.

18. Editors of Encyclopaedia Britannica, "Phonograph," *Encyclopaedia Britannica*, www.britannica.com/technology/phonograph; and D. Hochfedler, "Alexander Graham Bell: American Inventor," *Encyclopaedia Britannica*, February 28, 2020, www.britannica.com/biography/Alexander -Graham-Bell.

19. "The meaning and origin of the expression: Standing on the shoulders of Giants," The Phrase Finder, www.phrases.org.uk/meanings /268025.html.

20. D. K. Murray, *Borrowing Brilliance: The Six Steps to Business Innovation by Building on the Ideas of Others* (New York: Gotham Books, 2009).

21. L. M. Fisher, "Company News; Xerox Sues Apple Computer Over Macintosh Copyright," *New York Times*, December 15, 1989, www .nytimes.com/1989/12/15/business/company-news-xerox-sues-apple -computer-over-macintosh-copyright.html; *Apple Computer, Inc., vs. Microsoft Corporation*, US Court of Appeals for Ninth Circuit—35 F.3d 1435, 1994, Justia US Law, law.justia.com/cases/federal/appellate-courts /F3/35/1435/605245/; and G. Edwards, "Led Zeppelin's 10 Boldest Rip-Offs," *Rolling Stone*, June 22, 2016, www.rollingstone.com/music/music -news/led-zeppelins-10-boldest-rip-offs-223419/.

22. "Charles Lyell: Principles of Geology," Nova Evolution, PBS, www .pbs.org/wgbh/evolution/library/02/4/l_024_01.html; S. Brin and L. Page, "The anatomy of a large-scale hypertextual web search engine," *Computer Networks and ISDN Systems* 30, no. 1–7 (1998): 107–117; and L. Page, S. Brin, R. Motwani, and T. Winograd, *The PageRank citation ranking: Bringing order to the web*, Technical Report, Stanford InfoLab, January 29, 1998, ilpubs.stanford.edu:8090/422/1/1999-66.pdf.

23. D. J. Simons and C. F. Chabris, "Gorillas in our midst: Sustained inattentional blindness for dynamic events," *Perception* 28, no. 9 (1999):

1059–1074; and C. Chabris interview, "Paying Attention," Alumni, Research, Harvard University: The Graduate School of Arts and Sciences, July 25, 2017, gsas.harvard.edu/news/colloquy/summer-2017/paying-attention.

24. D. J. Simons, "Monkeying around with the gorillas in our midst: Familiarity with an inattentional-blindness task does not improve the detection of unexpected events," *i-Perception* 1, no. 1 (2010): 3–6.

25. D. Memmert, "The effects of eye movements, age, and expertise on inattentional blindness," *Consciousness and Cognition* 15, no. 3 (2006): 620–627.

26. T. Drew, M. L. H. Võ, and J. M. Wolfe, "The invisible gorilla strikes again: Sustained inattentional blindness in expert observers," *Psychological Science* 24, no. 9 (2013): 1848–1853.

27. R. Wiseman, *The Luck Factor: Changing Your Luck, Changing Your Life—the Four Essential Principles* (New York: Miramax Books, 2003); and G. Klein, *Seeing What Others Don't: The Remarkable Ways We Gain Insights* (New York: Public Affairs, 2013). In a recent book, Nick Chater argues that people are mistaken if they think that their minds can keep working on problems that they are not actively considering, that is, there is no such unconscious thought. Achieving solutions, he argues, results from finding new perspectives when attacking problems after a rest period or being engaged in other tasks. See N. Chater, *The Mind Is Flat: The Illusion of Mental Depth and the Improvised Mind* (London: Allen Lane, 2018); and D. J. Cai, S. A. Mednick, E. M. Harrison, J. C. Kanady, and S. C. Mednick, "REM, not incubation, improves creativity by priming associative networks," *Proceedings of the National Academy of Sciences* 106, no. 25 (2009): 10130–10134.

28. K. Duncker and L. S. Lees, "On problem-solving," *Psychological Monographs* 58, no. 5 (1945): i–113; and R. E. Adamson, "Functional fixedness as related to problem solving: A repetition of three experiments," *Journal of Experimental Psychology* 44, no. 4 (1952): 288–291.

29. H. Rahmandad, N. Repenning, and J. Sterman, "Effects of feedback delay on learning," *System Dynamics Review* 25, no. 4 (2009): 309–338, 310.

30. M. Csíkszentmihályi, *Flow: The Psychology of Optimal Experience* (New York: Harper and Row, 1990).

31. K. Robinson and L. Aronica, *The Element: How Finding Your Passion Changes Everything* (London: Penguin, 2010).

32. T. M. Amabile, *How to Kill Creativity* (Boston: Harvard Business School Publishing, 1998); and D. H. Pink, *Drive: The Surprising Truth About What Motivates Us* (London: Penguin, 2011).

33. "Rules of the Dojo," Student Handbook, Aikido Schools of Ueshiba, August 31, 2016, asu.org/student-handbook/proper-dojo-etiquette/.

34. M. Schrage, "Just How Valuable Is Google's '20% Time'?," *Harvard Business Review*, August 20, 2013, hbr.org/2013/08/just-how-valuable-is -googles-2-1; and V. Govindarajan and S. Srinivas, "The Innovation Mindset in Action: 3M Corporation," *Harvard Business Review*, August 6, 2013, hbr.org/2013/08/the-innovation-mindset-in-acti-3.

35. S. H. Seggie, E. Soyer, and K. H. Pauwels, "Combining big data and lean startup methods for business model evolution," *AMS Review* 7, no. 3–4 (2017): 154–169.

36. "Mary Phelps Jacob: Brassiere," Historical Inventors, Lemelson-MIT Progam, lemelson.mit.edu/resources/mary-phelps-jacob; M. E. Ruane, "Caresse Crosby, Who Claimed the Invention of the Bra, Was Better Known for Her Wild Life," *Washington Post*, November 11, 2014; P. Lyle, "The Crosbys: Literature's Most Scandalous Couple," *Telegraph* (London), June 19, 2019, www.telegraph.co.uk/culture/5549090/The-Crosbys-literatures -most-scandalous-couple.html; and "Bibliographic data: US1115674 (A) —1914-11-02, Brassiere," Espacenet: Patent Search, worldwide.espacenet .com/publicationDetails/biblio?FT=D&date=19141103&DB=&locale =en_EP&CC=US&NR=1115674A&KC=A&ND=1.

37. J. Swearingen, "An Idea That Stuck: How George de Mestral Invented the Velcro Fastener," The Vindicated, *New York*, November 2016, nymag.com/vindicated/2016/11/an-idea-that-stuck-how-george-de-mestral -invented-velcro.html.

38. J. M. Benyus, *Biomimicry: Innovation Inspired by Nature* (New York: Morrow, 1997); "The World Is Poorly Designed: But Copying Nature Helps," Vox, YouTube, 6:49, November 9, 2017, www.youtube.com/watch ?v=iMtXqTmfta0; and T. McKeag, "How One Engineer's Birdwatching Made Japan's Bullet Train Better," The Biomimicry Column (blog), GreenBiz, October 19, 2012, www.greenbiz.com/blog/2012/10/19/how-one -engineers-birdwatching-made-japans-bullet-train-better.

39. E. Dane, "Reconsidering the trade-off between expertise and flexibility: A cognitive entrenchment perspective," *Academy of Management Review* 35, no. 4 (2010): 579–603. There's a working paper that analyzes the relationship between interests and creativity: L. Niemi and S. Cordes, "The Arts and Economic Vitality: Leisure Time Interest in Art Predicts Entrepreneurship and Innovation at Work," working paper, 2015, www .arts.gov/sites/default/files/Research-Art-Works-BostonCollege.pdf. There's also a study on Nobel Prize winners and how they are more likely to have interests in arts and crafts with respect to their peers. R. Root-Bernstein et al., "Arts foster scientific success: Avocations of nobel, national

academy, royal society, and sigma xi members," *Journal of Psychology of Science and Technology* 1, no. 2 (2008): 51–63.

40. D. Shah, "By the Numbers: MOOCS in 2017," Class Central: MOOC Report, January 18, 2018, www.class-central.com/report/mooc-stats -2017/.

41. A. Sliwka, "The Contribution of Alternative Education," in *Innovating to Learn, Learning to Innovate* (Paris: OECD/CERI, 2008), 93; "What Is a Flipped Classroom?" (blog post), Panopto, September 17, 2018, www.panopto.com/blog/what-is-a-flipped-classroom/; M. Resnick, "Kindergarten for Our Whole Lives," TEDxBeaconStreet, YouTube, 16:03, November 30, 2017, www.youtube.com/watch?v=IfvgVpQI56I; and K. Dickinson, "How does Finland's top-ranking education system work?," Big Think, February 8, 2019, bigthink.com/politics-current-affairs /how-finlands-education-system-works.

42. E. G. Pitcher, "An evaluation of the Montessori method in schools for young children," *Childhood Education* 42, no. 8 (1966): 489–492; C. Marshall, "Montessori education: a review of the evidence base," *npj Science of Learning* 2, no. 1 (2017), 11; and J. C. Manner, "Montessori vs. Traditional Education in the Public Sector: Seeking Appropriate Comparisons of Academic Achievement," *Forum on Public Policy Online* 2007, no. 2 (2007).

43. Additional operational details for a possible escape to passion mechanism: Schools could determine a certain minimum amount of core courses that cannot be dropped. They could make sure that parts of the advanced versions of these classes may be dropped, once again after a successful midterm. Classes with more contact hours could be dropped later in the semester to ensure that everyone has similar conditions. Schools could set minimum GPAs necessary for students to be eligible for the program. Students can be allowed to do the projects in small teams. Because the program requires a successful midterm, students who wish to drop a course would have to learn the basic material they might have largely ignored were they taking the class in the traditional way. They'd have incentives to work hard at the beginning of the semester to escape from the course after a midterm. The mechanism could even improve class environments for some courses. It would eliminate from sessions those who are least interested as the content progresses to more advanced topics within the semester. The mechanism might involve a few additional challenges. For instance, each school would have to monitor the whole process to some degree. Students who escape would need to be accommodated in a room

and someone would have to supervise them. Families would need to be informed in detail about the mechanism. Ultimately, the method should be tested and tweaked accordingly.

44. J. Hirsch, "Pixar's Secret for Giving Feedback (Communication)," Leadx, June 20, 2017, leadx.org/articles/pixar/.

Chapter 3: Blinded to Risk

1. P. Schulte et al., "The Chicxulub asteroid impact and mass extinction at the Cretaceous-Paleogene boundary," *Science* 327, no 5970 (2010): 1214–1218; R. A. DePalma et al., "A seismically induced onshore surge deposit at the KPg boundary, North Dakota," *Proceedings of the National Academy of Sciences* 116, no. 17 (2019): 8190–8199; R. Smith, "Here's What Happened the Day Dinosaurs Died," *National Geographic*, June 11, 2016, news.nationalgeographic.com/2016/06/what-happened-day-dinosaurs -died-chicxulub-drilling-asteroid-science/; and D. Preston, "The Day the Dinosaurs Died," *The New Yorker*, March 29, 2019, www.newyorker.com /magazine/2019/04/08/the-day-the-dinosaurs-died. Asteroid impact, also known as the K-T event, is currently the main hypothesis behind the extinction that took place approximately sixty-six million years ago. There is another theory that involves increased volcanic activity in India, called the Deccan Traps hypothesis. Both events might have happened and contributed to the global catastrophe. But this does not change the value of the analogy we are presenting in the chapter: B. Bosker, "The Nastiest Feud in Science," *The Atlantic*, September 2018, www.theatlantic.com/magazine /archive/2018/09/dinosaur-extinction-debate/565769/.

2. N. N. Taleb, *The Black Swan: The Impact of the Highly Improbable* (New York: Random House, 2007).

3. "1918 Pandemic (H1N1 virus)" (web page), Centers for Disease Control and Prevention, National Center for Immunization and Respiratory Diseases (NCIRD), March 20, 2019, www.cdc.gov/features/1918-flu -pandemic/index.html.

4. "The Effects of Climate Change" (web page), Global Climate Change, NASA, climate.nasa.gov/effects/; and D. J. Wuebbles et al., eds., *Climate Science Special Report: Fourth National Climate Assessment*, vol. 1 (Washington, DC: US Global Change Research Program, 2017), doi: 10.7930 /J0J964J6.

5. D. Ferber, "Livestock feed ban preserves drugs' power," *Science* 295, no. 5552 (2002): 27–28; and "Antimicrobial Resistance" (web page),

World Health Organization, February 15, 2018, www.who.int/news-room /fact-sheets/detail/antimicrobial-resistance.

6. "We'll Live to 100—How Can We Afford It?" (white paper), World Economic Forum, May 2017, www3.weforum.org/docs/WEF_White _Paper_We_Will_Live_to_100.pdf.

7. R. Hertwig et al., "Decisions from experience and the effect of rare events in risky choice," *Psychological Science* 15 (2004): 534–539; R. Hertwig and I. Erev, "The description-experience gap in risky choice," *Trends in Cognitive Sciences* 13, no. 12 (2009): 517–523; R. Hau et al., "The description-experience gap in risky choice: The role of sample size and experienced probabilities," *Journal of Behavioral Decision Making* 21, no. 5 (2008): 493–518; and A. de Palma et al., "Beware of black swans: Taking stock of the description-experience gap in decision under uncertainty," *Marketing Letters* 25 (2014): 269–280. For an alternative view, check out also: A. Glöckner et al., "The reversed description-experience gap: Disentangling sources of presentation format effects in risky choice," *Journal of Experimental Psychology: General* 145, no. 4 (2016): 486–508.

8. The opposite could also happen. If someone experiences a rare event, the subsequent perception could be different than expert estimates. In particular, it could feel more probable than it actually is. But in the case of rare disasters, this opposite case would be less observed and would affect a smaller proportion of a given population.

9. There are 365 days in a year. The approximate probability of a birthday match between any two specific people is $1/365$. The probability of a no match is thus $364/365$. The probability of two no matches in a row is $(364/365)^2 = .9972$. The probability of n no matches in a row is $(364/365)^n$. There are three hundred different combinations of two people in a group of twenty-five; the probability of three hundred no matches in a row is $(364/365)^{300} = 44\%$. The probability that there is at least one match $= 1 - 44\% = 56\%$.

10. R. Meyer and H. Kunreuther, *The Ostrich Paradox: Why We Underprepare for Disasters* (Philadelphia: Wharton Digital Press, 2017).

11. ESF #14, ed., *Hurricane Ike Impact Report* (Washington, DC: FEMA, December 2008), www.fema.gov/pdf/hazard/hurricane/2008/ike /impact_report.pdf; and D. F. Zane et al., "Tracking deaths related to hurricane Ike, Texas, 2008," *Disaster Medicine and Public Health Preparedness* 5, no. 1 (2011): 23–28.

12. E. Michel-Kerjan, S. Lemoyne de Forges, and H. Kunreuther, "Policy tenure under the US national flood insurance program (nfip)," *Risk Analysis* 32, no. 4 (2012): 644–658.

13. B. M. Barber and T. Odean, "All that glitters: The effect of attention and news on the buying behavior of individual and institutional investors," *The Review of Financial Studies* 21, no. 2 (2007): 785–818; I. Erev and E. Haruvy, "Learning and the Economics of Small Decisions," in *The Handbook of Experimental Economics*, vol. 2, ed. J. H. Kagel and A. E. Roth (Princeton, NJ: Princeton University Press, 2016), 1–136; D. Fudenberg and A. Peysakhovich, "Recency, records, and recaps: Learning and non-equilibrium behavior in a simple decision problem," *ACM Transactions on Economics and Computation (TEAC)* 4, no. 4 (2016): 23; and T. Lejarraga, J. K. Woike, and R. Hertwig, "Description and experience: How experimental investors learn about booms and busts affects their financial risk taking," *Cognition* 157 (2016): 365–383.

14. "What Would Happen If We Stopped Vaccinations?" (web page), Vaccines & Immunizations, National Center for Immunization and Respiratory Diseases, Centers for Disease Control and Prevention, June 29, 2018, www.cdc.gov/vaccines/vac-gen/whatifstop.htm; and A. Kata, "Anti-vaccine activists, Web 2.0, and the postmodern paradigm: An overview of tactics and tropes used online by the anti-vaccination movement," *Vaccine* 30, no. 25 (2012): 3778–3789.

15. "Ebola Virus Disease" (web page), Regional Office for Africa, World Health Organization, www.afro.who.int/health-topics/ebola-virus-disease; "Ebola virus disease—Democratic Republic of the Congo" (Disease outbreak news: Update), Emergencies preparedness, response, World Health Organization, April 25, 2019, www.who.int/csr/don/25-april-2019-ebola-drc /en/; and J. Golding, "Ebola: How a Killer Disease Was Stopped in Its Tracks," BBC News, July 23, 2018, www.bbc.com/news/health-44872418.

16. M. Molteni, "Ebola Is Now Curable: Here's How the New Treatments Work," *Wired*, December 8, 2019, www.wired.com/story/ebola-is-now -curable-heres-how-the-new-treatments-work/.

17. B. Brende et al., "CEPI: A new global R&D organisation for epidemic preparedness and response," *Lancet* 389, no. 10066 (2017): 233–235.

18. E. Wilson, "Thank You Vasili Arkhipov, the Man Who Stopped Nuclear War," *Guardian* (Manchester, UK), October 27, 2012, www .theguardian.com/commentisfree/2012/oct/27/vasili-arkhipov-stopped -nuclear-war.

19. P. Aksenov, "Stanislav Petrov: The Man Who May Have Saved the World," BBC News, September 23, 2013, www.bbc.com/news/world -europe-24280831; P. Hoffman, "I Had a Funny Feeling in My Gut," *Washington Post*, February 10, 1999, www.washingtonpost.com/wp-srv /inatl/longterm/coldwar/soviet10.htm; and A. Nagesh, "Stanislav Petrov—

the Man Who Quietly Saved the World—Has Died Aged 77," *Metro* (London), September 18, 2017, metro.co.uk/2017/09/18/stanislav-petrov -the-man-who-quietly-saved-the-world-has-died-aged-77-6937015/.

20. P. Anthony, director, *The Man Who Saved the World*, documentary about Stanislav Petrov (Denmark: Statement Film, Light Cone Pictures, 2014); and "The Nobel Prize in Chemistry 1995," www.nobelprize.org /prizes/chemistry/1995/summary/.

21. N. Aizenman, "The Doctor Killed in Friday's Ebola Attack Was Dedicated—But Also Afraid," NPR, April 23, 2019, www.npr.org/sections /goatsandsoda/2019/04/23/716121928/the-doctor-killed-in-fridays-ebola -attack-was-dedicated-but-also-afraid; and G. Sume, "Remembering Dr. Richard Valery Mouzoko Kiboung: 1977–2019" (statement), World Health Organization, May 4, 2019, www.who.int/news-room/detail/04 -05-2019-remembering-dr-richard-valery-mouzoko-kiboung.

22. K. W. Morrison, "Reporting Near Misses," *Safety + Health*, August 24, 2014, www.safetyandhealthmagazine.com/articles/10994-reporting -near-misses; C. H. Tinsley, R. L. Dillon, and P. M. Madsen, "How to avoid catastrophe," *Harvard Business Review* 89, no. 4 (2011): 90–97; and S. Jones, C. Kirchsteiger, and W. Bjerke, "The importance of near miss reporting to further improve safety performance," *Journal of Loss Prevention in the Process Industries* 12, no. 1 (1999): 59–67.

23. T. Harford, "Mental bias leaves us unprepared for disaster," *Financial Times*, August 1, 2017.

24. S. Laska, "What if Hurricane Ivan had not missed New Orleans?," *Sociological Inquiry* 78, no. 2 (2008): 174–178. This article first appeared in *Natural Hazards Observer,* November 2004, 5–6, hazards.colorado.edu /uploads/observer/2004/nov04/nov04.pdf. See also S. Laska and B. H. Morrow, "Social vulnerabilities and Hurricane Katrina: An unnatural di-saster in New Orleans," *Marine Technology Society Journal* 40, no. 4 (2006): 16–26; and S. Laska, "Shirley Laska Award Statement," American Sociolog-ical Association, www.asanet.org/news-and-events/member-awards/public -understanding-sociology-asa-award/shirley-laska-award-statement.

25. T. M. Nichols, *The Death of Expertise: The Campaign Against Estab-lished Knowledge and Why It Matters* (Oxford, UK: Oxford University Press, 2017).

26. G. J. Velders et al., "The importance of the Montreal Protocol in protecting climate," *Proceedings of the National Academy of Sciences* 104, no. 12 (2007): 4814–4819; and A. R. Douglass, P. A. Newman, and S. Solomon, "The Antarctic ozone hole: An update," *Physics Today* 67, no. 7 (2014): 42.

27. K. K. Wallman, "Enhancing statistical literacy: Enriching our society," *Journal of the American Statistical Association* 88, no. 421 (1993): 1–8; and M. Schield, "Statistical literacy: Thinking critically about statistics," *Of Significance* 1, no. 1 (1999): 15–20.

28. H. Rosling, *Factfulness: 10 Reasons We're Wrong About the World—and Why Things Are Better Than You Think* (New York: Flatiron Books, 2018); and "Almost Nobody Knows the Basic Global Facts" (web page), Gapminder, www.gapminder.org.

29. There are many accomplished scholars and practitioners who dedicate a significant amount of their time and effort to discuss and enlighten the public about complex statistical issues. The following constitutes a nonexhaustive list (in no particular order): Gerd Gigerenzer has authored several popular books, including *Gut Feelings*, *Risk Savvy*, and *Reckoning with Risk*, offering insights on better understanding and using probability and statistics when making decisions; Howard Wainer has been writing books on how evidence can be misinterpreted because of faulty analyses and presentations in domains such as education, economics, and medicine. His popular works include *Truth or Truthiness*, *Uneducated Guesses*, *Medical Illuminations*, and *Visual Revelations*; Nassim Taleb wrote and has been expanding his five-volume treatise *Incerto*, which is an "investigation of opacity, luck, uncertainty, probability, human error, risk, and decision making when we don't understand the world"; David Spiegelhalter writes accessible articles in a variety of popular outlets and contributes to broadcasts to improve "the way that uncertainty and risk are discussed in society, and show how probability and statistics can be both useful and entertaining"; Ben Goldacre has been discussing a wide variety of statistical and decision-making issues in the medical domain. His books on the subject include *Bad Pharma* and *Bad Science*. There's also a collection of his articles and arguments in *I Think You'll Find It's a Bit More Complicated Than That*; Philip Tetlock has been measuring and analyzing people's abilities to forecast important political, social, and economic events. The Good Judgment Project he has been comanaging provides insights on how different experts make predictions and express their opinions about the future. He has cowritten *Superforecasting: The Art and Science of Prediction*; Andrew Gelman writes a blog on "statistical modeling, causal inference, and social science," where he and his insightful commentators discuss the implications of a wide variety of influential research published by scientists all around the world; John Allen Paulos has been writing books on the importance of mathematical

and statistical literacy. His book *Innumeracy* is a good starting point to understand how an accurate understanding of basic mathematics is crucial for making informed decisions; Sam Savage wrote *The Flaw of Averages* and founded the organization Probability Management, where he and his team are "rethinking uncertainty through communication, calculation, and credible estimates"; Edward Tufte is a statistician and an artist who is considered a pioneer in data visualization and information design. His main books on the subjects are *Beautiful Evidence*, *The Visual Display of Quantitative Information*, *Envisioning Information*, and *Visual Explanations*; and Spyros Makridakis is a statistician specializing in forecasting. Together with colleagues, he has conducted several M-Competitions since the 1970s, where a wide variety of statistical methods and professionals compete to determine the relative accuracy of different approaches. He has recently cowritten a book on luck: *Dance with Chance*.

30. T. O'Riordan, *Interpreting the Precautionary Principle* (Abingdon, UK: Routledge, 2013); and N. N. Taleb et al., "The precautionary principle (with application to the genetic modification of organisms)," Extreme Risk Initiative, NYU School of Engineering Working Paper Series, 2014, arXiv preprint arXiv:1410.5787. For counterarguments and further discussions, see also C. R. Sunstein, *Laws of Fear: Beyond the Precautionary Principle*, vol. 6 (Cambridge, UK: Cambridge University Press, 2005); and A. Bell, "What's All the Fuss About the Precautionary Principle?," *Guardian* (Manchester, UK), July 12, 2013, www.theguardian.com/science/political-science/2013/jul/12/precautionary-principle-science-policy.

31. "On Human Gene Editing: International Summit Statement" (news release), National Academies of Sciences, Engineering, Medicine, December 3, 2015, www8.nationalacademies.org/onpinews/newsitem.aspx?Record ID=12032015a; and G. O. Schaefer, "Why Treat Gene Editing Differently in Two Types of Human Cells?," Biomedicine & Biochemistry, December 18, 2015, scitechconnect.elsevier.com/treat-gene-editing-differently-human -cells/.

32. C. Zimmer, "Genetically Modified People Are Walking Among Us," *New York Times*, December 1, 2018, www.nytimes.com/2018/12/01/sunday-review/crispr-china-babies-gene-editing.html; and "One of CRISPR's Inventors Has Called for Controls on Gene-Editing Technology," *MIT Technology Review*, November 15, 2019, www.technologyreview.com/f/614719/crispr-has-made-jennifer-doudna-rich-now-she-says-it -must-be-controlled/.

Chapter 4: Free Choice That Isn't

1. E. H. L. Aarts and S. Marzano, eds., *The New Everyday: Views on Ambient Intelligence*. (Rotterdam, Netherlands: Uitgeverij 010, 2003); M. E. Pullman and M. A. Gross, "Ability of experience design elements to elicit emotions and loyalty behaviors," *Decision Sciences* 35, no. 3 (2004): 551–578; M. Hassenzahl, *Experience Design: Technology for All the Right Reasons* (San Rafael, CA: Morgan and Claypool, 2010); H. McLellan, "Experience design," *Cyberpsychology and Behavior* 3, no. 1 (2000): 59–69; and M. Hassenzahl et al., "Designing moments of meaning and pleasure. Experience design and happiness," *International Journal of Design* 7, no. 3 (2013): 21–31.

2. A. Toffler, *Future Shock* (New York: Bantam, 1971).

3. B. J. Pine II and J. H. Gilmore, *The Experience Economy* (Boston: Harvard Business School Press, 2011).

4. E. Fromm, *To Have or to Be?* (New York: Harper and Row, 1976), 11.

5. E. Claparède, "Recognition and 'Me-ness,'" in *Organization and Pathology of Thought: Selected Sources*, ed. and trans. D. Rapaport (New York: Columbia University Press, 1965).

6. J. LeDoux, *The Emotional Brain: The Mysterious Underpinnings of Emotional Life* (New York: Simon and Schuster, 1998); J. S. Feinstein, M. C. Duff, and D. Tranel, "Sustained experience of emotion after loss of memory in patients with amnesia," *Proceedings of the National Academy of Sciences* 107, no. 17 (2010): 7674–7679; and N. H. Frijda, *The Emotions* (Cambridge, UK: Cambridge University Press, 1986).

7. A. R. Damasio, *Descartes' Error* (New York: Harper Perennial, 1995), 193–194. These patients reportedly had bilateral damage of the ventromedial sector of the prefrontal cortex that effectively prevented communication between the amygdala and the prefrontal cortex.

8. FORA.tv, "When Emotions Make Better Decisions—Antonio Damasio," A. Damasio in conversation with D. Brooks, Aspen Ideas Festival, YouTube, 3:22, July 4, 2009, www.youtube.com/watch?v=1wup_K2WN0I; and Aspen Institute, "This Time with Feeling: David Brooks and Antonio Damasio," Aspen Ideas Festival, YouTube, 1:05:35, 2009, posted January 29, 2015, www.youtube.com/watch?v=IifXMd26gWE.

9. J. S. Lerner et al., "Emotion and decision making," *Annual Review of Psychology* 66 (2015): 799–823.

10. J. P. Forgas, "Why Bad Moods Are Good for You: The Surprising Benefits of Sadness," The Conversation, May 14, 2017, theconversation

.com/why-bad-moods-are-good-for-you-the-surprising-benefits-of
-sadness-75402; and A. Roberts, "Sadness makes us seem nobler, more
elegant, more adult. Which is pretty weird, when you think about it,"
Aeon, March 14, 2014, aeon.co/essays/why-does-sadness-inspire-great
-art-when-happiness-cannot.

11. G. S. Berns et al., "Neurobiological substrates of dread," *Science* 312,
no. 5774 (2006): 754–758.

12. J. Haidt, *The Righteous Mind: Why Good People Are Divided by Politics
and Religion* (New York: Vintage, 2012); and H. H. Ong et al., "Moral
judgment modulation by disgust is bi-directionally moderated by individual sensitivity," *Frontiers in Psychology* 5 (2014), 194.

13. A. I. Abramowitz and S. W. Webster, "The rise of negative partisanship and the nationalization of US elections in the 21st century," *Electoral
Studies* 41 (2016): 12–22; and A. I. Abramowitz and S. W. Webster, "Negative partisanship: Why Americans dislike parties but behave like rabid
partisans," *Political Psychology* 39 (2018): 119–135.

14. T. Brader, *Campaigning for Hearts and Minds: How Emotional Appeals
in Political Ads Work* (Chicago: University of Chicago Press, 2006); M. T.
Parker and L. M. Isbell, "How I vote depends on how I feel: The differential impact of anger and fear on political information processing," *Psychological Science* 21, no. 4 (2010): 548–550; N. A. Valentino et al., "Election
night's alright for fighting: The role of emotions in political participation,"
Journal of Politics 73, no. 1 (2011): 156–170; and F. Passarelli and G. Tabel-
lini, "Emotions and political unrest," *Journal of Political Economy* 125, no. 3
(2017): 903–946.

15. D. Ariely and T. S. Wallsten, "Seeking subjective dominance in
multidimensional space: An explanation of the asymmetric dominance
effect," *Organizational Behavior and Human Decision Processes* 63, no. 3
(1995): 223–232; and J. E. Slaughter, E. E. Kausel, and M. A. Quiñones,
"The decoy effect as a covert influence tactic," *Journal of Behavioral Decision
Making* 24, no. 3 (2011): 249–266.

16. D. Ariely, *Predictably Irrational: The Hidden Forces That Shape Our
Decisions* (New York: HarperCollins, 2008).

17. R. Kivetz, O. Netzer, and V. Srinivasan, "Alternative models for
capturing the compromise effect," *Journal of Marketing Research* 41, no.
3 (2004): 237–257; S. Frederick, L. Lee, and E. Baskin, "The limits of
attraction," *Journal of Marketing Research* 51, no. 4 (2014): 487–507;
S. Yang and M. Lynn, "More evidence challenging the robustness and
usefulness of the attraction effect," *Journal of Marketing Research* 51,

no. 4 (2014): 508–513; and J. Huber, J. W. Payne, and C. P. Puto, "Let's be honest about the attraction effect," *Journal of Marketing Research* 51, no. 4 (2014): 520–525.

18. A. Tversky and D. Kahneman, "Judgment under uncertainty: Heuristics and biases," *Science* 185, no. 4157 (1974): 1124–1131; N. Epley and T. Gilovich, "The anchoring-and-adjustment heuristic: Why the adjustments are insufficient," *Psychological Science* 17, no. 4 (2006): 311–318; and A. Furnham and H. C. Boo, "A literature review of the anchoring effect," *Journal of Socio-Economics* 40, no. 1 (2011): 35–42.

19. B. S. Nichols, "The development, validation, and implications of a measure of consumer competitive arousal (CCAr)," *Journal of Economic Psychology* 33, no. 1 (2012): 192–205; S. Gupta and J. W. Gentry, "The behavioral responses to perceived scarcity—the case of fast fashion," *International Review of Retail, Distribution and Consumer Research* 26, no. 3 (2016): 260–271; and H. Park, A. K. Lalwani, and D. H. Silvera, "The impact of resource scarcity on price-quality judgments," *Journal of Consumer Research* 46, no. 6 (2020): 1110–1124.

20. There's research on how number of options may affect our choices. In some contexts, having more options can create complications. For discussions on the subject, see B. Scheibehenne, R. Greifeneder, and P. M. Todd, "Can there ever be too many options? A meta-analytic review of choice overload," *Journal of Consumer Research* 37, no. 3 (2010): 409–425; B. Schwartz, *The Paradox of Choice: Why More Is Less* (New York: Harper Perennial, 2005); A. Chernev, U. Böckenholt, and J. Goodman, "Choice overload: A conceptual review and meta-analysis," *Journal of Consumer Psychology* 25, no. 2 (2015): 333–358; and E. Soyer and R. M. Hogarth, "The size and distribution of donations: Effects of number of recipients," *Judgment and Decision Making* 6, no. 7 (2011): 616.

21. A. Berger et al., "Gamified interactions: Whether, when, and how games facilitate self-brand connections," *Journal of the Academy of Marketing Science* 46, no. 4 (2018): 652–673.

22. N. Scheiber, "How Uber Uses Psychological Tricks to Push Its Drivers' Buttons," *New York Times*, April 2, 2017.

23. E. Costa and D. Halpern, "The behavioural science of online harm and manipulation, and what to do about it," The Behavioural Insights Team, 2019, www.bi.team/wp-content/uploads/2019/04/BIT_The-behavioural-science-of-online-harm-and-manipulation-and-what-to-do-about-it_Single.pdf; and T. Mirsch, C. Lehrer, and R. Jung, "Digital nudging: Altering user behavior in digital environments," *Proceedings*

der 13. Internationalen Tagung Wirtschaftsinformatik (WI 2017) (2017): 634–648.

24. E. Pariser, *The Filter Bubble: What the Internet Is Hiding from You* (London: Penguin, 2011); C. Sunstein, "The Daily We: Is the Internet Really a Blessing for Democracy?," *Boston Review*, June 1, 2001; and C. Sunstein, "The Rise of the Daily Me Threatens Democracy," *Financial Times*, June 10, 2008, www.ft.com/content/3e2ee254-bf96-11dc-8052-0000779fd2ac.

25. S. Vosoughi, D. Roy, and S. Aral, "The spread of true and false news online," *Science* 359 (2018): 1146–1151; H. Allcott and M. Gentzkow, "Social media and fake news in the 2016 election," *Journal of Economic Perspectives* 31, no. 2 (2017): 211–236; and G. L. Ciampaglia and F. Menczer, "Misinformation and Biases Infect Social Media, Both Intentionally and Accidentally," The Conversation, June 20, 2018, theconversation.com /misinformation-and-biases-infect-social-media-both-intentionally -and-accidentally-97148.

26. P. Noor, "There Are Plenty More Like Cambridge Analytica. I Know—I've Used the Data," *Guardian* (Manchester, UK), March 23, 2018, www.theguardian.com/commentisfree/2018/mar/23/plenty-more -like-cambridge-analytica-data-facebook; N. Bowles, "After Cambridge Analytica, Privacy Experts Get to Say 'I Told You So,'" *New York Times*, April 12, 2018, www.nytimes.com/2018/04/12/technology/privacy -researchers-facebook.html; J. Isaak and M. J. Hanna, "User data privacy: Facebook, Cambridge Analytica, and privacy protection," *Computer* 51, no. 8 (2018): 56–59; and E. L. Andrews, "The Science Behind Cambridge Analytica: Does Psychological Profiling Work?," *Stanford Business (Insights)*, April 12, 2018, www.gsb.stanford.edu/insights/science-behind -cambridge-analytica-does-psychological-profiling-work.

27. T. Harris, "How a Handful of Tech Companies Control Billions of Minds Every Day," TED Talks, April 2017, www.ted.com/talks/tristan _harris_the_manipulative_tricks_tech_companies_use_to_capture_your _attention?language=en.

28. R. H. Thaler and C. R. Sunstein, *Nudge: Improving Decisions About Health, Wealth, and Happiness* (New York: Penguin, 2009).

29. H. Cronqvist and R. H. Thaler, "Design choices in privatized social -security systems: Learning from the Swedish experience," *American Economic Review* 94, no. 2 (2004): 424–428; S. Benartzi and R. H. Thaler, "Behavioral economics and the retirement savings crisis," *Science* 339, no. 6124 (2013): 1152–1153; J. J. Choi et al., "Optimal defaults," *American Economic*

Review 93 no. 2 (2003): 180–185; P. Rozin et al., "Nudge to nobesity I: Minor changes in accessibility decrease food intake," *Judgment and Decision Making* 6 no. 4 (2011): 323–332; and E. Dayan and M. Bar-Hillel, "Nudge to nobesity II: Menu positions influence food orders," *Judgment and Decision Making* 6, no. 4 (2011): 333–342. For a more generic perspective on business applications, see D. G. Goldstein et al., "Nudge your customers toward better choices," *Harvard Business Review* 86, no. 12 (2008): 99–105.

30. P. W. Schultz et al., "The constructive, destructive, and reconstructive power of social norms," *Psychological Science* 18, no. 5 (2007): 429–434; P. W. Schultz et al., "The constructive, destructive, and reconstructive power of social norms: Reprise," *Perspectives on Psychological Science* 13, no. 2 (2018): 249–254; and D. L. Costa and M. E. Kahn, "Energy conservation 'nudges' and environmentalist ideology: Evidence from a randomized residential electricity field experiment," *Journal of the European Economic Association* 11, no. 3 (2013): 680–702.

31. P. John, *How Far to Nudge? Assessing Behavioural Public Policy* (Cheltenham, UK: Edward Elgar Publishing, 2018); T. Grüne-Yanoff and R. Hertwig, "Nudge versus boost: How coherent are policy and theory?," *Minds and Machines* 26, no. 1–2 (2016): 149–183; and S. Reijula et al., "Nudge, boost, or design? Limitations of behaviorally informed policy under social interaction," *Journal of Behavioral Economics for Policy* 2, no. 1 (2018): 99–1055.

32. O. G. Leon, "Value-focused thinking versus alternative-focused thinking: Effects on generation of objectives," *Organizational Behavior and Human Decision Processes* 80, no. 3 (1999): 213–227; and S. D. Bond, K. A. Carlson, and R. L. Keeney, "Generating objectives: Can decision makers articulate what they want?," *Management Science* 54, no. 1 (2008): 56–70.

33. D. Goleman, *Emotional Intelligence* (New York: Bantam, 2006).

34. R. B. Cialdini, *Influence: The Psychology of Persuasion* (New York: HarperCollins, 2007).

35. J. B. Singer, "Five Ws and an H: Digital challenges in newspaper newsrooms and boardrooms," *International Journal on Media Management* 10, no. 3 (2008): 122–129. In addition to our own suggestions, we also recommend Ralph Keeney's work on value-focused thinking: R. L. Keeney, *Value-focused Thinking: A Path to Creative Decision Making* (Cambridge, MA: Harvard University Press, 1992).

36. B. Schwartz et al., "Maximizing versus satisficing: Happiness is a matter of choice," *Journal of Personality and Social Psychology* 83, no. 5 (2002): 1178.

Chapter 5: If It Feels Good, Do It

1. We were inspired by Raj Patel's book as we made the connection to Oscar Wilde's quote: R. Patel, *The Value of Nothing: How to Reshape Market Society and Redefine Democracy* (London: Portobello Books, 2011).

2. Glossary of Industrial Organisation Economics and Competition Law, compiled by R. S. Khemani and D. M. Shapiro, commissioned by the Directorate for Financial, Fiscal and Enterprise Affairs, OECD, 1993, stats.oecd.org/glossary/detail.asp?ID=3215.

3. "Stress, overtime, disease, contribute to 2.8 million workers' deaths per year, reports UN labour agency," UN News, April 18, 2019, news.un.org/en /story/2019/04/1036851; "Poor working conditions are main global employment challenge," Newsroom, International Labour Organization, February 13, 2019, www.ilo.org/global/about-the-ilo/newsroom/news/WCMS_670171 /lang--en/index.htm; and International Labour Organization, *Safety and Health at the Heart of the Future of Work: Building on 100 Years of Experience* (Geneva, Switzerland: ILO, 2019), www.ilo.org/wcmsp5/groups/public/--- dgreports/---dcomm/documents/publication/wcms_686645.pdf.

4. R. A. Matthew, O. Brown, and D. Jensen, *From Conflict to Peacebuilding: The Role of Natural Resources and the Environment* (Nairobi, Kenya: United Nations Environment Programme, 2009), postconflict.unep.ch/ publications/pcdmb_policy_01.pdf; X. Sala-i-Martin and A. Subramanian, "Addressing the natural resource curse: An illustration from Nigeria," *Journal of African Economies* 22, no. 4 (2013): 570–615; and A. J. Venables, "Using natural resources for development. Why has it proven so difficult?," *Journal of Economic Perspectives* 30, no. 1 (2016): 161–184.

5. L. Lebreton et al., "Evidence that the Great Pacific Garbage Patch is rapidly accumulating plastic," *Scientific Reports* 8, no. 4666 (2018); J. Hammer, M. H. Kraak, and J. R. Parsons, "Plastics in the marine environment: The dark side of a modern gift," *Reviews of Environmental Contamination and Toxicology* 220 (2012): 1–44; UNEP, *Marine Plastic Debris and Microplastics: Global Lessons and Research to Inspire Action and Guide Policy Change* (Nairobi, Kenya: United Nations Environment Programme, 2016), doi.org/10.18356/0b228f55-en; and S. Sharma and S. Chatterjee, "Microplastic pollution, a threat to marine ecosystem and human health: A short review," *Environmental Science and Pollution Research* 24, no. 27 (2017): 21530–21547.

6. N. Rodríguez-Eugenio, M. McLaughlin, and D. Pennock, *Soil Pollution: A Hidden Reality* (Rome: FAO, 2018), 142.

7. J. A. Manik and J. Yardley, "Building Collapse in Bangladesh Leaves Scores Dead," *New York Times*, April 24, 2013, https://www.nytimes.com/2013/04/25/world/asia/bangladesh-building-collapse.html; J. Moulds, "Child Labor in the Fashion Supply Chain: Where, Why and What Can Be Done," *Guardian* (Manchester, UK), 2016, labs.theguardian.com/unicef-child-labour/; and International Labour Office, *Marking Progress Against Child Labour: Global Estimates and Trends 2000–2012* (Geneva, Switzerland: ILO/IPEC, 2013).

8. M. Springmann et al., "Options for keeping the food system within environmental limits," *Nature* 562, no. 7728 (2018): 519–525; and G. Eshel et al., "Land, irrigation water, greenhouse gas, and reactive nitrogen burdens of meat, eggs, and dairy production in the United States," *Proceedings of the National Academy of Sciences* 111, no. 33 (2014): 11996–12001.

9. M. Contag et al., "How They Did It: An Analysis of Emission Defeat Devices in Modern Automobiles," in *2017 IEEE Symposium on Security and Privacy (SP)* (San Jose, CA: Institute of Electrical and Electronics Engineers, 2017), 231–250; and D. Carrington, "Wide Range of Cars Emit More Pollution in Realistic Driving Tests, Data Shows," *Guardian* (Manchester, UK), 2015, www.theguardian.com/environment/2015/sep/30/wide-range-of-cars-emit-more-pollution-in-real-driving-conditions-tests-show.

10. Featured in M. Heffernan, *Willful Blindness: Why We Ignore the Obvious* (New York: Simon and Schuster, 2011). The quote can be seen directly in the Senate hearing transcript: "An overview of the ENRON collapse," Senate Hearing 107–724, December 18, 2001 (Washington, DC: US Government Printing Office, 2015), www.govinfo.gov/content/pkg/CHRG-107shrg82282/html/CHRG-107shrg82282.htm.

11. M. H. Bazerman and A. E. Tenbrunsel, *Blind Spots: Why We Fail to Do What's Right and What to Do About It* (Princeton, NJ: Princeton University Press, 2011).

12. Heffernan, *Willful Blindness*.

13. BadfishKoo, "The Hitchhiker's Guide to the Galaxy—Point of View Gun" (2005), YouTube, 2:58, posted June 11, 2014, www.youtube.com/watch?v=zxo3Jy3p8zo.

14. P. Bloom, *Against Empathy: The Case for Rational Compassion* (London: Penguin, 2018).

15. P. Slovic et al., "Iconic photographs and the ebb and flow of empathic response to humanitarian disasters," *Proceedings of the National Academy of Science* 114 (2017): 640–644; and D. Västfjäll et al., "Compassion fade: Affect and charity are greatest for a single child in need," *PLoS One* 9, no. 6 (2014): e100115.

16. In his book *Against Empathy*, psychologist Paul Bloom defines and discusses in detail the more generic notion of rational compassion. Our notion of informed compassion would constitute a first and essential part of such an approach. It involves gathering ethically relevant information about a given situation that may be hidden from immediate observation.

17. M. V. Halter, M. C. C. De Arruda, and R. B. Halter, "Transparency to reduce corruption?," *Journal of Business Ethics* 84, no. 3 (2009): 373.

18. "Poverty headcount ration at $1.90 a day (2011 PPP) (% of population)" (table), Poverty, The World Bank, data.worldbank.org/topic /poverty; "Global Health Observatory (GHO) data" (web page), World Health Organization, www.who.int/gho/mortality_burden_disease/life _tables/en/; and M. Roser and E. Ortiz-Ospina, "Global Extreme Poverty," Our World in Data, published 2013, updated 2019, ourworldindata.org /extreme-poverty.

Chapter 6: Magic Bullets

1. There are countless resources, both online and offline, that offer advice based on successful people and organizations. We have previously discussed the problems with learning from these in detail: E. Soyer and R. M. Hogarth, "Stop Reading Lists of Things Successful People Do," *Harvard Business Review*, March 13, 2017, hbr.org/2017/03/stop-reading-lists-of-things -successful-people-do. The list of strategies featured in the beginning of the chapter come from many popular sources: J. Goudeau, "14 Things Successful People Do Before Breakfast," World Economic Forum and Business Insider, November 2, 2015, wef.ch/1GXNYzF; M. Schwantes, "Warren Buffett Says This 1 Simple Habit Separates Successful People from Everyone Else," *Inc.*, January 18, 2018, www.inc.com/marcel-schwantes /warren-buffett-says-this-is-1-simple-habit-that-separates-successful -people-from-everyone-else.html; S. R. Covey, *The 7 Habits of Highly Effective People: Powerful Lessons in Personal Change* (New York: Simon and Schuster, 2004); H. Grant-Halvorson, *Nine Things Successful People Do Differently* (Boston: Harvard Business Press, 2012); K. Kruse, *15 Secrets Successful People Know About Time Management* (Philadelphia: Kruse Group, 2015); B. Spall and M. Xander, *My Morning Routine: How Successful People Start Every Day Inspired* (New York: Portfolio/Penguin, 2018); M. Ward, "9 Habits of Highly Successful People, from a Man Who Spent 5 Years Studying Them," CNBC, March 28, 2017, www.cnbc.com/2017/03/28/9- habits-of-highly-successful-people.html; L. Ho, "How to Be Successful in Life? 13 Tips from the Most Successful People," Lifehack, July 4, 2019,

www.lifehack.org/articles/lifestyle/how-to-be-successful-in-life.
html; B. Wiest, "13 Things Highly Successful People Do Not Waste
Their Mental Energy On," *Forbes*, July 23, 2018, www.forbes.com/sites
/briannawiest/2018/07/23/13-things-highly-successful-people-do-not
-waste-their-mental-energy-on; R. LoCascio, "Why the Most Successful
People Fail Most Often," *Inc.*, August 23, 2016, www.inc.com/rob-locascio
/4-spectacular-failures-from-the-most-successful-entrepreneurs.html; and
D. Schwabel, "4 Things Every Successful Person Has in Common," *Forbes*,
December 17, 2013, www.forbes.com/sites/danschawbel/2013/12/17/14
-things-every-successful-person-has-in-common/.

2. D. Fincher, director, *The Social Network* (Culver City, CA: Sony Pictures Home Entertainment, 2010; and T. Schwartz, "The Social Network:
Separating fact from fiction," MTV, Oct 4, 2010, mtv.com/news/2437629.

3. L. Vanderkam, "Um, about that World Economic Forum tweet and
infographic," Laura Vanderkam: Writer, Author, Speaker, January 21, 2016,
lauravanderkam.com/2016/01/um-about-that-world-economic-forum
-tweet-and-infographic/.

4. N. J. Roese and K. D. Vohs, "Hindsight bias," *Perspectives on Psychological Science* 7, no. 5 (2012): 411-426.

5. Z. Church, "Uber CEO's Eight Traits of Great Entrepreneurs," Ideas
Made to Matter (blog), MIT Management Sloan School, December 3,
2015, mitsloan.mit.edu/newsroom/articles/uber-ceo-eight-traits-of-great
-entrepreneurs/.

6. M. J. Mauboussin, *Think Twice: Harnessing the Power of Counterintu-
ition* (Boston: Harvard Business Review Press, 2012).

7. In *The Black Swan*, Taleb refers to the unobservable failures as "silent
evidence." N. N. Taleb, *The Black Swan: The Impact of the Highly Improbable*
(New York: Random House, 2007).

8. R. H. Frank, *Success and Luck: Good Fortune and the Myth of Meritocracy*
(Princeton, NJ: Princeton University Press, 2016).

9. M. Shermer, "Surviving statistics," *Scientific American* 311, no. 3 (2014):
94; J. Denrell, "Vicarious learning, undersampling of failure, and the myths
of management," *Organization Science* 14, no. 3 (2003): 227–243 ; and G. Le
Mens and J. Denrell, "Rational learning and information sampling: On the
'naivety' assumption in sampling explanations of judgment biases," *Psychological review* 118, no. 2 (2011): 379.

10. Grant-Halvorson, *Nine Things Successful People Do Differently*.

11. R. M. Hogarth and E. Soyer, "Simulated experience: Making intuitive sense of big data," *MIT Sloan Management Review* 56, no. 2 (Winter
2015): 49–54.

12. A. Duckworth, *Grit: The Power of Passion and Perseverance* (New York: Scribner, 2016).

13. Two sources that credit Dylan for the quote: Expecting Rain, www .expectingrain.com/discussions/viewtopic.php?f=6&t=89999&sid=f631 ecbe520af16796a92b5c75ca2ad1&view=print; and subreddit: r/bobdylan, Reddit, 2018, www.reddit.com/r/bobdylan/comments/6ynj1e/bob_dylan_ really_said_the_sentence_a_man_is_a/.

14. "success," Lexico, Oxford, en.oxforddictionaries.com/definition/success.

15. E. J. Langer, "The illusion of control," *Journal of Personality and Social Psychology* 32, no. 2 (1975): 311–328; J. Klayman, "Varieties of Confirmation Bias," in *Psychology of Learning and Motivation*, vol. 32 (New York: Academic Press, 1995), 385–418; and R. S. Nickerson, "Confirmation bias: A ubiquitous phenomenon in many guises," *Review of General Psychology* 2, no. 2 (1998): 175–220.

16. M. R. Leary and D. R. Forsyth, "Attributions of Responsibility for Collective Endeavors," in *Review of Personality and Social Psychology: Vol. 8. Group processes*, ed. C. Hendrick (Newbury Park, CA: Sage, 1987), 167–188; and J. Schroeder, E. M. Caruso, and N. Epley, "Many hands make overlooked work: Over-claiming of responsibility increases with group size," *Journal of Experimental Psychology: Applied* 22, no. 2 (2016): 238.

17. R. M. Arkin, A. J. Appelman, and J. M. Burger, "Social anxiety, self-presentation, and the self-serving bias in causal attribution," *Journal of Personality and Social Psychology* 38, no. 1 (1980): 23; T. S. Duval and P. J. Silvia, "Self-awareness, probability of improvement, and the self-serving bias," *Journal of Personality and Social Psychology* 82, no. 1 (2002): 49; and J. Shepperd, W. Malone, and K. Sweeny, "Exploring causes of the self-serving bias," *Social and Personality Psychology Compass* 2, no. 2 (2008): 895–908.

18. M. Syed, *Black Box Thinking: The Surprising Truth About Success* (London: Hachette, 2015).

19. R. Byrne, *The Secret* (New York: Simon and Schuster, 2008); and "What Is the Secret? The Secret by Rhonda Byrne," The Law of Attraction, www.thelawofattraction.com/the-secret/.

20. Cochrane Complementary Medicine: "The Field was established in 1996 to support and promote systematic reviews of complementary, alternative, and integrative therapies and to function as a link between Cochrane, a worldwide organization that prepares systematic reviews of all kinds of healthcare therapies, and practitioners, researchers, and consumers with an interest in complementary medicine," cam.cochrane.org.

21. T. Gilovich, *How We Know What Isn't So* (New York: Simon and Schuster, 2008); D. Graham-Rowe, "Biodiversity: Endangered and in

demand," *Nature* 480, no. 7378 (2011): S101–S103; and Y. Feng et al., "Bear bile: dilemma of traditional medicinal use and animal protection," *Journal of Ethnobiology and Ethnomedicine* 5, no. 2 (2009).

22. W. H. Starbuck and B. Hedberg, "How Organizations Learn from Success and Failure," in *Handbook of Organizational Learning and Knowledge*, ed. M. Dierkes et al. (Oxford: Oxford University Press, 2001).

23. Success rate and base rate are similar concepts. For example, in a certain job application scenario, base rate would be how many people would be talented enough to get that job within the population. Success rate is about the proportion of people admitted to the job. M. Bar-Hillel, "The base-rate fallacy in probability judgments," *Acta Psychologica* 44, no. 3 (1980): 211–233; and M. McDowell et al., "A simple tool for communicating the benefits and harms of health interventions: A guide for creating a fact box," *Medical Decision Making Policy & Practice* 1 (2016): 1–10.

24. J. Denrell, C. Fang, and C. Liu, "Perspective—Chance explanations in the management sciences," *Organization Science* 26, no. 3 (2014): 923–940.

25. Another important issue here is to acknowledge one's reference class. The success rate should be calculated using the prevalence of projects that are similar to the one we are considering. For instance, in this example, if we think we are better than half of those projects to begin with, the success rate would become 10 in 100.

26. G. Gigerenzer, *Reckoning with Risk: Learning to Live with Uncertainty* (London: Penguin, 2003).

27. D. McRaney, "Survivorship Bias," You Are Not So Smart: A Celebration of Self-Delusion" (blog), May 23, 2013, youarenotsosmart.com /2013/05/23/survivorship-bias/.

28. "FailCon Goes Global" (web page), FailCon, thefailcon.com; "We Live Without Filters: By Sharing Stories of Failure" (web page); and Fail Festival (website), failfestival.org.

29. M. Stefan, "A CV of failures," *Nature* 468, no. 7322 (2010): 467. Houshofer's regular CV and CV of Failures can both be found at www .princeton.edu/haushofer/.

30. E. Ries, *The Lean Startup: How Today's Entrepreneurs Use Continuous Innovation to Create Radically Successful Businesses* (New York: Crown Business, 2011), 56.

31. Peter Skillman Design (spaghetti tower design challenge), www.peter skillmandesign.com/spaghetti-tower-design-challenge; and "Draw Toast" (web page), Tom Wujec, www.tomwujec.com/marshmallowchallenge.

Chapter 7: Happiness Foiled

1. K. M.Sheldon and R. E. Lucas, eds., *Stability of Happiness: Theories and Evidence on Whether Happiness Can Change* (Amsterdam: Elsevier, 2014); D. Kahneman, E. Diener, and N. Schwarz, eds., *Well-being: The Foundations of a Hedonic Psychology* (New York: Russell Sage Foundation, 1999).

2. R. E. Lucas, "Adaptation and the set-point model of subjective well-being: Does happiness change after major life events?," *Current Directions in Psychological Science* 16, no. 2 (2007): 75–79; S. Fredrick and G. Loewenstein, "Hedonic Adaptation," in *Well-being: The Foundations of a Hedonic Psychology*, 302–329; and A. Tversky and D. Griffin, "Endowment and Contrast in Judgments of Well-being," in *Subjective Well-being: An Interdisciplinary Perspective*, ed. F. Strack, M. Argyle, and N. Schwarz (Oxford, UK: Pergamon Press, 1991), 101–118.

3. P. Brickman and D. T. Campbell, "Hedonic Relativism and Planning the Good Society," in *Adaptation Level Theory: A Symposium* , ed. M. H. Appley (New York: Academic Press, 1971), 287–302; D. Myers, *The Pursuit of Happiness* (New York: Morrow, 1992); and E. Diener, R. E. Lucas, and C. N. Scollon, "Beyond the Hedonic Treadmill: Revising the Adaptation Theory of Well-being," in *The Science of Well-being* (Dordrecht, UK: Springer, 2009), 103–118.

4. We had discussed this issue (recency effect) in Chapter 3, where it caused problems. If experience with catastrophes get diluted, we may fail to prepare effectively. In the context of happiness, experiences could gradually lose their effect in time on how people feel.

5. D. Kahneman, J. L. Knetsch, and R. H. Thaler, "Anomalies: The endowment effect, loss aversion, and status quo bias," *Journal of Economic Perspectives* 5, no. 1 (1991): 193–206; and N. Novemsky and D. Kahneman, "The boundaries of loss aversion," *Journal of Marketing Research* 42, no. 2 (2005): 119–128.

6. P. M. Groves and R. F. Thompson, "A dual-process theory of habituation: Neural mechanisms," *Habituation*, vol. 2 (New York: Academic Press, 1973), 175–205; R. Zajonc, "Attitudinal effects of mere exposure," *Journal of Personality and Social Psychology Monograph Supplement* 9, no. 2, pt., 2 (1968): 1–32; and A. Heingartner and J. V. Hall, "Affective consequences in adults and children of repeated exposure to auditory stimuli," *Journal of Personality and Social Psychology* 29, no. 6 (1974): 719–723.

7. N. D. Weinstein, "Community noise problems: Evidence against adaptation," *Journal of Environmental Psychology* 2, no. 2 (1982): 87–97; D. Weinhold, "The happiness-reducing costs of noise pollution," *Journal*

of Regional Science 53, no. 2 (2013): 292–303; and R. W. Novaco and O. I. Gonzalez, "Commuting and Well-being," in *Technology and Psychological Well-being*, ed. Y. Amichai-Hamburger (Cambridge, UK: Cambridge University Press, 2009), 174–205.

8. C. Lewis, N. Wardrip-Fruin, and J. Whitehead, "Motivational Game Design Patterns of 'ville Games," in *Proceedings of the International Conference on the Foundations of Digital Games* (New York: ACM, 2012), 172–179; and D. McRaney, "The Sunk Cost Fallacy," You Are Not So Smart: A Celebration of Self-Delusion (blog), March 25, 2011, youarenotsosmart .com/2011/03/25/the-sunk-cost-fallacy/.

9. B. M. Staw, "Knee deep in the big muddy: A study of escalating commitment to a chosen course of action," *Organizational Behavior and Human Performance* 16 (1976): 27–44; and R. H. Thaler, "Toward a positive theory of consumer choice," *Journal of Economic Behavior and Organization* 1 (1980): 39–60.

10. V. Liberman et al., "Happiness and memory: Affective significance of endowment and contrast," *Emotion* 9, no. 5 (2009): 666.

11. D. Kahneman, *Thinking, Fast and Slow* (New York: Farrar, Straus and Giroux, 2011).

12. B. L. Fredrickson and D. Kahneman, "Duration neglect in retrospective evaluations of affective episodes," *Journal of Personality and Social Psychology* 65, no. 1 (1993): 45–55; A. M. Do, A. V. Rupert, and G. Wolford, "Evaluations of pleasurable experiences: The peak-end rule," *Psychonomic Bulletin & Review* 15, no. 1 (2008): 96–98; and D. Kahneman et al., "When more pain is preferred to less: Adding a better end," *Journal of Personality and Social Psychology* 65, no. 1 (1993): 401–405.

13. Someone who has been to the same ski resort several times in the past may not be affected by the same view in the same way, however spectacular it may be. Similarly, someone who had previously lost a wallet or suffered similar skiing accidents before may have a different perception of the final blunder. One's personal experience would also influence expectations of a ski trip, which in turn would shape one's ultimate satisfaction.

14. Photo by Brian Snyder, copyright Reuters.

15. "Disappointment on the podium: `Silver medalists" (web page), Yahoo! Sports, August 6, 2012, sports.yahoo.com/photos/olympics -silver-medal-expressions-slideshow/olympics-day-9-gymnastics -artistic-photo-1344256222.html; and V. H. Medvec, S. F. Madey, and T. Gilovich, "When less is more: Counterfactual thinking and satisfaction among Olympic medalists," *Journal of Personality and Social Psychology* 69, no. 4 (1995): 603–610.

16. R. H. Frank, *Luxury Fever: Why Money Fails to Satisfy in an Era of Excess* (New York: Simon and Schuster, 2001). M. Harron and G. Turner, screenwriters, American Psycho, film (Muse Productions, Lionsgate Films, 2000), based on B. E. Ellis, *American Psycho* (Vintage Books, 1991).

17. M. Konnikova, "How Facebook makes us unhappy," *The New Yorker*, Setpember 10, 2013; P. Verduyn et al., "Passive Facebook usage undermines affective well-being: Experimental and longitudinal evidence," *Journal of Experimental Psychology: General* 144, no. 2 (2015): 480–488; H. Krasnova et al., "Envy on Facebook: A hidden threat to users' life satisfaction?" Paper presented at International Conference on Wirtschaftsinformatik (WI), Leipzig, Germany, 2013; C. Seife, *Virtual Unreality: Just Because the Internet Told You, How Do You Know It's True?* (London: Penguin, 2014); and P. Steel, *The Procrastination Equation* (Sydney, Australia: Murdoch Books, 2011).

18. S. Valenzuela, N. Park, and K. F. Kee, "Is there social capital in a social network site?: Facebook use and college students' life satisfaction, trust, and participation," *Journal of Computer-Mediated Communication* 14, no. 4 (2009): 875–901; M. Burke, C. Marlow, and T. Lento, "Social Network Activity and Social Well-being," in *Proceedings of the SIGCHI Conference on Human Factors in Computing Systems* (New York: ACM, 2010), 1909–1912; and M. D. Lieberman, *Social: Why Our Brains Are Wired to Connect* (Oxford, UK: Oxford University Press, 2013).

19. A. Alter, *Irresistible: The Rise of Addictive Technology and the Business of Keeping Us Hooked* (London: Penguin, 2017); and N. Eyal and R. Hoover, *Hooked: A Guide to Building Habit-Forming Products* (New York: Portfolio/Penguin, 2013).

20. M. Duggan, "Online Harassment 2017," Pew Research Center: Internet & Technology, July 11, 2017, www.pewinternet.org/2017/07/11/online-harassment-2017/; and M. Duggan, "Experiencing Online Harassment," Pew Research Center: Internet & Technology, July 11, 2017, www.pewinternet.org/2017/07/11/experiencing-online-harassment/.

21. Cardigan Mountain School, "Cardigan's Commencement Address by Chief Justice John G. Roberts, Jr.," YouTube, 18:03, June 6, 2017, www.youtube.com/watch?time_continue=627&v=Gzu9S5FL-Ug.

22. O. Burkeman, *The Antidote: Happiness for People Who Can't Stand Positive Thinking* (New York: Farrar, Straus and Giroux, 2012).

23. D. Gilbert, *Stumbling on Happiness* (New York: Knopf, 2006).

24. S. Lyubomirsky, *The Myths of Happiness: What Should Make You Happy, but Doesn't, What Shouldn't Make You Happy, but Does* (London: Penguin, 2014).

25. A. Kumar and T. Gilovich, "Some 'thing' to talk about? Differential story utility from experiential and material purchases," *Personality and Social Psychology Bulletin* 41, no. 10 (2015): 1320–1331; T. Gilovich, A. Kumar, and L. Jampol, "A wonderful life: Experiential consumption and the pursuit of happiness," *Journal of Consumer Psychology* 25, no. 1 (2015): 152–165; L. Van Boven and T. Gilovich, "To do or to have? That is the question," *Journal of Personality and Social Psychology* 85, no. 6 (2003): 1193–1202; and E. Fromm, *To Have or to Be?* (New York: Harper and Row, 1976).

26. S. Davidai and T. Gilovich, "The headwinds/tailwinds asymmetry: An availability bias in assessments of barriers and blessings," *Journal of Personality and Social Psychology* 111, no. 6 (2016): 835–851; S. Plous, *The Psychology of Judgment and Decision Making* (New York: McGraw-Hill, 1993); and A. Tversky and D. Kahneman, "Availability: A heuristic for judging frequency and probability," *Cognitive Psychology* 5, no. 2 (1973): 207–232.

27. Behavior Studio, "Hillel Einhorn on Happiness: Happiness Is a 2 x 2," YouTube, 1:13, December 5, 2016, www.youtube.com/watch?v=f 6BALquQ_Bo; and R. M. Hogarth and J. Klayman, "Hillel J. Einhorn 1941–1987," *American Psychologist* 43, no. 8 (1988): 656.

Conclusion: The Wisdom of the Experience Coach

1. D. J. Clark, director, *Behind the Curve*, documentary (Aliso Viejo, CA: Delta-v Productions, 2018).

2. D. Epstein, *Range: Why Generalists Triumph in a Specialized World* (New York: Riverhead Books, 2019).

3. M. B. Holbrook and R. M. Schindler, "Age, sex, and attitude toward the past as predictors of consumers' aesthetic tastes for cultural products," *Journal of Marketing Research* 31 (1994): 412–422.

4. D. Lovallo and D. Kahneman, "Delusions of success," *Harvard Business Review* 81, no. 7 (2003): 56–63.

5. E. Kross and I. Grossmann, "Boosting wisdom: Distance from the self enhances wise reasoning, attitudes, and behavior," *Journal of Experimental Psychology: General* 141 (2012): 43–48.

6. A. Tversky and D. Kahneman, "Availability: A heuristic for judging frequency and probability," *Cognitive Psychology* 5, no. 2 (1973): 207–232.

7. A. Furnham and H. C. Boo, "A literature review of the anchoring effect," *Journal of Socio-Economics* 40, no. 1 (2011): 35–42; and N. Epley and T. Gilovich, "The anchoring-and-adjustment heuristic: Why the adjustments are insufficient," *Psychological Science* 17, no. 4 (2006): 311–318.

8. J. K. Phillips, G. Klein, and W. R. Sieck, "Expertise in judgment and decision making: A case for training intuitive decision skills," *Blackwell Handbook of Judgment and Decision Making* 297 (2004): 315; G. Klein, "Developing expertise in decision making," *Thinking & Reasoning* 3, no. 4 (1997): 337–352; and D. Kahneman and G. Klein, "Conditions for intuitive expertise: A failure to disagree," *American Psychologist* 64, no. 6 (2009): 515–526.

INDEX

EMRE SOYER is a behavioral scientist and an entrepreneur. After working in and establishing several startups, he completed his PhD under Robin Hogarth's supervision. Since then, he has been conducting research and working with a variety of companies and sectors, building tools and methods to improve individual and team decisions. He's also been a visiting lecturer at INSEAD and ESSEC in France, Cass Business School in the United Kingdom, TUM in Germany, SDA Bocconi and Politecnico di Milano in Italy, USI in Switzerland, and Ozyegin University in Turkey, among others.

ROBIN M. HOGARTH became hooked in his twenties on questions involving how people make decisions. That fascination still exists five decades later and has led to a career that, sparked by a PhD at the University of Chicago, involved academic positions at INSEAD in France, the University of Chicago, and Pompeu Fabra University in Barcelona, where he is currently an emeritus professor. He has published a wide range of studies on judgment and decision-making in leading scholarly journals and several books (including *Educating Intuition*, 2001). He has advised and inspired generations of researchers in the field of judgment and decision-making.

PublicAffairs is a publishing house founded in 1997. It is a tribute to the standards, values, and flair of three persons who have served as mentors to countless reporters, writers, editors, and book people of all kinds, including me.

I. F. STONE, proprietor of *I. F. Stone's Weekly*, combined a commitment to the First Amendment with entrepreneurial zeal and reporting skill and became one of the great independent journalists in American history. At the age of eighty, Izzy published *The Trial of Socrates*, which was a national bestseller. He wrote the book after he taught himself ancient Greek.

BENJAMIN C. BRADLEE was for nearly thirty years the charismatic editorial leader of *The Washington Post*. It was Ben who gave the *Post* the range and courage to pursue such historic issues as Watergate. He supported his reporters with a tenacity that made them fearless and it is no accident that so many became authors of influential, best-selling books.

ROBERT L. BERNSTEIN, the chief executive of Random House for more than a quarter century, guided one of the nation's premier publishing houses. Bob was personally responsible for many books of political dissent and argument that challenged tyranny around the globe. He is also the founder and longtime chair of Human Rights Watch, one of the most respected human rights organizations in the world.

·   ·   ·

For fifty years, the banner of Public Affairs Press was carried by its owner Morris B. Schnapper, who published Gandhi, Nasser, Toynbee, Truman, and about 1,500 other authors. In 1983, Schnapper was described by *The Washington Post* as "a redoubtable gadfly." His legacy will endure in the books to come.

Peter Osnos, *Founder*